D0121817

The
Father
of SPIN

Even so, the spirit and electricity that had fueled countless campaigns were vibrantly there. I wanted to know more about this man so as to understand how PR had influenced my profession of journalism and how it had shaped our culture.

This, then, is a book about Edward L. Bernays. But it also is a book about America. It is about how public thought is routinely shaped or, some might say, manipulated by singular powers in our culture. And so it is by necessity a book about democracy in the era of the spinmeister.

The
Father
of SPIN

Starting with SYMBOLS

1

IT WAS SUPPOSED TO BE A SECRET.

Eddie and Doris had settled on a modern marriage, one that was more merger than old-fashioned romance and ritual. A coming-together in the austere marriage chapel in the New York Municipal Building. No family or friends to bear witness. No gown or tuxedo, no band or bouquet. Not even a wedding ring—a symbol, to such free-thinking youth in 1922, of the spousal slavery they were determined to resist.

Even the timing was chosen with a concern for privacy. As the bride and groom arrived, the city-issued clock registered five minutes to noon, just moments before the chapel would close, almost ensuring that, no matter how esteemed the couple, the nuptials would not be reported in the next day's papers.

They'd already managed to hide their attachment from colleagues at the publicity office they shared on Fifth Avenue. Eddie's family, meanwhile, was so convinced of his commitment to bachelordom that, when his sister married five years before, her husband assumed the name Bernays as the only way to perpetuate a proud line in which Eddie was the only male heir. This humble ceremony would clinch it, letting them spring the surprise some days or weeks later, showing off their cunning and casualness.

In the end, however, all the stealth and subterfuge were for naught, as the young publicity agent couldn't keep the secret, even if it was his own marriage.

"Directly we reached the Waldorf-Astoria, where we were to honeymoon, all desire for secrecy blew away like a mist in the sunny breeze," Doris recalled years later. "My husband grasped the telephone and called hundreds of his most intimate friends to tell them about our secret marriage."[1]

Some already knew, having read the matrimonial item that an enterprising reporter had dug up for the paper that evening of September 16. And the groom's father, who had long anticipated this occurrence, had stashed a box of jewelry in a vault five years before with a letter marked "For Doris, when she shall have married Edward."

For those who were still in the dark, Eddie offered up the sort of inspired strategy that was quickly becoming his trademark. He persuaded his new bride to register with him at the Waldorf under her maiden name. He knew this would trigger a policy that he as hotel PR man had instituted where the press would immediately be notified of anything newsworthy. In this case the news was of a married couple who were about to occupy a suite recently vacated by the king and queen of Belgium and who had signed in as "Edward L. Bernays and wife, Doris E. Fleischman."

The result: headlines, here and overseas, proclaiming, "This Bride Registers Under Her Maiden Name," or, more simply, "Independent." More than 250 newspapers ran stories explaining how, for the first time, a married woman had registered at the Waldorf with her husband, using a different name, and the elegant old hotel had permitted it.

So much for their secret. But why save the surprise, Eddie reasoned, when the marriage could become a major story now, one that might help him, his hotel client, and the women's movement? "Doris didn't like the publicity," he acknowledged forty years later, "but I liked it. In retrospect, I was crowing. I married the girl I loved, and everyone ought [to] know about it. I was ego projecting, I supposed, and boasting about the woman I had captured.

"Doris, overnight, had become the new symbol of women's rights throughout the United States—and the world. But I really didn't mind. In fact I liked it. . . . And as far as the Waldorf was concerned, they liked it too, for here was an old hotel that stood for feminism in the public mind, the most modern and contemporary of current ideas."[2]

· · ·

Eddie had been polishing his powers of persuasion for more than a decade by the time of his marital coup. He began, in a way, when he stepped onto a lonely railroad platform on the flats of Cayuga Lake in 1908. The decision to enroll at Cornell's august College of Agriculture had been a joint one by his father, Ely, an ardent disciple of Teddy Roosevelt's back-to-the-soil movement, and his mother, Anna, who worshiped nature. They believed Cornell, with its scientific approach to farming and its remote setting in the overgrown village of Ithaca, was just the place for Eddie to sever his ties to Manhattan and learn to earn his living from the land.

But the roots never took. He was short and wiry, while his farm-bred classmates were tall and strapping. He'd been raised in a New York City brownstone and reared on the Broadway theater and on books. He spent his summers at a spa near Wiesbaden or at an Adirondack Mountain retreat, and when the weather turned cold he dug in to declensions in Latin, Greek, and German. His fellow students—most of them, anyway—had sprung from the soil. They were the kinds of boys who'd gone barefoot until November and ordered their one pair of shoes from the Sears, Roebuck catalog; who knew the agricultural life they were destined for because their parents and grandparents had lived it; and who had no use for city boys or Jews although, except for Eddie, they didn't know many of either.

His culture shock was even more pronounced in the classroom. He stayed awake just enough to get passable grades in courses like General Comparative Morphology and Physiology of Plants,

Physiography of the Campus and Immediate Vicinity, and Animal Husbandry, which involved "the principles of feeding, care, selection and management of dairy and beef cattle, sheep and swine." Equally frustrating was how removed Cornell seemed from the Progressive movement that was sweeping America at the turn of the century, promising to bust up trusts, eliminate slums, reform corrupt cities, and otherwise harness the runaway forces of industrialization and urbanization.

His disappointment was still evident fifty-three years later when Eddie rendered his verdict on his higher education: "My three and a half years at the Cornell University College of Agriculture gave me little stimulation and less learning."[3]

As he stopped to reflect, however, he realized he had learned more than he thought. There was his work on the *Cornell Countryman*, which confirmed that he wasn't a gifted writer but could be a masterful communicator. Membership in the Cosmopolitan Club had won him friends from China, South Africa, Cuba, and other far-off nations he would someday work with, while involvement in the theater and chorus taught him about actors and singers, if not about acting and singing. And knowing he didn't fit in with conventional thinking on campus got him accustomed to thinking unconventionally, to operating at the edge and pushing the boundaries, which became his trademark over a career that lasted more than eighty years.

As for his complaints about fellow students, he managed to find enough attractive young women to let him indulge his growing fascination with females. "Some of my few pleasant memories of Cornell," he conceded in his memoirs, "are my drives with coeds over snow-covered dirt roads overlooking silvery Lake Cayuga, to the accompanying sound of horses' hoofs as they crunched the packed snow."

"Perhaps Cornell was the right place for me after all," he decided later, "because it furnished, in a negative way, a test for aptitudes and adjustments. . . . I was looking for something that was not there and found something better."

Important insights, but they didn't make it any easier for Eddie to decide what to do when Cornell handed him his degree in February

1912. Trained in agriculture, but not wanting to dirty his hands on another animal or plant, the twenty-year-old with the wavy mustache and close-cropped hair accepted a professor's offer to write for the *National Nurseryman* journal. He hadn't studied journalism but he'd practiced it in grammar school, high school, and summer camp, as well as in college. And he loved it now, relishing the way "German-American proprietors of nurseries in Danville, New York, greeted me as if I were a rich uncle, inviting me to lunch and dinner at their homes, where we discussed Goethe, Schiller, and fruit-tree stock." The job might have lasted if there'd been more time for Goethe and Schiller and less need to come up with stories about apples, peaches, and pears.

From there he tried filling out bills of lading on hay and oats at New York City's Produce Exchange, where his father worked. Then he booked himself as supercargo on a freighter bound for Rotterdam and from there made his way to Paris. The City of Light was indeed illuminating, letting Eddie practice his French on coachmen, muse about life with waiters serving aperitifs, and, best of all, stroll the narrow streets near the Place Vendôme with his latest amour, stopping occasionally "to embrace and kiss passionately." The problem, again, was work. For a time he tried decoding cables concerning grain trades for the venerable Louis Dreyfus and Company, a job that proved even more tedious than his previous posts.

His way out appeared by accident, and as he liked to tell the story, "it all started with sex."

Back in Manhattan after quitting his Paris job, Eddie at first pined for Europe's charm and sophistication, dismissing New York as a "dirty little village on the Hudson." But he soon got caught up in the spirit of Woodrow Wilson's New Freedom, with its promise of rising economic opportunity and falling cultural inhibitions. Although he was unemployed, his father's success as a grain dealer let him settle in to a relatively carefree existence, one where he could contemplate his future without worrying about it. Still, it felt good to bump into an old friend like Fred Robinson when he boarded the Ninth Avenue trolley on a brisk December morning in 1912.

Years earlier Fred and Eddie had been coeditors of the school paper at Public School 184, and Fred's father had just turned over to him two monthly journals he owned, the *Medical Review of Reviews* and the *Dietetic and Hygienic Gazette*. Fred asked Eddie, "How'd you like to help me run the *Review* and the *Gazette*?"

Eddie accepted the offer on the spot and began work the next morning. Neither he nor Fred knew much about medicine or nutrition, and neither had any real experience in publishing, unless you count the *Echo* at P.S. 184. But both were ambitious and enterprising, which was all most entrepreneurs of the era began with, and both were willing to do everything from writing and editing to promotion and office errands. They used the *Medical Review* to argue against women wearing corsets with stays and to encourage shower baths; they published expert opinions on health controversies, a relatively novel approach; and they tried something even newer to promote the journal and its advertisers: distributing free copies to most of the 137,000 licensed physicians in the United States.

Their real break came two months after they joined forces, when a doctor submitted a glowing review of *Damaged Goods*, a work by French playwright Eugène Brieux. The play—about a man with syphilis who marries, then fathers a syphilitic child—attacked the prevailing standards of prudery. It was taboo back then to openly discuss sexually transmitted disease, and even worse to talk about public health remedies, but *Damaged Goods* did both.

Eddie and his partner published the doctor's review—a bold step, given their conservative audience. Then they went a step further. They'd read that Richard Bennett, a leading actor (and the father of soon-to-be movie star Joan Bennett), was interested in producing *Damaged Goods*. So Eddie wrote him, saying, "The editors of the *Medical Review of Reviews* support your praiseworthy intention to fight sex-pruriency in the United States by producing Brieux's play *Damaged Goods*. You can count on our help."[4]

Bennett quickly accepted the offer, pumping up the young editor with visions of a crusade against Victorian mores, promising to recruit actors who would work without pay and prodding him to raise money for the production. Eddie was so excited that he volunteered to underwrite the production.

There were two problems with his generosity. He was earning just $25 a week at the journals, and another $25 tutoring the scions of fashionable New York families, and neither he nor his partner could conceive of how they'd come up with the money to rent a theater and pay other expenses. Even more imposing were the New York City censors who several years before had shut down a George Bernard Shaw play about prostitution and who were not likely to approve one that featured such frank treatment of syphilis.

Eddie took those hurdles as challenges. Anything could be accomplished, he believed, if people could be made to see what looked like an obstacle as an opportunity. All that was required was a bit of insight into how people defined obstacles and opportunities, along with some creative prodding to get them to rethink those definitions.

The key with *Damaged Goods*, he realized, was to transform the controversy into a cause and recruit backers who already were public role models. The twenty-one-year-old editor formed a *Medical Review of Reviews* Sociological Fund Committee, then attracted members with an artful appeal that played on Bennett's reputation as an artist as well as the worthiness of battling prudishness. Among those who signed up were John D. Rockefeller Jr., Mrs. William K. Vanderbilt Sr., Mr. and Mrs. Franklin D. Roosevelt, Dr. William Jay Schieffelin, whose company had recently brought to America a treatment for syphilis, and the Reverend John Haynes Holmes of New York's Unitarian Community Church. Each committee member was asked to contribute four dollars, which entitled him to one ticket, and many were asked for endorsements designed to head off police intervention.

The committee was more effective than anyone dreamed. Hundreds of checks poured in, and testimonials were offered by luminaries like Rockefeller. "The evils springing from prostitution cannot be understood," the oil magnate said in a letter, "until frank discussion of them has been made possible." This was the first time that Eddie, or anyone else, had assembled quite such a distinguished front group. And its success ensured not only that he would use this technique repeatedly but also that it would continue to be employed today, when it takes a detective to unmask the interests behind such innocuous-sounding groups as the Safe Energy Communication Council (antinuclear), the Eagle Alliance (pronuclear), and the Coalition Against Regressive Taxation (trucking industry).

Damaged Goods, meanwhile, was a huge hit, presented before overflow audiences in New York, then heading to the National Theater in Washington and a performance before Supreme Court justices, members of the president's cabinet, and congressmen from across the country. Its success at the box office was even more impressive given that most reviewers agreed with the *New York American*, which pronounced the play "dull and almost unendurable." What mattered more was that the production, in the words of one editorial on March 15, 1913, made it strike "sex-o'clock in America"—precisely the note the boy editors were aiming for.

Bernays and Robinson dreamed of a string of similar productions— on narcotics, the white slave trade, and other social evils that begged for redress. "There were no limits to what we could accomplish," Eddie recalled later. Unfortunately, Richard Bennett had other ideas. Having quietly acquired all American rights to the play, the actor bade Eddie and Fred good-bye. "I don't need you or your damn sociological fund anymore," he told his would-be partners. "I'll start my own fund. I own all the rights to *Damaged Goods*. Ta, ta."[5]

. . .

Eddie's adrenaline was flowing too fast for him to waste time licking his wounds, and he was too pumped up by his brush with the brave new worlds of theater and promotion to return to his dull medical magazines. So he arranged to deliver a young boy to his mother in Paris as a way of earning ship's fare, then headed to Carlsbad in what is now the Czech Republic to talk over his recent exploits with his uncle, Sigmund Freud.

The novice promoter had strong familial ties to the venerated psychoanalyst: His mother was Freud's sister, and his father's sister was Freud's wife. And when Eddie and his parents left Vienna when the boy was barely one, his two older sisters remained behind with Freud and Freud's parents until Ely Bernays got established in New York. All of which gave Eddie an intimate connection to the Father of Psychoanalysis, a connection he capitalized on every chance he got.

On this trip he and Freud took long walks in the woods, where they must have made quite a sight—the Austrian uncle, walking stick in hand, wearing his familiar green Tyrolean hat with a feather and a ram's horn stuck in the hatband, salt-and-pepper knickers, and brown brogues, and his American nephew fitted out in a Brooks Brothers suit. It's not known what the pair talked about. All Eddie could remember more than fifty years later was his uncle's playful explanation in a restaurant that "these brook trout are swimming in the order of their price range," and Freud's gentle admonition that his nephew not swat an insect on the tablecloth, preferring to "let the fly take its prome-nade on the high plateau." He also recalled Freud's "pleasant and easy attitude, his understanding sympathy, more candid and relaxed in his attitude to me than any other older man I had ever known. It was as if two close friends were exchanging confidences instead of a famous uncle of fifty-seven and an unknown nephew of twenty-two."

Whatever the specifics of their conversation, it is clear that when Eddie returned to New York in the fall of 1913 he was more taken than ever with the Viennese doctor's novel theories on how uncon-scious drives dating to childhood make people act the way they do. And Eddie was convinced that understanding the instincts and sym-bols that motivate an individual could help him shape the behavior of the masses.

He didn't waste any time testing that understanding. For starters, there was his work on Broadway, where he had signed on with Klaw and Erlanger, the General Motors of theatrical booking agents. His job was to help make hits out of plays like Jean Webster's *Daddy Long-Legs*, a precursor to "Little Orphan Annie." *Daddy* is a comedy about a twelve-year-old girl whose irrepressible spirit first helps her endure a grim orphanage, then assists her in coping with the world of wealth into which she's thrust by an anonymous benefactor.

Eddie's approach was straightforward: take techniques that had worked with *Damaged Goods* and, as he would do over and over, push them several steps further. That meant linking *Daddy Long-Legs* to a worthwhile activity, one that made theatergoers feel they were doing more than indulging in entertainment. Eddie called it hitching private interests to public ones. He joined forces with New York's State Charities Aid Association to organize a network of *Daddy Long-Legs* funds. Groups formed on college campuses and in high schools would raise money that private families could use to take in orphans.

The results were impressive. A dollmaker manufactured ten thousand *Daddy Long-Legs* dolls dressed in orphan-blue checkered gingham, and the proceeds went to the Aid Association. A famous race car driver retired his lucky Kewpie doll in favor of a *Daddy Long-Legs* doll, and other drivers did the same. As always, the achievements were chronicled in newspapers across New York State and eventually the nation, with one story crediting the campaign with spawning "a small upheaval in clubdom" and noting that the Sophia Fund of Bronxville had renamed itself the *Daddy Long-Legs* Sewing Club.

Another pattern emerged in this campaign that would resurface repeatedly. Eddie had decided that prim and proper Vassar College was an ideal place from which to launch his promotion. He arranged a meeting with influential undergraduates, got the gathering written up on the front page of the *Poughkeepsie Evening Enterprise*, and placed stories in five New York City papers: the *Times, World, Sun, Tribune,* and *Post*—all based on 15 cents collected from the students.

Officials at Vassar were not amused. "It could never have been inferred by any readers that it was a joke collection of fifteen cents, made, as the girls supposed, for a joke and nothing else," Elizabeth Hazelton Haight, head of the Vassar Alumnae Council's publicity committee, wrote Eddie several days after the stories appeared. In a separate letter to the Aid Society she wrote, "I surmise Mr. Bernays' advertising methods have simply run away with him without your cognizance, and I hope that you will check his use of the name of the college until there are facts here that warrant it."[6]

Eddie was chagrined, but he insisted later that he had learned a lesson: "That it is sound to find out beforehand what people's reactions may be." His reason for finding out, however, was so he could adjust his tactics rather than change course. As he continued in his memoirs, "Vassar's timidity didn't slow my ardor. I was able to make arrangements for several Vassar alumnae nights at *Daddy Long-Legs*. . . . The Friday after Thanksgiving, there was a greater demand for tickets than the house could fill."[7]

The up-and-coming press agent made an even bigger stir in the rarefied world of dance, handling publicity for the U.S. tour of Sergei Diaghilev's Ballet Russe. Diaghilev, a Russian aristocrat and veteran of the acclaimed Imperial Russian Theater, had assembled a company blending classical ballet with the modern dance of Isadora Duncan. He featured the most sought-after European dancers, including Waslaw Nijinsky; dazzled audiences with his use of music, set decoration, color, costume, light, and story; and revitalized a theatrical form that had become ponderous and stereotyped. Rave reviews poured in across Europe, and now, in the summer of 1915, it was announced that the Ballet Russe would make its American debut the following January.

It was left to a twenty-three-year-old agriculture student to sell the Ballet Russe to a country that didn't care much for European culture, knew and cared even less about Russia, and thought men had no business dancing on the stage wearing slippers and tights.

But Eddie was coming to thrive on just this sort of challenge. He began by acknowledging that he was as ignorant about the ballet as the public he sought to enlighten, then set out toward self-enlightenment. That meant digging up all the information he could from the library, secondhand bookstores, and the Metropolitan Opera Company, which was sponsoring the Ballet Russe tour. It also meant eliciting bits of dance wisdom from Fred A. King, the arts editor of *Literary Digest*, and from budding ballerina Natasha Rambova, who later married Rudolph Valentino. And it meant conducting what is today called opinion research, but in 1915 Bernays's research consisted mainly of chatting with people and forming educated guesses about what they thought of the ballet and why.

Having roughly determined what the public didn't know or didn't like about ballet, Eddie set out to educate them and alter their attitude. The packet he prepared for the press suggests the inventive slants he used to get skeptical editors interested in the ballet. It featured "4 pages sketch of Nijinsky's life, 2 pages Choreography Becomes Chirography, 3 pages Nijinsky's mother-in law brands him a spy, 3 pages Are American Men Ashamed of Being Graceful? 1 page World's Greatest Dancer Walks Broadway Unnoticed, 2 pages Dreaming a Ballet Into Being, 1 page Nothing Like a Stencil To Keep My Lady Warm, 1 page Life of Ballet Girl, 1 page It's Safety Pins that Keeps the Ballet Russe Together, 21 pages (15 stories) of fashions, novelties, and influence of the Ballet on modern dress."[8]

Eddie's stints in journalism had also shown him where he could cut corners. Would a reader recognize that the ballet's press person had written the *Vanity Fair* story about the ballet? No problem, he would shuffle the letters of his name around and become Aybern Edwards. The *Ladies' Home Journal* wouldn't run promotional photographs for fear its readers might be offended by skirts that didn't reach below the knees? No problem. For $600 Eddie engaged a pair of painters to add some length to the ballerinas' skirts, and the pictures ran in a two-page color spread that reached millions of unknowing subscribers.

Then there was the problem of how to make the press pay attention to Flores Revalles, the principal ballerina in *Scheherazade*. He tried calling a press conference, but only the *Morning Telegraph* showed up. So a short time later Eddie had Revalles photographed in a tight-fitting fringed gown at the Bronx Zoo with a long, harmless snake draped around her body. The seductive shot was distributed across the country, with a caption saying the subject had selected a cobra, but through her charm and beauty had rendered it harmless, and that she could be seen almost every day in Bronx Park musing over the reptile's sinuous movements.

Newspapers ran that story on page one, which Eddie thought splendid. "I urged Revalles to make a pet snake her trademark and never to travel without one," he recalled. "She hesitated, but agreed—show people intuitively adjust themselves to getting publicity for themselves, whatever the method. When I saw how easily Revalles became a national celebrity, I recognized how necessary it was to look behind a person's fame to ascertain whether the basis was real or fictitious. Public visibility had little to do with real value.

"Without the snake or some equivalent, Flores Revalles, an attractive, provocative and talented girl, might well have had to wait years for national recognition. The snake took up a long lag time."[9]

Stunts like that were standard for press agents of the day as they promoted popular movie stars like Douglas Fairbanks, Mary Pickford, and Norma Talmadge. But Eddie had a flair few could rival. He worked for clients with profiles high enough to ensure that his gimmicks would assume mythic dimensions, and unlike most of his contemporaries, he learned from and grew with each new client. And recognizing that press coverage wasn't the only way to draw attention to clients like the ballet company, he enticed manufacturers of jewelry, handbags, lampshades, table linens, and other products to introduce models inspired by the color and design of Ballet Russe sets and costumes.

Adella Hughes, founding director of the Cleveland Symphony Orchestra, watched Bernays's machinations as the ballet prepared to visit the Midwest. "No project was ever better prepared for in the matter of publicity and promotion," she wrote in her 1947 autobiography, *Music Is My Life.* "The Metropolitan Opera people had placed this in the hands of Edward L. Bernays. The value and quality of the promotional material that came from his office have never been equalled by any other organization within my experience."[10]

The *New York Dramatic Mirror* agreed, writing in its December 4, 1915, issue: "Congratulations are due Edward L. Bernays, general press representative of the Serge de Diaghilew Imperial Ballet Russe, for the excellent showing he has made in recent numbers of magazines. In these days of world crises it is, indeed, no easy task to secure publicity for mere amusements. One can scarcely pick up a periodical of late without finding illustrated articles about Karsavina, Nijinsky, Bohn and other leading members of the famous organization."[11]

There were, of course, hitches, including some major ones that threatened to sabotage the tour. Nijinsky, who'd been ballyhooed more than anyone else in the company, was arrested in Hungary as an enemy alien and missed the whole first season. When he finally was freed, he sprained his ankle and missed most of the follow-up tour. French conductor Pierre Monteux also was missing in action at first, in his case fighting Germans on the French front during World War I. And it seemed everyone on the tour was romantically entangled with everyone else. The most titillating and tumultuous of those relationships, according to Bernays, involved Diaghilev; his longtime lover, Nijinsky; Nijinsky's new wife, Romola; and Diaghilev's new lover, Léonide Massine, who had replaced Nijinsky during the first U.S. tour.

What kind of impression did those affairs of the heart and of high culture have on the young promoter? His three years with the ballet "taught me more about life than I have learned from politics, books, romance, marriage and fatherhood in the years since," he wrote five decades later. "I had never imagined that the interpersonal relations of the members of a group could be so involved and complex, full of medieval intrigue, illicit love, misdirected passion and aggression. But while it happened, I took it all for granted as part of a stimulating job."[12]

And it wasn't just Bernays who was profoundly affected by the whole ballet experience. A nation that was used to chortling over Charlie Chaplin or rejoicing with the high-stepping Ziegfeld girls found itself drawn to this more refined, decidedly European entertainment. "The whole country was discussing the ballet," Eddie wrote. "The ballet liberated American dance and, through it, the American spirit. It fostered a more tolerant view toward sex; it changed our music and our appreciation of it. . . . The ballet scenarios made modern art more palatable; color assumed new importance. It was a turning point in the appreciation of the arts in the United States."

While he was wrapping up his work with the Ballet Russe in 1917, Eddie was presented with another European artistic sensation to introduce to America: Enrico Caruso, the greatest tenor of his time and one of the music world's greatest characters.

Plugging Caruso meant following what was becoming a familiar pattern. First came the press releases, then the visits to editors and publishers. He also coined phrases aimed at capturing public atten-tion, dubbing Caruso "the man with the orchid-lined voice." What dis-tinguished this assignment from earlier ones was the amount of time Eddie spent observing the artist up close, staying in the same hotels and remaining on call twenty-four hours a day during a swing through Pittsburgh, Cincinnati, and Toledo.

Being on call sometimes meant handling crises—like the time when, at the banquet following a nine-encore performance in Cincinnati, the great singer suddenly slid under the table and wouldn't come out until Eddie ordered someone to shut a nearby window, the source of a draft that Caruso worried would give him a cold. Or when, at Pittsburgh's Shenley Hotel, the tenor insisted on two extra mattresses and seven-teen more pillows. With help from the hotel manager Eddie dug up the extra bedding, and Caruso supervised the construction of a triple-tiered bed with pillows placed around the edges to keep out breezes.

Then there was the time a hotel wedding party on the floor below was keeping Caruso awake. He called Eddie, who called the manager, who called the revelers, who, when they heard who the complainant was, willingly agreed to be relocated nine floors down.

Of course, Eddie was well compensated for his labors as advance man and nursemaid. The Metropolitan Musical Bureau, which had hired him, took 15 percent of all concert receipts, and he earned 25 percent of the bureau's profits, which meant thousands of dollars. What really thrilled the twenty-five-year-old promoter, however, was Caruso's acceptance of him as an equal.

"We acted like two boys toward each other—boys who like and understand each other," Eddie recalled. "We never had to translate our feelings into words. After I had seen him several times he called me by what I suppose was an Italian diminutive added to my name—Bernaysi."[13]

Eddie also was fascinated by the public's adoration of Caruso. And, in a lesson he'd learned while working with the Ballet Russe and that he would later apply in behalf of corporate moguls and American presidents, he realized that such impressions could easily be fashioned or reshaped. "The overwhelming majority of the people who reacted so spontaneously to Caruso had never heard him before," Eddie wrote. "The public's ability to create its own heroes from wisps of impressions and its own imagination and to build them almost into flesh-and-blood gods fascinated me. Of course, I knew the ancient Greeks and other early civilized peoples had done this. But now it was happening before my eyes in contemporary America."

The press agent's own image got a lift from Caruso's American visit. In a tribute repeated by other profilers, music critic Pitts Sanborn of the *New York Globe* referred to Eddie as "the Caruso of press agents and the press agent of Caruso."

While most of his time in those early days was taken up boosting the careers of other artists, he also experimented, at a time when anything seemed possible, with composing his own art. His proudest was a ten-poem set that ran in *The Broadway Anthology*, a sixty-page book of poetry by four press agents.

Like his other verses, the one about Caruso, titled "The Pillow Cases," sought to make press-agentry seem poetic, but it also underscored the thin line between cleverness and chicanery:

> On the platform patiently nestled were twenty-six pieces of luggage,
> Twenty-six pieces of luggage, containing more than their content,
> Twenty-six pieces of luggage would get him the story, he had not given himself.
> Craftily, one lured the reporters to look on this bulging baggage.
> "Pillows and pillows and pillows," was whispered, "Tonight he will sleep on them."
> Vulture-like swooped down the porters,
> Bearing them off to the taxis.
> Next morning the papers carried the story: "Singer Transports His Own Bedding,"
> But the artist slept soundly on Ostermoors that night.
> The baggage held scores for the orchestra.[14]

· · ·

The war raging in Europe affected Eddie, as it did most Americans, long before America joined in.

First there was its dampening effect on grain exports, which effectively shut down Ely Bernays's lucrative grain-trading business. Americans' demand for news about the war also complicated the job of Broadway press agents, who fought even more fiercely for the meager space that remained. And the enmity from the battlefields spilled over even to the Ballet Russe, where Pierre Monteux, Diaghilev's French conductor, agreed to conduct the works of dead German composers like Beethoven but not live ones like Richard Strauss, whose *Till Eulenspiegel* Monteux was scheduled to conduct.

Eddie launched his campaign to enlist on April 6, 1917, the very day America declared war on Germany. He signed up for the army, then wrote to top army and navy officers to press his case. Finally he used a contact from the music world to reach a colonel at the recruiting office, who scheduled him for a physical.

The verdict: flat feet and defective vision. He demanded and received a second exam, which produced the same results, and was officially turned down for active duty.

Rejection only made him more determined. He'd always been a bit insecure about his Austrian roots, his Jewishness, and most of all his diminutive 5-foot-4-inch stature. Now he was determined to prove he was a true American capable of defending his country. A string of successful publicity campaigns had taught him how to get his way, so he decided to conduct a campaign in his own behalf. He wrote to the Red Cross in France asking for "any position for which you believe my qualifications and past experience fit me." He wrote to the Commission on Military Training offering to get musicians to perform at army camps. He even helped out at his local draft board, organizing its statistical and clerical functions.

When none of that produced results, Eddie helped sell U.S. bonds and war saving stamps, promoted recruitment rallies, and arranged publicity for a patriotic music festival. He also outlined in *Musical America* what the journal called a "vivid, dramatic, convincing" plan for musicians to pitch in to the war effort. Whenever singers performed, he advised, they should include a song about the military. Same for orchestras and songwriters, while music store owners were urged to donate instruments for the troops. And "naval recruiting would take on tremendous impetus if there were daily parades of bluejackets through the city streets, headed by the ship's band."[15]

Being involved on the periphery was frustrating, however, and he finally wangled an interview with Ernest Poole, head of the Foreign Press Bureau of the U.S. Committee on Public Information (CPI), the closest thing to a propaganda bureau the government had back then. Poole seemed impressed by a stack of testimonial letters Eddie brought along, but he insisted, given Eddie's birth in an enemy country, that any assignment with the CPI await a complete investigation by Military Intelligence.

The probe took several months, but the result was a letter from the chief of Military Intelligence attesting that Eddie's "abilities are unquestionably remarkable. We have nothing in our files to indicate any disloyal activity and the suspicions that might arise from his infancy in Austria and his Austrian parentage are far outweighed by the extremely cordial vouchers for his loyalty contained in letters from Captain F. P. Adams, Earl Derr Biggers, Frank Crowninshield, and many others, all well aware of his Austrian nativity but convinced of his desire to serve this country."[16]

Finally given his chance to serve, Eddie recruited Ford, International Harvester, and scores of other American firms to distribute literature on U.S. war aims to foreign contacts and post U.S. propaganda in the windows of 650 American offices overseas. He distributed postcards to Italian soldiers at the front so they could boost morale at home, and he planted propaganda behind the German lines to sow dissent. He organized rallies at Carnegie Hall featuring freedom fighters from Poland, Czechoslovakia, and other states that were anxious to break free of the Austro-Hungarian Empire. And to counter German propaganda he had American propaganda printed in Spanish and Portuguese and inserted into export journals sent across Latin America.

In short, he helped win America over to an unpopular war using precisely the techniques he'd used to promote *Daddy Long-Legs* and the Ballet Russe.

Eddie wasn't part of the CPI brain trust, as some of his reminiscences suggest; he was head of the Export Section and co-head of the Latin American Section of the Foreign Press Bureau, which was one of several bureaus of the CPI. Still, with most bureau staffers plucked from newspapers or universities, he was one of the few versed in the hard-nosed tactics needed to capture and keep the attention of the war-weary public in America and abroad. And, as always, he outhustled almost everyone else and exhibited more flashes of inspired salesmanship. Poole later remembered him as "one of the ablest and most devoted younger workers on our staff."[17] And in 1918, when there was question about Eddie's being drafted for a military clerkship, CPI Chairman George Creel drafted a letter saying, "As you know, our policy is not to interfere with military service in any degree, but it is most certainly the case that Mr. Bernays' present position is far more important to the Government than any clerkship that he might fill."[18]

When it came to his role at the Paris Peace Conference, where he was part of a sixteen-person CPI press team, the reviews were less glowing. Before the team set sail, Eddie put out a press release announcing the mission, and the *New York World* ran a story saying the "announced object of the expedition is 'to interpret the work of the Peace Conference by keeping up a worldwide propaganda to disseminate American accomplishments and ideals.'"[19]

That set off a firestorm, with Republicans in Congress charging that Creel and the CPI were perpetuating their censorship of the press even though the war was over and skewing coverage to favor the Democratic president, Woodrow Wilson. Creel insisted the mission was never intended to influence coverage by American reporters, and in a book published two years later he blamed the whole mess on Eddie's statement, although he didn't name him specifically.[20] James R. Mock and Cedric Larson, in *Words That Won the War,* confirmed that "Creel was not uniformly pleased with the post-Armistice work of Bernays."[21]

The battles over Paris can only be understood in terms of a wider disillusionment in America over the bloody war the nation was emerging from. Many Americans still weren't sure why they had fought or what they'd achieved, and they didn't want to get further entangled overseas. The Senate, sensing those sentiments, voted down the Treaty of Versailles and repudiated the League of Nations, which President Wilson had passionately promoted and which Eddie had enthusiastically embraced.

Eddie was convinced he was being made a scapegoat for the failures in Paris, and he sought to set the record straight in his autobiography. Poole, he wrote, had okayed his statement to the press. And Creel was "tired or disheartened by the criticism of the senators and the press. But whatever it was, it finally wore him down. I can't understand his giving up; he had always been a fighter. But it is tragically clear that he did not fight to maintain the functioning of our press mission, which he himself had created to serve as a press relations body."[22]

Historians still debate those conflicting interpretations, but whoever's right, the controversy offers insights into the way Eddie operated then and until his death seventy-seven years later. He viewed activities with which he was involved in epic terms, as events that helped shape American and world culture, whether it was the Paris Peace Conference or the U.S. tours of Caruso and the Ballet Russe. He was exceedingly proprietary about his role in those events, seeing himself as having battled for the public good as others succumbed to temptation, and doing all he could to ensure that history would see him in the same heroic light. And he always got the last word because he outlived contemporaries like Creel, who died twelve years before Eddie wrote his autobiography and therefore was unable to defend himself.

Then there was Eddie's temper. He prided himself on his mild-mannered disposition, on speaking from fact rather than emotion, and on responding with reason rather than anger, but he was not one to be lightly crossed. Or, as Creel discovered, to play the patsy. It's apparent in his memoirs, in the many interviews he granted, and in his relationships at the office and at home that if you punched him, you'd best be prepared for a counterpunch or a barrage of blows. Question his motives or effectiveness, and he'd marshal all his tactical and creative resources to prove you wrong, doing so effectively enough to make you wonder whether you were wrong and to make you think twice about questioning him in the future.

All those personality traits were on full display in his battle with Creel and the others, which he described in his memoirs with a vigor that suggested it had transpired months or weeks before, rather than forty-seven years earlier. "I believe that Creel's failure to insist on effective handling of Peace Conference press relations—that is, to maintain liaison with the public—helped to lose the peace for us," Eddie wrote. "In 1918 I was concerned about the future of the world. I still am. Lack of effective public relations between President Wilson and the people of the United States, historians confirm, was one of the reasons for the rejection of the League of Nations by the United States. The final breakdown of the League in the early Thirties was due in large part to the same lack of good public relations."

His experience in Paris may have left Eddie disillusioned about his government's failure to grasp the power of publicity, but it reinforced his belief in his new vocation and how it could mold the public mind. He had an opportunity to test those tenets even before he got back to America.

At one of many cocktail parties he attended in Paris after the breakup of the CPI press mission, he met Haisan Kendry, an aide to Arabia's Emir Feisal, who fought alongside the fabled Lawrence of Arabia in the war against the Turks. Kendry and Feisal wanted Eddie's help in rallying Arab-Americans to push for U.S. recognition of Arabia as an independent state, one of the few hopes they saw for forestalling British and French bids to carve up the land.

Eddie did eventually talk to lots of Arabs in New York, who "were strong for independence for their homeland but had no inclination to dig into their pockets and back their enthusiasm with necessary funds." While things didn't work out with the emir, the experience planted in Eddie's mind an idea that "doing publicity for other nations, applying my experience to other countries, might be a fascinating, constructive career"—an idea he would later carry forward from Lithuania to Guatemala and from India to Israel.

That was one of many dreams he brought back from Paris. The world was changing, he realized, and he saw himself on the cusp of that change, ready to exploit the new optimism and opportunities infecting America and the world.

"I knew that musical and theatrical press-agentry and publicity would not satisfy me, after my experiences in the broader theater of world affairs," he wrote, looking back. "I was intent on carrying forward what I had learned in my work with *Damaged Goods*, the Russian Ballet, Caruso and the Committee on Public Information. The impact words and pictures made on the minds of men throughout Europe made a deep impression on me. I recognized that they had been powerful factors in helping win the war.

"Paris became a training school without instructors, in the study of public opinion and people. . . . The process was as fortuitous as the flight of windswept pollen."

Lighting Up AMERICA

2

U.S. TOBACCO TYCOONS SCORED NEARLY AS STUNNING A TRIUMPH as did U.S. troops during World War I. When America joined the war, cigarettes were considered unsavory, if not unmanly; most men preferred cigars, pipes, or chewing tobacco. But cigarettes proved more convenient in the trenches, new blended tobaccos produced a milder and more appealing product, and Uncle Sam began putting cigarettes in soldiers' rations, with the result that many doughboys changed their smoking habits. Cigarettes were manly things now, the stuff of warriors. And as their use among men soared, so did the profits of the companies making them. All of which convinced cigarette makers that the time was ripe to open a second front, this time targeting females.

In 1928, just as they were beginning that push, Edward L. Bernays began working for George Washington Hill, head of the American Tobacco Company, which made America's fastest-growing brand of cigarettes, Lucky Strikes. "Hill," Bernays recalled later, "became obsessed by the prospect of winning over the large potential female market for Luckies. 'If I can crack that market, I'll get more than my share of it,' he said to me one day. 'It will be like opening a new gold mine right in our front yard.'"[1]

The war and changing social mores already were helping Hill tap that lode. Many women who'd replaced men in factories or served abroad had taken up the habit, defying the taboo against female smoking, and college coeds were trying to tear down barriers against women smoking in public places. The share of cigarettes consumed by women more than doubled from 1923 to 1929, but it still was just 12 percent, far lower than Hill had hoped.

The quickest way to rally more women to his cause, the tobacco man believed, was to zero in on their waistlines. His theory was simple: slimness was coming into vogue, and cigarettes could be sold to the public, and especially to women, as a fat-free way to satisfy their hunger. He'd already settled on a slogan—"Reach for a Lucky Instead of a Sweet"—and to bring it to life he turned to the thirty-six-year-old Bernays, whom he'd been paying $25,000 a year just to be available.

It was a wise choice. Bernays didn't invent fashions like the pursuit of a svelte figure, but he was becoming the acknowledged master of accentuating such trends and capitalizing on them for his clients, a process he termed "crystallizing public opinion." And during his eight-year association with the tobacco tycoon he would make clear his willingness to employ whatever antics or deceptions it took to do that crystallizing, including trying to discredit new research linking smoking to deadly diseases.

Bernays launched the campaign against sweets with his tried-and-true tactic of enlisting "experts," in this case convincing Nickolas Muray, a photographer friend, to ask other photographers and artists to sing the praises of the thin. "I have come to the conclusion," Muray wrote, "that the slender woman who, combining suppleness and grace with slenderness, who instead of overeating sweets and desserts, lights a cigarette, as the advertisements say, has created a new standard of female loveliness. . . . I am interested in knowing if my own judgment concurs with that of others, and should be most happy to have your opinion on this subject."[2] Who could argue that thin wasn't better than fat? Few did, and the results were forwarded to newspapers, with similar "surveys" readied for actors, athletes, "beautiful girls," society women, and male dancers.

Magazines and newspapers also were furnished with the latest findings on the get-thin trend. For fashion editors, that meant photo after
photo of slender Parisian models in haute couture dresses. For news
editors, it meant testimonials like one from the former chief of the
British Association of Medical Officers of Health warning that sweets
caused tooth decay and advising that "the correct way to finish a meal
is with fruit, coffee and a cigarette. The fruit," Dr. George F. Buchan
continued, "hardens the gums and cleans the teeth; the coffee stimu-
lates the flow of saliva in the mouth and acts as a mouth wash; while
finally the cigarette disinfects the mouth and soothes the nerves."[3]

Bernays even persuaded dancing-school entrepreneur Arthur
Murray to sign a letter testifying that "on the dance floor, results of
over-indulgence are quickly revealed—causing embarrassment not
only to one's dancing partner but also to other dancers by encroaching
on more than a fair share of space on a crowded or, as is often the case,
on a dance floor of limited proportions. Dancers today, when tempted
to overindulge at the punch bowl or the buffet, reach for a cigarette
instead."[4]

Not content to rely on the press or on the influence of experts, he
also worked directly to change the way people ate. Hotels were urged
to add cigarettes to their dessert lists, while the Bernays office widely
distributed a series of menus, prepared by an editor of *House and
Garden*, designed to "save you from the dangers of overeating." For
lunch and dinner they suggested a sensible mix of vegetables, meats,
and carbohydrates, followed by the advice to "reach for a cigarette
instead of dessert."

And he proposed that homemakers hire kitchen cabinetmakers to
provide special spaces to hold cigarettes the same as they did for flour
and sugar, urged container makers to provide labeled tins for smokes
just as they did for tea and coffee, and encouraged home economics
writers to "stress the importance of cigarettes in home-making. . . .
Just as the young and inexperienced housewife is cautioned not to let
her supplies of sugar or salt or tea or coffee run low, so she should be
advised that the same holds true of cigarettes."[5]

Seldom if ever had a publicity campaign been carried out on so many fronts, and seldom if ever again will those responsible save, and make public, the details of their orchestrations the way Bernays did when he left to the Library of Congress twenty-four boxes of records pertaining to the American Tobacco Company.

Those records also reveal that, as the anti-sweet campaign was catching on, the Bernays office even took to writing jokes. "A moment in the mouth and ten years upon the hips" was one sent to *The New Yorker, Life,* and the *Harvard Lampoon.* Then there was a series of "Candy Advertisements of the Future," with entries like this one: "A little fat guy smoking a Lucky? Yeh, he was here about ten minutes ago but he disappeared. Where did he go? Nowhere. I'm telling you, he just smoked the Lucky and disappeared."[6]

The sugar companies and other enterprises weren't amused. Hill got angry letters from cocoa brokers and peanut butter makers, from the manufacturers of salted nuts and of candy, including one who charged that American Tobacco's attacks were "unfair, unsportsman-like and absolutely avaricious." And Senator Reed Smoot of Utah, a big beet sugar state, struck back from the Senate floor, calling the tobacco company campaign "an orgy of buncombe, quackery, and downright falsehood and fraud."

Bernays responded by casting the controversy in the favorable glow of what he called "the new competition." In a letter he drafted for business professors, to be signed by an esteemed economist, Bernays wrote, "A battle carried on fairly in this manner can serve the public in presenting both sides of a discussable question and in bringing the underlying democratic principle of free competition fairly to the front."[7]

He realized that controversy breeds coverage, which almost always was good for his client. And he knew that the high ground was the best place from which to wage any battle—an assumption borne out by responses to his letters on the "new competition" from bank presidents and leading lawyers, along with the chairmen of economics departments at schools as diverse as Tufts University and the Utah Agricultural College. All this seemed to delight Hill, who wrote to

Bernays, "I think the record shows that we have 'shut them up' pretty well."[8]

A month after the first campaigns to attract women smokers, Hill ordered up a second series, this time stressing moderation. The "moderation" he had in mind, of course, meant consuming fewer sweets and more cigarettes. Bernays responded with an intricate proposal for a Moderation League, one that, ironically, he wanted to model on the "the Anti-Tuberculosis Association, Anti-Cancer Associations, Cardiac Associations etc."[9]

Hill balked at the long-range program, but loved Bernays's proposal to sign up the glamorous Ziegfeld Girls. Six of the dancers formed the Ziegfeld Contour, Curve and Charm Club, signing a pledge to "renounce the false pleasure of the table—fattening foods, drinks, and cloying sweets. But I make no sacrifices: I shall smoke cigarettes."

One thing led to another on the moderation front, and Bernays recalled that "what we did had all the effect of a long-range program, for as soon as one action was gaining momentum we proposed another and carried that out. Hill was happy."[10] Which isn't surprising since, as Hill exulted in a December 1928 letter to Bernays, American Tobacco's revenues rose by $32 million that year, and Luckies "show a greater increase than all other Cigarettes combined."[11]

Bernays himself never smoked, although his wife Doris did for several years. And the man who helped persuade tens of thousands of Americans to give up sweets in favor of cigarettes admitted later in an interview, "I didn't like the taste [of tobacco]. I prefer chocolate."[12]

· · ·

Hill didn't especially care what his PR man liked personally so long as he continued peddling tobacco products as if he meant it. Selling cigarettes was more passion than occupation for Hill, a rawboned, diminutive figure who presided from behind a desk that seemed to take up half of the corner office he had inherited from his father. Wearing a tilted Stetson with fishhooks protruding from the brim, he'd hold court in a plainspoken, reasoned manner. Then, without warning, he would explode in a tirade at his stenographer, advertising executive, or anyone else who happened to be there. He insisted on being chauffered around in an open Cadillac, bodyguard at his side, and demanded the car be stationed at the curb outside his Fifth Avenue office in case he needed it. His greatest pleasure, however, revolved around the Lucky Strikes he would eventually elevate to America's best-selling cigarette brand. There were Luckies stuffed in all four compartments of the cigarette box on his desk, Luckies secured by clamps to the windows of his car, and two dachshunds, Mr. Lucky and Mrs. Strike, roaming his estate in the Hudson Valley.

Hill loved the way Bernays used the anti-sweets campaign to promote Luckies, but that only whetted his appetite to crack the female market. So early in 1929 he summoned Bernays and demanded, "How can we get women to smoke on the street? They're smoking indoors. But, damn it, if they spend half the time outdoors and we can get 'em to smoke outdoors, we'll damn near double our female market. Do something. Act!"[13]

Bernays understood they were up against a social taboo that cast doubt on the character of women who smoked, but he wasn't sure of the basis of the inhibition or how it could be overcome. So he got Hill to agree to pay for a consultation with Dr. A. A. Brill, a psychoanalyst and disciple of Bernays's uncle, Dr. Sigmund Freud.

"It is perfectly normal for women to want to smoke cigarettes," Brill advised. "The emancipation of women has suppressed many of their feminine desires. More women now do the same work as men do. Many women bear no children; those who do bear have fewer children. Feminine traits are masked. Cigarettes, which are equated with men, become torches of freedom."[14]

That rang a bell for Bernays. Why not organize a parade of prominent women lighting their "torches of freedom"? And do it on Easter Sunday, a holiday symbolizing freedom of spirit, on Fifth Avenue, America's most prestigious promenade?

He gathered a list of thirty debutantes from a friend at *Vogue*, then sent each of them a telegram signed by his secretary, Bertha Hunt. "In the interests of equality of the sexes and to fight another sex taboo I and other young women will light another torch of freedom by smoking cigarettes while strolling on Fifth Avenue Easter Sunday," the dispatch explained. "We are doing this to combat the silly prejudice that the cigarette is suitable for the home, the restaurant, the taxicab, the theater lobby but never, no, never for the sidewalk. Women smokers and their escorts will stroll from Forty-Eighth Street to Fifty-Fourth Street on Fifth Avenue between Eleven-Thirty and One O'Clock."[15]

A similar appeal was made through an advertisement in New York newspapers, this one signed by Ruth Hale, a leading feminist and wife of *New York World* columnist Heywood Broun.

The script for the parade was outlined in revealing detail in a memo from Bernays's office. The object of the event, it explained, would be to generate "stories that for the first time women have smoked openly on the street. These will take care of themselves, as legitimate news, if the staging is rightly done. Undoubtedly after the stories and pictures have appeared, there will be protests from non-smokers and believers in 'Heaven, home and mother.' These should be watched for and answered in the same papers."

The memo also discussed prominent churches the parade would pass, and from which it would like marchers to join up, including Saint Thomas's, Saint Patrick's, and "the Baptist church where John D. Rockefeller attends."

What kind of marchers would be best? "Because it should appear as news with no division of the publicity, actresses should be definitely out. On the other hand, if young women who stand for feminism— someone from the Women's Party, say—could be secured, the fact that the movement would be advertised too, would not be bad. . . . While they should be goodlooking, they should not look too 'model-y.' Three for each church covered should be sufficient. Of course they are not to smoke simply as they come down the church steps. They are to join in the Easter parade, puffing away."

The memo made it clear that not much would be left to chance: "On Monday of Holy Week, the women should be definitely decided upon. On the afternoon of Good Friday, they should be in this office, by appointment, and given their final instructions. They should [be] told where and when they are to be on duty Easter morning and furnished with Lucky Strikes. As the fashionable churches are crowded on Easter, they must be impressed with the necessity of going early. 'Business' must be worked out as if by a theatrical director, as for example: one woman seeing another smoke, opens her purse, finds cigs but no matches, asks the other for a light. At least some of the women should have men with them."

Finally, there was the matter of ensuring that the march would be preserved for posterity: "We should have a photographer to take pictures for use later in the roto sections, to guard against the possibility that the news photographers do not get good pictures for this purpose."[16]

The actual march went off more smoothly than even its scriptwriters imagined. Ten young women turned out, marching down Fifth Avenue with their lighted "torches of freedom," and the newspapers loved it.

Two-column pictures showed elegant ladies, with floppy hats and fur-trimmed coats, cigarettes held self-consciously by their sides, as they paraded down the wide boulevard. Dispatches ran the next day, generally on page one, in papers from Fremont, Nebraska, to Portland, Oregon, to Albuquerque, New Mexico. Typical was this one from the United Press: "Just as Miss Federica Freylinghusen, conspicuous in a tailored outfit of dark grey, pushed her way thru the jam in front of St. Patrick's, Miss Bertha Hunt and six colleagues struck another blow in behalf of the liberty of women. Down Fifth Avenue they strolled, puffing at cigarettes. Miss Hunt issued the following communiqué from the smoke-clouded battlefield: 'I hope that we have started something and that these torches of freedom, with no particular brand favored, will smash the discriminatory taboo on cigarettes for women and that our sex will go on breaking down all discriminations.'"[17]

Go on they did. During the following days women were reported to be taking to the streets, lighted cigarettes in hand, in Boston and Detroit, Wheeling and San Francisco. Women's clubs, meanwhile, were enraged by the spectacle, and for weeks afterward editorial writers churned out withering prose, pro and con. "Thumbs down," said the *News* in Everett, Massachusetts, while John A. Schaffer, editor and publisher of the *Chicago Evening Post*, the *Indianapolis Star*, the *Terre Haute Star*, and the *Muncie Star*, agreed that "it is always a regret to me to see women adopt the coarser attitudes and habits of men." But the headline in the Ventura, California, *Star*, "Swats Another Taboo," suggested the march may have achieved its aim, and a few weeks later Broadway theaters created a stir by admitting women to what had been men-only smoking rooms.

The uproar he'd touched off proved enlightening to Bernays. "Age-old customs, I learned, could be broken down by a dramatic appeal, disseminated by the network of media," he wrote in his memoirs. "Of course the taboo was not destroyed completely. But a beginning had been made."[18]

· · ·

The Torches of Freedom campaign remains a classic in the world of public relations, one still cited in classrooms and boardrooms as an example of ballyhoo at its most brilliant and, more important, of creative analysis of social symbols and how they can be manipulated.

Yet there's another, more troubling side to the story of Bernays's bid to get women smoking, one not discussed in his 849-page autobiography and never mentioned in his countless tellings and retellings of the American Tobacco tale over the subsequent sixty-six years.

For starters, he almost always concealed the fact that American Tobacco was behind his initiatives. Letters soliciting support from specialists came from other, seemingly independent experts like Muray the photographer or Murray the dancer. Discerning readers might have suspected that a commercial interest had prompted the campaign, but it would have taken a detective to pinpoint the company. The connection was further masked as it moved down the ladder from "expert" to press to public.

That was just what Bernays envisioned, judging from memos to American Tobacco officials. In May 1929 he wrote Hill suggesting that letters drumming up support for the "new competition" initiative "be sent through a disinterested organization—for instance, a business syndicate."[19] And a February 1930 memo to another top tobacco company official advises working through "a disinterested public-spirited citizen who would issue releases, statements, and letters just because he likes to. . . . There are many such people. We could find one."[20]

One way he found such citizens and specialists was by offering money. Sometimes it came as an honorarium, like the $100 he proposed paying a "dietician [who] talks on diet as the best means to produce moderate curves" and a "physiologist induced to comment on benefits of modern trend to reasonable figure." Then there was the $5,000 he offered to donate to the favorite charity of Mrs. Charles Dana Gibson, wife of the creator of the renowned Gibson Girl illustrations, if she would agree to sign a statement saying "she smoked Luckies and that they were kind to her throat."

After he made the offer, Bernays wrote years later, "I watched her face. I thought she would reject my offer with hauteur. I listened intently for what she would say. She said quietly, 'Why, of course, I'll be delighted.' That was all."[21]

People who received letters signed by Mrs. Gibson and the others could call the offices that mailed them to find out who was behind them. And many did, which was why Bernays left written instructions with one such office that "under no circumstances is the name or telephone number of Edward L. Bernays to be given to anyone who calls."[22]

It may have been concerns like that—about secrecy or duplicity, bribes and backpedaling—that led the *American Bankers Association Journal* to turn down Bernays's request to sign a letter on the "new competition." James E. Clark, editor of the journal, replied that "after due consideration we find that this is a matter in which we cannot participate in any way."[23]

To be fair, there's disagreement in the public relations community even today on what level of masking a client's identity is permissible, as contemporary controversies over cigarette promotions make clear, and there was far less consensus when Bernays was working for American Tobacco. Yet he set his own high standard in many an interview, then and later, such as when he told a public relations historian in 1959 that whenever he enlisted experts "we did it in an open or overt way."

Nowhere did his actions seem to contradict his words more overtly than at the Easter Parade down Fifth Avenue on March 31, 1929. His secretary, Bertha Hunt, was quoted in newspapers nationwide about her participation, but she failed to mention her connection to Bernays, American Tobacco, or Lucky Strikes. She told New York's *Evening World* that she "first got the idea for this campaign when a man with her in the street asked her to extinguish her cigaret [*sic*] as it embarrassed him. 'I talked it over with my friends, and we decided it was high time something was done about the situation.'"[24] A Shreveport, Louisiana, newspaper, meanwhile, wrote that "Miss Hunt says she is not connected with any firm."[25] And the communiqué she issued said pointedly that she and her co-marchers had "no particular brand favored."[26]

Before the parade, when women who'd been solicited to march called to ask how their names had surfaced, secretaries and other members of Bernays's staff knew just what they were expected to do: stonewall, which was what they did. And the telegram that went to *Vogue*'s debutantes apparently made no mention of the march's actual sponsors.

The outcome was one that most publicity men can only dream about: an irresistible script for a stunt, flawlessly executed, covered in nearly every paper in America, with no one detecting the fingerprints of either Bernays or his tobacco company client.

If he began by disguising his role in the battle to get women smoking, Bernays more than made up for that in later years. The parade story in particular became part of his repertoire on the speaking circuit and in scores of interviews he granted up until his death in 1995, and with each retelling the tale got more colorful and his claims more sweeping. In his 1965 memoirs, for instance, he discussed the slow process of breaking down conventions like the taboo against women smoking. But by 1971 he was telling an oral historian at Columbia University that "overnight the taboo was broken by one overt act," the 1929 Easter Sunday march.

"I was interested in this as a manifestation of leadership," Bernays continued during the Columbia session. "Hill was elated. Up to that time, no advertising had ever mentioned a woman smoking."[27] In fact as early as 1926, a year before Bernays went to work for Hill and three years before the Easter Parade, the makers of Chesterfields were displaying posters in which a woman asked her cigarette-smoking lover to "blow some my way." The next year Marlboro took up the entire back cover of *Bon Ton*, a woman's magazine, with this ad: "Women—when they smoke at all—quickly develop discerning taste. That is why Marlboros now ride in so many limousines, attend so many bridge parties, repose in so many handbags." Even American Tobacco had cautiously ventured into the fray by 1927, with a series of testimonials from opera stars and actresses that Luckies were soothing to the throat.[28]

Michael Schudson, a professor of communications and sociology at the University of California at San Diego, argues that attitudes toward women smoking in public started to shift substantially long before ads began appearing, thanks to milder cigarettes, social changes brought on by World War I, and the fact that, for many women, cigarettes had become a symbol of liberation. By the time the admen and Bernays weighed in, Schudson adds, "this was an old story."[29]

Other historians give American Tobacco a larger role in persuading women to smoke—but they say that was largely due to the efforts of Albert Lasker, a trailblazing advertising consultant who together with Hill dreamed up the notion of reaching for a Lucky instead of a sweet. They also credit public relations pioneer Ivy Lee, whose firm went to work for Hill a year before Bernays, continued there for decades afterward, and was paid $15,000 more a year than Bernays.

Allan M. Brandt, who teaches the history of science and medicine at Harvard, acknowledges those other twists and turns of smoking history but still concludes that no single event crystallized and exploited the wider trends as effectively as Bernays's parade. Calling it "a publicity stunt of genuine historical significance," Brandt writes that "Bernays had successfully reinvigorated the controversies of the previous decade, enlisting the cultural tensions over women's public smoking. . . .

"Hill and Bernays shaped and promoted the cigarette's status as the symbol of the independent feminist and the bold, glamorous flapper."[30]

· · ·

The image of elegance that Bernays shaped for the smoking woman was one that, not long before, he'd made fun of.

Back in the summer of 1927, a year before he hooked up with Hill, Bernays got a call for help from the ad agency representing Liggett and Myers, the makers of Chesterfields, Luckies' archrival. How, they asked, would Bernays counter Hill's pitch that Lucky Strikes were so "kind to your voice" that even Metropolitan Opera stars smoked them? Since it was just the kind of slogan that Bernays himself might have concocted, the admen reasoned, he was the perfect person to refute it.

His response was a familiar one—he suggested the establishment of a front group, the same sort he'd created to promote *Damaged Goods*, the play about syphilis—only this incarnation for Liggett and Myers was mainly intended to be fun. The mission of the Tobacco Society for Voice Culture would be "so to improve the CORDS of the THROAT through cigarette smoking that the public will be able to express itself in SONGS OF PRAISE or more easily to swallow anything." Free membership would be offered to "all lovers of the weed, including students of MUSIC, therapeutics, elocution or dentistry." And its "ULTI-MATE GOAL" would be "a smoking TEACHER for every SINGER."[31]

When a New York judge ruled the society too frivolous to be incorporated, newspapers wrote about the decision just the way Bernays hoped they would. He was even more delighted when a judge in New Jersey said it was okay to open there. As a sign of its goodwill the new society vowed to "establish homes for singers, senators, and sensationalists whose voices have cracked under the weight and strain of their numerous cigaret testimonials."

Coverage for serious causes often is tough to come by, but the press, then as now, loved a good joke—which was why *The New Yorker* ran an item in "Talk of the Town" poking fun at the Lucky ads and the *New York Post* was inspired by the Tobacco Society to run a satire noting, "Whether It's Egg-Plant, Soccer or Dr. Stratton You Oppose, Mr. Johnson Finds an Organization Exists to Collect Your Dues." The *Medical Review of Reviews*, which Bernays had once edited, took a more serious slant, but one that served Liggett at least as well: it surveyed leading physicians who, as expected, confirmed that it was impossible for one cigarette to do a better job than all the rest at preventing throat irritation.[32]

How did Hill take the taunts?

First he investigated Bernays; then he hired him. "During the course of our campaign rough-looking characters slithered into our office from time to time and asked for a list of our clients," Bernays recalled, adding that he later learned the characters were detectives hired by Hill. Then David Schulte, owner of the Schulte cigar store chain, called to contract his services. Bernays was told to name his price for handling an unspecified project—with one catch: "Not advising any tobacco interests but ours." Bernays agreed, severing his ties with Liggett and signing on with Schulte for twice as long and 50 percent more money. It was another nine months before he learned that Schulte had been fronting for Hill.[33]

"'You've been on the American Tobacco payroll for nine months,'" Bernays recalls Hill crowing. "'You were working for Liggett and Myers, weren't you? And we got you from them, didn't we? And you didn't know anything about it. That's why Lucky Strike is on top.'"

Hill also failed to mention that he had hired Bernays's competitor, Ivy Lee, years before. Neither of the public relations pioneers knew the other was working for American Tobacco, Bernays says, although Hill did eventually tell Bernays why he'd hired them both: "If I have both of you, my competitors can't get either of you." And while Hill was generous with his PR advisers, their retainers looked chintzy next to what he paid himself: in 1930, the year Luckies rose to number one, Hill's salary and bonuses totaled $2.5 million.

"I deplored the methods he used," Bernays recounted in 1965, "but I reasoned that if Hill's highly respected company behaved that way, it must be part of the accepted pattern of corporate behavior. Possibly business was always conducted like a war. Hill acted like a general, intent on confounding an enemy."[34] Several years later Bernays offered an even harsher judgment: "In retrospect, Mr. Hill was a troglodyte, a dictator, intent on exerting the monopoly principle to the limit of his power to be the dominant figure in his field."[35]

Those assessments almost certainly were colored by the harsh way historians had judged Hill, and by Bernays's desire to distance himself from the tobacco man and the increasingly tainted tobacco industry. Regardless of what he said after the fact, Bernays had spent eight years deeply absorbed in the strange and intoxicating world of George Washington Hill, riding the waves of a soaring, swashbuckling enterprise, reveling in the fact that Hill was paying him an annual retainer that in today's terms would amount to $300,000, and not seeming to mind Hill's disregard for people deceived and rules broken. In fact Bernays was the one who pointed the way in much of that deception and rule breaking. And while Hill affected the attitudes of a cowboy and Bernays feigned an intellectual air, the two were a lot alike: Bernays was thirty-six when he went to work for American, Hill just seven years older. Both had an abiding faith in American capitalism and the rewards it could offer them, both had demanding fathers before whom they were determined to prove themselves, both sensed they were at the cutting edge of an evolving profession, and both were anxious to test the limits.

It's unlikely the two ever became real friends, but they offered each other something valuable. Bernays's gift for promotion helped Hill push Lucky Strikes past its archcompetitors, Camels and Chesterfields, while Hill enthusiastically endorsed Bernays's most outlandish and expensive schemes.

"I doubt whether a serious business committee today would permit me to retain a psychoanalyst to evaluate billboards [and] parade women on Fifth Avenue lighting cigarettes as symbolic torches of freedom,"

Bernays reflected decades later. "These ideas would be regarded as far out, remote or risky. Or if by chance they were accepted, they would be so diluted by the time they got into the works that they would be worn thin and possibly ineffective."[36]

. . .

And what would today's buttoned-down executives say about Bernays's proposal to conduct a propaganda campaign in behalf of a color?

That crusade seemed a bit far-fetched even in 1934. Hill remained determined to win over women smokers, but company surveys showed that many women wouldn't smoke Luckies because its green package with the red bull's-eye clashed with their favorite clothing. "What do you suggest?" Bernays remembered Hill asking. The PR man replied, "Change the Lucky package to a neutral color that will match anything they wear." That was all Hill needed to set him off: "I've spent millions of dollars advertising the package. Now you ask me to change it. That's lousy advice."

At which point Bernays offered advice that kicked off a campaign almost as legendary as the Torches of Freedom parade. "If you won't change the color of the package," he reasoned, "change the color of fashion—to green."[37]

Change an entire nation's taste in colors? This was an idea so egocentric and eccentric that few public relations executives then or now would suggest it and fewer still would have any notion how to make it work. But Bernays's specialty was determining why the public preferred certain things, then reengineering those preferences to coincide with his clients' needs, and he set off on his six-month task with supreme confidence.

First he analyzed the color itself, much as his uncle Sigmund might have done. A book entitled *The Language of Color* told him that green was "an emblem of hope, victory, and plenty" and "symbolical of solitude and peace." Those were upbeat themes to build on. Even more encouraging were statistics showing that green already made up about 20 percent of the current lines being turned out by French fashion houses.

What Bernays needed was a big event to light up the world of fashion—maybe an Emerald Ball, he thought, a Bal Vert or a Mermaid Ball. He settled on a Green Ball, to be held at the stately Waldorf-Astoria and attended by New York's leading debutantes, with proceeds going to some deserving charity. And he found the ideal hostess: Mrs. Frank A. Vanderlip, chairwoman of the Women's Infirmary of New York and wife of the former chairman of the National City Bank.

All Mrs. Vanderlip needed to know, Bernays decided, was that proceeds would buy milk for undernourished kids, furnish clothing to cardiac patients, and support other projects at the infirmary. "I explained," he wrote later, "that a nameless sponsor would defray the costs up to $25,000; our client would donate our services to promote the ball; the color green would be the ball's motif and the obligatory color of all the gowns worn at the ball.

"I added, 'I can assure you the cause is not Paris green, a poison.'"[38]

The fashion and accessories industries were his next target. A Green Ball would require not just green gowns but also, Bernays insisted, green gloves and green shoes, green handkerchiefs, green bandeaux, and, yes, green jewelry. He began by approaching the Onondaga Silk Company, filling in its enterprising president, Philip Vogelman, on plans for the ball and suggesting he could be at the leading edge of the move to green—if he moved fast.

Vogelman signed up and invited fashion editors to the Waldorf for a Green Fashions Fall Luncheon with, of course, green menus featuring green beans, asparagus-tip salad, broiled French lamb chops with haricots verts and olivette potatoes, pistachio mousse glacé, green mints, and crème de menthe. The head of the Hunter College art department gave a talk entitled "Green in the Work of Great Artists," and a noted psychologist enlightened guests on the psychological implications of the color green. The press took note, with the *New York Sun* headline reading, "It Looks Like a Green Winter." The *Post* predicted a "Green Autumn," and one of the wire services wrote about "fall fashions stalking the forests for their color note, picking green as the modish fall wear."

But what if the new green clothing clashed with people's drapes, curtains, or other house decor? A Color Fashion Bureau, organized under the auspices of Onondaga Silk, was there with advice, sending 1,500 letters on the up-and-coming color to interior decorators, home-furnishings buyers, art industry groups, and clubwomen. The bureau also sent 5,000 announcements to department stores and merchandise managers.

Wouldn't green clash with people's summertime skin color? Not at all, according to this campaign advisory: Green "is most becoming to all degrees of burns—from the first strawberry flush to the last Indian brown. Since beach life provides the highest degree of visibility for (and of) ladies, green is naturally highly successful for bathing suits and beach ensembles."[39]

By now the bandwagon seemed to be rolling on its own. Mrs. Vanderlip enlisted for her invitation committee luminaries like Mrs. James Roosevelt, Mrs. Walter Chrysler, Mrs. Irving Berlin, and Mrs. Averell Harriman. Altman's and Bonwit Teller filled their Fifth Avenue windows with green gowns, suits, and accessories, and *Vogue* ran two pages of sketches of the green dresses to be brought to New York from Paris. Bernays was particularly delighted when "the unsuspecting opposition gave us a boost: the November magazine advertisements for Camel cigarettes showed a girl wearing a green dress with red trimmings, the colors of the Lucky Strike package. The advertising agency had chosen green because it was now the fashionable color."[40]

Just months after opening, the Color Fashion Bureau was besieged with requests for information—from 77 newspapers, 95 magazines, 29 syndicates, 301 department stores, 145 women's clubs, 175 radio stations, 83 manufacturers of furniture and home decorations, 64 interior decorators, 10 costumers, and 49 photographers and illustrators.

The lesson, Bernays wrote years afterward, is that "emphasis by repetition gains acceptance for an idea, particularly if the repetition comes from different sources."[41]

Another lesson seemed to be that if you trod softly you could keep a secret this big. The official ball program danced around the issue of who was behind it by saying, "Since the fashion trend seemed to point toward green and since green is a gay color for a fete, this ball is called The Green Ball." A woman's page editor in Philadelphia tried to learn more about where all the greenery was coming from; when she couldn't, she sent in this good-natured plea: "Let me know what you are plugging. It is so adroit that even I, hard-boiled old she-dragon, can't detect it. If, as I suspect, it is glazed chintz, I will add a description with place to buy, including prices."[42]

The Green Ball came off as planned, maybe better. It was "a gay, vivid night, something to remember," *Vogue* reported. Later in the same issue: "We thought the lovely ladies who were all done up in green to take part in the pageant of paintings looked unusually lovely. 'Green,' we were murmuring to ourselves, 'is a pretty difficult colour to wear, taken by and large,' when we discovered that each lady, before she went out into the limelight, had been made up by Marie Earle so that her face and her dress made a beautiful harmony." And then this: "The Waldorf did the graceful thing, as usual, and put a flourishing finish on The Green Ball last week by setting a Continental *boîte de nuit*. They called it the Casino Vert and carried out the colour motif of the ball by flooding the crystal chandeliers and the mirrored walls with a green-blue light."[43]

But did Hill, who attended the ball, think it and the accompanying campaign benefited him and his prized Lucky Strikes?

Bernays says the tobacco tycoon seldom offered praise, and in the case of the Green Ball "I don't recall bothering to check Hill's reaction." Still, he adds, "the color green was so omnipresent that he could not escape it. . . . [The ball] firmly established green's predominance."[44]

Other, more neutral observers disagree over the success of the green campaign. Edwin P. Hoyt, in his book *The Supersalesmen*, says the whole episode was a great example of the "phenomenal mistakes" Hill made during his career. "He wanted to establish green that year as the color for women's fashions. He failed dismally."[45] But sixteen years later author Robert Sobel reached a decidedly different conclusion: "Green did become the 'in color' that year. Hill was pleased. Bernays received a bonus."[46]

· · ·

Bernays's crusade in behalf of the color green was a precursor to today's promotions by Macy's and other retailers of products featuring the "Colors of van Gogh" and the "Palette of Picasso." Similarly, his bids to link smoking to popular causes like women's liberation and the stay-thin movement helped inspire contemporary efforts to sell cigarettes by linking them to the macho Marlboro Man and super-cool Joe Camel.

But not all of Bernays's labors for Hill reached those levels of legend, or of controversy.

There were, for instance, the billboards Hill wanted to display depicting a woman offering a package of Luckies to two men. Bernays objected, saying they made him "queasy" and recommending that, before the billboards were put up, they should be viewed by Dr. Brill, the psychiatrist who dreamed up the "torches of freedom" concept. Brill worried that having three people in the picture would confuse observers. "'Two people should appear, one man and one woman. That is life,'" Bernays recalled the psychologist saying. "'Nor should a woman offer two men a package of cigarettes. The cigarette is a phallic symbol, to be offered by a man to a woman. Every normal man or woman can identify with such a message.'

"The use of psychoanalysis as the basis of advertising is common today," Bernays added, but Brill's "lightning analysis" of the cigarette poster "may have been the first instance of its application to advertising."[47]

Bernays also proposed that, for the first time, a U.S. tobacco company aggressively court black customers. "Has any one ever found out what the likes of the colored people of the U.S. are in regard to cigarettes?" he asked in a 1931 memo to a top official at the American Tobacco Company. "I find that five million negroes are church members in the U.S. I find there are a million negro farmers in the U.S. We have just developed a close contact with the negro press, and if Luckies are the favored cigarettes, it may be possible to develop some propaganda along these lines."[48] But officials at the tobacco company declined, fearing, they said, that to take the Associated Negro Press up on its offer to do a story on American Tobacco's black employees would obligate American to run ads in papers read by a primarily black readership. And that, the officials apparently worried, might offend the company's white clients.

Quashing gossipmongering was another area where Bernays was becoming an expert. One rumor in the 1930s had Lucky Strike firing all its salesmen, an especially inflammatory charge in the midst of the depression. Bernays's first rule in deflating rumors was never to repeat them publicly, for fear of fanning them. A related precept held that the best antidote was to publicize facts and figures showing the rumor couldn't be true, which in this case meant letting people know about the large number of salesmen still working for American.

A more vexing falsehood was that American Tobacco workers had the dreaded disease leprosy and that Luckies were being contaminated. The rumor was traced to a taxi stand on New York's West Forty-second Street, but knowing who initiated it didn't help end it. That took getting the top health official in Raleigh, North Carolina, to give American an award for "the scrupulous cleanliness of its Raleigh factory."

The whispering campaign where he really got to flex his powers of persuasion began near the end of 1930, when word spread that American Tobacco had fired its Jewish workers.

Knowing the rumor was unfounded, Bernays decided to take his response directly to Jewish cigar store owners across New York City. His emissaries would be American Tobacco salesmen, but it was key that they know just what to do and say. He outlined his instructions in a December 1930 memo: "The salesman should enter a shop and gauge the character of the shop. He should then say, dependent upon the character of the shop, in Yiddish, in English with a Yiddish accent, or in straight English, 'Good morning. My name is Mehr. How is business?'

"If the answer is 'bad,' as it will pretty surely be, the salesman should say in Yiddish 'Well, we Jewish boys certainly have nothing to worry about with the American Tobacco Company. Fortunately, in this depression there is one high spot—and that is tobacco. Whether times are good or times are bad, everybody wants to smoke. Now that's true of Salisburys. Why don't you stock some of them?' Then plunge into sales talk about Salisburys. . . .

"If the attitude is questionable about the relationship of the Jews to the American Tobacco Company, the salesman should say this—'All I can tell you, like one gentleman to another gentleman—it's a lie. I've been with the American Tobacco Company. I'm a good Jew. My father was a rabbi. There are Jewish girls in the clerical department; there are Jewish boys in the order department. They got a Jewish lawyer, Louis Levy. They got a Jewish advertising man, Albert Lasker. They got me and a lot of other Jews selling. I know Blumberg, and Greenberg, and Stilberg.'

"Nothing more than that should be done," Bernays wrote. "There should be no emotion, no argument, no bets, no gathering of crowds. . . . After a day's such work, if the plan is followed out carefully, we will have a picture of the situation, and we will then make plans, dependent on what the situation is, to meet the situation."[49]

He also attacked the rumor on other fronts: getting the American Jewish Congress, the *Jewish Tribune*, and others to investigate and eventually repudiate the charges; showering the press with releases about high-ranking Jews at American Tobacco and how some of the firm's most notable innovations were "largely attributable to the business acumen of the Jew"; and dispatching staff members across the country to monitor the reaction and dispel fearmongering.

As the rumors began to fade, Hill, at Bernays's urging, let Jewish groups know how grateful he was for their help—sending donations to the Jewish Home for Children, the Jewish Philanthropic Societies of New York, the Jewish Telegraphic Agency, and the Jewish Welfare Federation; joining the Jewish Publication Society; and giving the Jewish War Veterans of the United States 5,000 Lucky Strikes to hand out to soldiers wounded in the war.

• • •

There was one "rumor," however, that wouldn't go away for Hill and his compatriots: that cigarettes could be killers.

The public in the 1920s and 1930s didn't have the kind of compelling evidence that's available today linking tobacco to cancer, heart disease, strokes, and other maladies. But people did know that smoking made them cough, irritated their throats, and had other unpleasant aftereffects. That, after all, was why American Tobacco had recruited opera stars to testify that Luckies soothed the throat, and the hollowness of that claim made it easy for Bernays to launch his campaign of ridicule for Liggett and Myers.

While he made fun of American's response, Bernays knew the company was smart to focus on public apprehension over the safety of its products, and when he went to work for Hill he made health issues a major target of his propaganda.

Spitting was an early test case. Traditionally, cigars had been rolled by hand, with factory workers twirling the end of the cigar between their lips to moisten and shape it. Cremos, made by a subsidiary of American, ended that practice when it mechanized its factory, and Hill wanted Bernays to ensure the company got credit.

"I remembered that Charles Dickens, in his notes on American travel, had complained of the nasty American habit of spitting in public, a practice that was still prevalent despite anti-spitting ordinances," Bernays wrote, looking back. "Spitting was a menace to health, since saliva could transmit tuberculosis and other diseases. I decided to draw the public's attention directly to the dangers of spitting and indirectly to the health-safety factor in Cremo cigars."[50]

The result was a massive campaign to get cities and towns to post signs warning against spitting, supplied by the tobacco company, and advertisements proclaiming, "We know spit is a horrid word but it is worse on the end of your cigar. . . . The war against Spitting is a crusade of decency . . . join it. Smoke Certified Cremo!"

American also sought to get out the word on its "toasting process," which bombarded tobacco used in Luckies with the era's latest elixir—ultraviolet rays. Bernays's claims about toasting were nearly identical to the ones he'd made light of four years earlier, when he was with Liggett. The toasting process, his releases proclaimed, "gives you a cigarette free from harsh irritants" and "kind to your throat."

He wasn't the only one making such pitches, of course. Old Gold promised "Not a cough in a carload," Camels countered with "They don't get your wind," and Chesterfields were said to be "much milder" and "will not harm nose and throat."

Which suggests a question: Did Bernays realize then the deadly nature of products he was peddling?

Absolutely not, he insisted in a letter to the *Boston Globe* in 1972. "When I worked with George Hill of the American Tobacco Co. no one had yet discovered that cigarettes caused cancer. Cigarettes four decades ago were considered 'kind to your throat.' Opera stars endorsed them."[51]

The opera star endorsements were, as he well knew, a sham, which was why he made fun of them at the time and why his citing them forty years later is disingenuous at best. Further, his papers at the Library of Congress, which became public upon his death in 1995, make clear he had good reason to suspect the perils of smoking as early as 1930, more than fifteen years before tobacco companies acknowledged that they suspected smoking was dangerous. The Bernays papers also make clear that he helped his client, American Tobacco, keep such doubts under wraps.

Consider the project he initiated to have a medical researcher produce abstracts of journal articles on the health effects of tobacco. One such summary, from a study in the early 1930s, referred to a "carcinoma that had developed after three years in a rabbit subjected to tobacco" and said "the cancer-producing property of tobacco has been determined in clinics."

Bernays attached that abstract to a May 22, 1933, letter to Paul Hahn, one of Hill's top aides, writing, "As you will see, certain of the material in these articles is unfavorable to tobacco. However, I do not feel that there is anything immediate to be done. I do feel that serious attention should be given to the problem of having ready a strong offensive in case the press should give prominence to the recurring articles which I note, from time to time, on the relationship of smoking and carcinoma. I believe that the American Tobacco Company and the tobacco interests generally should be fully prepared with authentic information if, as, and when the need for such information occurs."[52]

The next day Bernays sent Hahn another summary, this one discussing "two additional negative reports from important German medical magazines."

"The typical symptoms of acute [nicotine] poisoning are nausea, vomit, diarrhea, and blood pressure increase," the abstract warned. "Symptoms of chronic nicotine poisoning are extracardiac systoles, accelerated pulse with subsequent irregular cardiac activity; loss of appetite associated with gastric disturbance; vertigo, fatigue, nervousness, irritability. . . . It is assumed, though not definitely proved, that the nicotine tolerance of the habitual smoker is attributable to more rapid organic destruction, chiefly of the liver. Heavy smokers among nursing mothers excrete amounts of nicotine through the milk glands which can affect the baby. . . . Recent observations have shown that cases of angina pectoris on a purely nervous base [*sic*] in younger persons are not infrequently due to smoking tobacco."

"I personally believe that moderate smoking is a harmless pleasure, and a healthy person used to smoking can be allowed about four cigars and twelve cigarettes daily without harm," the author of the abstract said. But he or she went on to conclude that "the only reliable method of avoiding nicotine is by giving up smoking."[53]

In a memo to American Tobacco, Bernays said that the nicotine findings "indicate again what we must be prepared to answer." In fact, he was already helping to prepare that answer. One approach to newspaper stories on the dangers of smoking, he wrote Hahn, was to "lay down a barrage to the editors of the country, reflecting to them authoritative opinion on the cigarette in relation to the physiology of the human body—doing this not so much with the purpose of getting this material printed, but doing it rather to build up such a constructive picture of the cigarette in the minds of the editors that when a story of the type I am sending you comes along, they will hesitate to print it because they have been convinced of the contrary point of view."[54]

The cynicism of his approach is inescapable. As his memos to Hahn indicate, Bernays took seriously the medical evidence he was gathering on the dangers of smoking, yet he was urging American Tobacco to do all it could to ensure that newspaper editors dismiss that evidence.

Bernays also was working with several doctors who were willing to argue the tobacco company's side of the story. An article to be sent out under the signature of one of them, Dr. Clarence W. Lieb, observed that "men worship at various shrines: Venus (love), Bacchus (liquor), Mars (war), Ceres (sweets, starchy foods), and Lady Nicotine (tobacco). The least harmful is the latter.

"The benefits of tobacco are: (1) It is a pleasure. (2) A good laxative after breakfast. (3) Checks obesity by lessening the appetite. (4) Aids nutrition by stimulating the secretory functions of the stomach. (5) It consoles the lonely. (6) It aids contemplation. (7) It is a manual as well as oral activity. (8) It promotes sociability." The article concedes that "smoking is not good for: (1) The young. (2) The aged. (3) Those suffering from hyperacidity. (4) Those suffering from malnutrition. (5) Those having loose bowels. (6) Those having asthma. (7) Those having any chronic disease, except when tobacco acts as a placebo. (8) Those individuals, of whom there are some, who have an idiosyncrasy against strawberries or cucumbers."

The proposed article ends on the sort of upbeat note Bernays was trying to strike for his tobacco client and that the public back then listened to: "Nicotine is, of course, a mild poison. So is coffee or tea. So, too, do certain highly respected foods produce poison in the human system when taken to excess or in wrong combinations."[55]

Whatever his attitude in public, at home he did all he could to persuade his wife, Doris, to give up her pack-a-day habit. "He used to hide my mother's cigarettes and make us hide the cigarettes. He didn't think they were good for Mother," remembers his elder daughter, also named Doris. Anne, his younger daughter, recalls that when her father found a pack of her mother's Parliaments "he'd pull them all out and just snap them like bones, just snap them in half and throw them in the toilet. He hated her smoking."

Doris eventually gave up smoking after a physician warned her, in the late 1940s, that it was causing circulatory problems in her leg. "The doctor said she might need complete amputation," Anne remembers, "and that scared her sufficiently that she just stopped smoking. One day she was and the next she wasn't. She never had another cigarette."[56]

· · ·

Decades later, when the surgeon general and other medical authorities released incontrovertible evidence of the dangers of smoking, Bernays used his talents of persuasion to help undo addictions he'd help build.

In 1964 he unveiled a bold and detailed plan to transform smoking into "an antisocial action which no self-respecting person carries on in the presence of others." To do that, he proposed enlisting moviemakers and radio and television personalities, advertising executives, clergy and doctors, in a bid "to outlaw and eliminate cigarette smoking."[57] Those would be ambitious goals even for today's antismoking groups, with their extra resources, scientific backing, and public support, but when he unveiled it more than thirty years ago the Bernays plan was considered downright radical. He eventually joined in more realistic initiatives like one that got cigarette advertising banned from radio and television, a move he said "got rid of a sense of guilt" he had carried around for years.

To truly be absolved of that guilt, however, he would have had to admit that his memorable campaigns helped set the standard of no-holds-barred secretive tactics that the tobacco industry and its PR men have adhered to ever since. He would also have had to acknowledge the true extent of his suspicions, as early as the 1930s, about the risks of smoking. Instead, he insisted up until his death that he'd concocted schemes like the Torches of Freedom parade only because he didn't know back then that smoking was dangerous, and his claim seemed credible because that was the line tobacco companies were taking.

Why would he maintain a fiction belied by his own American Tobacco files, which he voluntarily donated to the Library of Congress?

He may not have remembered just how clearly his papers contradicted the story he was telling, especially since they were nearly forty years old by the time he left them to the library, and he probably didn't have the time or energy then to review all 805 boxes. He may not have felt the abstracts he received on health studies offered conclusive enough proof on smoking's dangers. Or he may not have believed the files could harm him, since the library had agreed not to make them public until after he died.

It's even more likely, however, that he understood public opinion well enough to know what a bombshell it would be, for him and for the tobacco industry, to reveal how early they had suspected smoking's deadly effects. He wouldn't actually destroy any of his files, either because that would be dishonest or because he felt they were too precious a record of his achievements. So he simply did what he'd done in so many campaigns for American Tobacco: he told only that part of the smoking story that served his interests and those of his former client, and he told it often enough, and in such convincing fashion, that he probably began to believe his own rhetoric.

The Big T H I N K

3

PUBLICITY MEN TRADITIONALLY SOLD THEIR SERVICES BASED ON their ability to chart the straightest course to their client's objective. If the aim was to sell more bacon, they would find ways to take a bite out of the business of other bacon-makers. If they were working for a book publisher, they would promote his titles and push the press for favorable reviews.

Eddie Bernays's approach was considerably more circuitous and infinitely more effective.

In the mid-1920s a huge bacon producer, Beechnut Packing Company, hired Bernays to help restore sales that had sagged as a country on the run trimmed its morning meal to juice, toast, and coffee. Deciding there was no point in trying to steal business from other ailing bacon producers, Bernays resolved to transform America's eating habits. He persuaded a famous New York doctor to write his colleagues asking whether they supported hearty or light breakfasts. Hearty won big, newspapers spread the word, people followed their physicians' advice, and sales soared of the two items most identified with big breakfasts—bacon and eggs. Thus the artery-clogging combination became forever linked in the American lexicon as well as on the American breakfast table.

He used a similar strategy in 1930 when he went to work for Simon and Schuster, Harcourt Brace, and other major book publishers. "Where there are bookshelves," he reasoned, "there will be books." So he got respected public figures to endorse the importance of books to civilization, and then he persuaded architects, contractors, and decorators to put up shelves on which to store the precious volumes—which is why so many homes from that era have built-in bookshelves.

The Bernays touch also shaped the world of medicine. Shortly after he signed on with the Multiple Sclerosis Society, he pointed out that the name of the illness was more of a mouthful than most Americans could digest. He urged pruning it back to MS, which the society did, helping transform an obscure ailment into a favorite cause.

Bernays's tactics differed, but his philosophy in each case was the same. Hired to sell a product or service, he instead sold whole new ways of behaving, which appeared obscure but over time reaped huge rewards for his clients and redefined the very texture of American life. Some analysts have referred to his methods as strategic or lateral thinking—mapping out a solution based on a client's standing in the wider economy and society rather than on narrow, vertical considerations like how they were faring against other bacon makers or booksellers. Bernays preferred the phrase "appeals of indirection," plotting a path to a client's goal that seemed roundabout but ultimately removed underlying as well as immediate impediments.

In retrospect we can pin an even simpler label on what he did: Big Think.

Big Think meant more than just refusing to be constrained by convention; Bernays consciously defied convention. He was convinced that ordinary rules didn't apply to him, and he repeatedly proved that he could reshape reality. He also took clients to places they had never dreamed of going, places that scared them at first but thrilled them when, as often happened, the public rallied, as he'd predicted. Sometimes his campaigns involved strategies so complex and oblique that even he had trouble following the script, which often involved front groups, letter-writing campaigns, and alliance after alliance; at other times his tactics were artfully simple, like reducing a name to its initials. Sometimes they appealed to the best instincts of clients and consumers; at other times he launched schemes he knew were wrong, and he willfully deceived the public. Always, however, there was a grand concept, the brash, bold, big thinking that grew out of his being more ingenious than his competitors, more cocksure, and generally more expensive. The big fees made him rich, but more important, they helped convince clients that his advice was worth its cost and that, since he was earning as much as their chief executive officer, it was with the CEO that he should be plotting strategy.

Big Think was part P. T. Barnum and part J. P. Morgan, blended in a way that was uniquely E. L. Bernays.

This new and evolving approach to publicity, its creator insisted, required new and evolving job titles. Before World War I he was content to call himself a press agent. By 1919, when he opened his first office in three rooms on East Forty-eighth Street, he'd decided "publicity direction" better conveyed the sweep of his labors. But something still was missing, something that would convey the seriousness of his advice and the range of his skills. So a year later, when he was testifying in a lawsuit involving his client Enrico Caruso and a reporter asked his profession, he tried yet another title, one he felt finally was worthy of his new enterprise: public relations counselor.

Those who caught his testimony that day could have been excused for mistaking the small man with the black mustache and gray demeanor for a traveling salesman or perhaps a new arrival from Central Europe. But if they looked closer they'd have noticed the passion with which he pleaded his case, the kind of passion that was redefining the fledgling field of public relations. Advertisers had always pressed consumers to pick one product over another, and press agents had shilled stories for clients, but now Bernays and a band of colleagues were skillfully manipulating symbols and trends in ways that affected what average Americans ate for breakfast, what sorts of homes they bought, and what colors they chose. And the PR men were doing it so adeptly that most people never realized it was happening and couldn't have conceived of how it was transforming the country.

Today, thanks to records made available upon Bernays's death in 1995, we can look backstage and see what strings he was pulling. And in the process we can better understand the dramatic world of public relations, a universe that has come to include hundreds of thousands of publicists, pollsters, advertising executives, and strategic planners, and that plays a more profound role than ever in our lives.

Most of what Bernays did at the beginning, when he was severing his ties to the Committee on Public Information and setting up his own practice, was aimed at helping American industry accommodate to the economic and social changes wrought by World War I. The pattern had been for firms to alter their product line or pitch to fit changing consumer tastes; Bernays believed that, approached the right way, consumers themselves could be made to do the adjusting.

That's what happened when Venida, a leading maker of hair nets, watched in horror as more and more women cut their hair so short they didn't need mesh to maintain it. Some had grown used to wearing short hair when they worked in wartime factories; others were aping dance idol Irene Castle, who'd bobbed her hair so it wouldn't interfere with her spins and dips. Bernays didn't panic, and he didn't try to sell more hairnets. Rather, he got health officials to urge, and occasionally order, food workers to wear nets to keep their hair out of the food. He got labor leaders to urge women factory workers to wear nets to prevent their curls from being caught in the machinery. And he got leading artists to proclaim that the standard for American beauty was long, flowing locks—which, of course, needed to be kept in place with a net.

Luggage makers were equally alarmed by changing tastes when they sought out Bernays in the late 1920s. Flapper fashions, which included scanties, short skirts, and cloche hats, took up less space than earlier multilayered styles. Staterooms on ships and trains allocated less and less room for luggage, and new-style traveling salesmen traveled light. The PR man counterattacked, again through the back door. He got magazines and newspapers to set a standard whereby well-bred travelers carried large wardrobes, and he urged architects to design more storage space, colleges to inform students of the many bags they needed to bring to campus, and health officials to explain why it was unsanitary to share a valise. Then he found a celebrity—singer-comedian Eddie Cantor—to pose while packing his big trunk for a concert tour.

The formula was simple: Bernays generated events, the events generated news, and the news generated a demand for whatever he happened to be selling.

"Not only God but counsels of public relations are masters of the mystic pulls of gravitation," *The Nation* observed in a 1927 issue. "Mr. Bernays holds, furthermore—and we cannot but agree with him—that the principle is applicable to *all* types of merchandise. . . . And so, happily, the consumer may forever cease from buying what he freely wants; and the Kingdom of Heaven of the Salesman will come upon earth."[1]

· · ·

Working that kind of otherworldly charm was easiest with major clients, who were less likely to be scared off by the machinations of Big Think and more likely to have the resources needed to pull it off.

The Bernays client list, which he said numbered 435 over his forty years of full-time practice, reads like a Who's Who in American commerce and culture of that era—General Electric, General Motors, Nash-Kelvinator, Philco Radio and Television, and U.S. Radium. From the world of art Bernays had the Ballet Theater and New York Philharmonic, playwright Eugene O'Neill, actor–theater manager Henry Miller, and painter Georgia O'Keeffe; from finance there was Mutual Benefit Life Insurance as well as Title Guarantee and Trust; and, from the communications industry, Columbia Broadcasting System, National Broadcasting Company, *Cosmopolitan, Fortune, Good Housekeeping, Ladies' Home Journal,* the *New Republic,* and *Time.* Hoteliers came to Bernays for advice, too, from the Waldorf and McAlpin in Manhattan, the Saint George in Brooklyn, and the Book-Cadillac in Detroit. Union clients included the Brotherhood of

Railroad Trainmen and the International Union of Electrical Workers, and retailers included the Great Atlantic and Pacific Tea Company, F. W. Woolworth, and R. H. Macy.

Procter and Gamble was one of Bernays's biggest clients and, after thirty years, his most loyal. Its problem in the early days was simple but vexing: children didn't care about keeping clean and had no use for P&G's primary product, Ivory soap. His solution was simple but brilliant: "Children, the enemies of soap, would be conditioned to enjoy using Ivory."

The idea came to him when a sculptor wrote to Procter and Gamble asking for big blocks of Ivory to carve in place of clay. Seizing on the publicity potential of this idea, Bernays set up a committee, which in 1924 organized a National Soap Sculpture Contest with cash awards and lots of press coverage. Sculptors, architects, and other artists over the years transformed blocks of soap weighing up to 1,000 pounds into likenesses of portly William Howard Taft and sinewy Charles Lindbergh, Alice in Wonderland, the Empire State Building, and a battle scene from the Middle Ages.

The focus eventually shifted to schoolchildren, who received brochures explaining that the only tools needed were "a pen knife or paring knife. Two orange sticks (such as ladies use for the care of their fingernails—you can get them at any drug store). A wire hair-pin about three inches long. A yard of string or covered wire." The leaflet also advised youngsters to "use discarded models for face, hands and bath. You will love the feeling of cleanliness that comes from an Ivory Soap bath once a day."[2]

The contests continued for more than thirty-five years, until 1961, using a million cakes of soap a year and inducing untold thousands of contestants from ages six to eighty-six to spend hour after hour whittling away at big white bars of Ivory. While its commercial success is tough to measure, Bernays's sculpting scheme clearly helped make Ivory the all-American soap, much as he'd established bacon and eggs as the all-American breakfast.

Not all of his grand conceptions for Procter and Gamble panned out so well, though, and some never made it to the drawing board.

Consider Bernays's plan of counterattack when P&G's archrival, Lever Brothers, tried to replace Ivory with its own floating soap—Swan. The way to sink Swan, Bernays argued, was to get reporters to write stories saying that swans were vicious creatures that attacked children. P&G executives didn't buy that tactic. "[Bernays] thought the only way to respond was tearing [Lever Brothers] down a little and hopefully destroying them, which of course [his tactic] never in the world would have done," recalls Oliver Gale, who ran P&G's public relations department from 1937 to 1957.[3]

Soap sculpting had its own rough moments. In the early years a prizewinner in New York was disturbed when his girlfriend jilted him. He sneaked into her home while she was out and, to calm his nerves, carved up bar after bar of soap. When she returned and refused to reconcile with him, he practiced his art of sculpting on her and her mother. A reporter who visited the murder scene tried to link the killer to the contest, but contest officials denied any connection and insisted the carvings were the work of young girls.[4]

Mack Trucks approached Bernays in 1949 with an even more imposing challenge. It could handle competition from other truck makers but not from the railroads. Fearful of losing their grip on shipping, train operators had launched a fierce campaign to convince the public that trucks were ruining the roads and to persuade states to levy road taxes high enough to price trucks out of the freight business.

The railroads, however, hadn't counted on Big Think. "Our population was growing," Bernays recalled later. "So was the number of passenger and truck automobiles. The static element was the highway system of the country. An idea hit me. Since no present solution was possible, maybe a future solution would assuage the frustrations of the public. If we could promise American motorists future satisfaction on their roads and work to bring that about, the gripe against the heavy trucks would be dissipated and tomorrow the problem would be solved." Promoting truck sales by building roads was, as the PR man acknowledged, "the most indirect kind of indirection," and while it seemed logical to him, it required all his skills of persuasion to get Mack to think that far ahead and delay gratification that long. Even tougher was getting Congress to commit the billions of dollars needed to construct a national highway system.[5]

But by now he'd worked out a recipe for solving problems like this, and as always with this man who was so consumed by symbols, new recipes demanded new names for the ingredients. His campaigns always began with an "overt act"—a stunt staged so cleverly that the press would think it was newsworthy—in this case a luncheon in the Waldorf-Astoria's grand ballroom at which the only speaker was Mack president E. L. Bransome and the sole topic his plan for paving the countryside. The next step was "segmenting," or identifying potential allies so they could be targeted with appeals. Bransome and colleagues obliged by barnstorming the nation, enlisting in their cause a curious collection of truck drivers, milk dealers, tire and rubber workers, and members of women's traffic clubs and men's driving clubs. Then he organized the "front groups"—the Trucking Information Service, the Trucking Service Bureau, and Better Living Through Increased Highway Transportation—which mailed out promotional letters and founded state associations to run local campaigns. Mack and Bernays brought Israeli ambassador Abba Eban onboard by agreeing to assemble trucks in Israel. They won over U.S. Army Chief of Staff William L. Barriger by convincing him that trucks were essential for warfare in the dawning atomic age. In all of this their aim was to get the attention of the public and, through it, the U.S. Congress.

It worked: Congress in 1950 approved $566 million in road-building funds for each of the next two years, and two years later it upped the ante to $652 million, the most it had ever authorized and a critical step toward completion of the interstate highway network. While several other forces were pushing for such a system, none was as determined as Mack and its allies. And while the railroads' share of the shipping business already was slipping, this helped cement the trend toward greater reliance on roads and less on rails.

Bernays's Mack campaign also set a model for lobbying that is still used in today's world of high-priced political action committees. He managed to unite disparate elements of an industry, in this case truck-ing, to battle a common enemy, the railroads. He realized that his greatest challenge was to rally the public to his cause, he knew the way to do that was to appeal to pocketbook issues, and he proved that in the face of such an onslaught, Congress could be persuaded to spend billions of taxpayer dollars.

Other clients required their own tailor-made approaches—some straightforward stunts, some more sophisticated manipulations of symbols, but all bearing the Bernays flair. For Cartier, the international jeweler, he inserted a plug in the 1931 movie *Fifty Million Frenchmen*, getting Maurice Chevalier to croon, "You've got those ways, those fetching ways, that make me rush out to Cartier's." That was sweet music to the Fifth Avenue jeweler and to what would become an entire industry devoted to product placement. For Dodge's 1928 Standard Six model he got Charlie Chaplin to record a radio ad. Worried that Chaplin's speaking role might give him stage fright, Bernays insured the actor's voice for $5,000 with Lloyd's of London, generating even more coverage. And for Dixie Cups he founded a Committee for the Study and Promotion of the Sanitary Dispensing of Food and Drink. One ad featuring a beautiful woman carried this caption: "Unwanted kisses are common enough in the lives of pretty girls. No wonder they avoid the rain of kisses promiscuously placed on the rims of publicly used and re-used glasses. Have your drinks in Individual Dixies and be exclusive. Be more than exclusive. Be safe! No lips ever touch a Dixie brim until it touches yours."[6]

America's brewers were more concerned about sanctimoniousness than safety. Prohibition was repealed in 1933, but it wasn't long before thousands of communities declared themselves dry, and the temperance movement picked up steam. So in 1935 the brewers picked up Bernays.

His strategy was familiar to every student of war, and of baseball: carefully analyze your opponent's game plan, and if you can't overcome it, co-opt it. That meant promoting beer as "the beverage of moderation" in a way that would distance it from distilled liquors and inoculate it against the temperance movement's argument that all alcohol posed the danger of overindulgence. He persuaded beer retailers to cooperate with law enforcement to ensure that their product was used responsibly, and he published "evidence" that beer was not fattening and had a caloric value equal to that of milk. He told homemakers that beer would make for a richer chocolate cake; told farmers that brewers were major buyers of their barley, corn, and rice; and told laborers that beer was the one alcoholic beverage they could afford. And he published booklets and wrote letters claiming that beer was the favorite drink of the ancient Babylonians and the monks of the Middle Ages as well as of George Washington, Thomas Jefferson, Patrick Henry, and the Pilgrims.

"Beer is a sort of vaccination against intemperance," argued a typical Bernays campaign brochure, this one urging people to vote for a Texas ordinance legalizing the sale of beer. "The 'bootleggers' thrive upon the stronger beverages, distilled spirits, those that carry the 'kick' in concentrated form, in small packages easy to conceal. . . . Where beer is accessible the liquor bottle 'on the hip' is not so much in evidence, whether that be in the home or at a public place, or—most important of all—in an automobile. Many sincere temperance workers believe that the best way to fight intemperance is to legalize the sale of beer everywhere."[7]

Such pearls of wisdom cost big dollars. In 1931 Bernays handled publicity for the first aviators to cross the Pacific nonstop, a brief assignment that netted him $4,000—which was $1,000 more than the lead pilot earned. In the 1940s the Columbia Rope Company paid him $40,000 a year for advice on "a multiplicity of problems, most of which I found insoluble." The Bank of America, meanwhile, solicited his advice on such matters as how to make reluctant regulators accept branch banking, advice they felt was worth $60,000 a year, which Bernays says was $10,000 more than the bank president's salary.

Fees like that quickly added up. Bernays's ledgers show that in 1931, at the height of the Great Depression, his income reached $98,513.55. Of that, profits were $60,183.17—the equivalent of more than $700,000 in 1997 dollars. And his earnings generally went up from there, with profits increasing as much as fivefold by 1935. In contemporary terms that means he was earning several million dollars a year.

His approach to money was simple, as he told an interviewer in 1985: "We decided that public relations advice is more important than legal advice, because legal advice is based on precedent but public relations advice might actually establish precedent. So we found out what lawyers charged, and we charged more. Up to then—1919, 1920—the most PR people received was $125 a week. Our first fees were $12,000 annual retainers and rose sharply from that."[8]

· · ·

Steep fees made it hard for any but the wealthiest to afford his counsel, but Bernays reduced and sometimes waived his charges for clients like the American Library Association, the Cardiac Committee of the Public Education Association, and the Mary Imogene Basset Hospital. He also served as chairman of the Citizens Committee for Better Schools of New York City and vice chairman of the Concert Committee of the New York Stadium, and he was a member of the boards of the Hospital for Joint Diseases of New York, the Metropolitan Educational TV Association, the New York Shakespeare Festival, and the Carnegie Hall Corporation. Beginning in 1946, he says in his memoirs, he committed half of his professional time to non-profit work.

Even when representing the rich, he was democratic in his sales pitches. He convinced blue-blooded Cartier's to institute $5 and $10 departments during the Depression, and he eventually terminated his relationship with the longtime client because, he said, "I gave serious thought to the wisdom of handling jewels during a depression and concluded that, in all conscience, I could not continue."[9]

At other times, he zeroed in on the elite of the elite, advising the Sherry Netherland Hotel to send solicitations to America's "1,000 wealthiest widows," owners of Rolls Royces, seniors at Ivy League colleges, and a "wide mailing list chosen from the social registers or blue books of New York and other leading cities."

Targeted mailings were one tactic he used on behalf of the Fifth Avenue hotel. This strategy is considered routine today, but it was pioneering in 1949. To analyze the hotel's clientele he ordered up a Dun and Bradstreet ratings check on one hundred guests who had paid with credit cards. And he commissioned a field study on how services at the Sherry Netherland stacked up against those at the Plaza, the Ritz-Carlton, and other top-of-the-line hostelries in Manhattan, checking on everything from whether the bellman opened the windows and adjusted the shades to whether a room had clean ashtrays, telegram blanks, a thermos, and running ice water.

Bernays even did his own review of the elegant Carnaval Room, unmasking deficiencies everywhere he turned. The two hostesses wore dresses that "looked a bit bedraggled, not freshly ironed. They didn't give a spritely impact to the eye." The principal headwaiter "was completely oblivious of us." The kitchen pantry was visible from his table and was "not immaculate. . . . Doors of pantry now painted red might be painted in stripes like the rest of decor to maintain pattern." As for the food, "my wife had a practically cold filet mignon and I had a warm—not hot—roast beef." The music might have soothed his raw nerves, but it was "no more or less pleasant than the dinner music one hears over the radio or in any place of equal or even less merit."[10]

That and other data generally went onto index cards, tens of thousands of them, stored in file drawers and referred to again and again, anytime he or an associate needed an address or phone number, a stored fact or tip to be followed up on—a sea of minutiae, swelled by a tide of simple tasks, that made up the big picture of Big Think. If one card didn't offer the answer, if one tactic didn't provide results, he moved on without pause to the next card or strategy.

An equally important maxim of Big Think was that extremism in defense of a client wasn't a vice and could be a virtue, even if it meant fighting dirty. In 1933, for example, Bernays helped Allied Chemical battle a bid by stockholders to make the company release data on its finances. One tactic was to suggest that the dissenting stockholders' ties to Belgium raised a threat of "foreign domination"—a strategy that should have been anathema to Bernays, who had been outraged when his Austrian roots were used to question his loyalty to America during World War I.

His methods often drew scathing criticism—*Editor and Publisher* branded him "the young Machiavelli of our time," and Supreme Court Justice Felix Frankfurter, in a letter to President Franklin Roosevelt, called Bernays and fellow PR pioneer Ivy Lee "professional poisoners of the public mind" who exploit "foolishness and fanaticism and self-interest."[11] But his hardball approach also attracted clients. Executives of the Jackson Heights Corporation told him they wanted his help with a new housing development, Bernays said, "because anyone who was a 'menace' of the proportions I was described by *Editor and Publisher* must be good." And *Printer's Ink* magazine, which like *Editor and Publisher* had skewered him over the years, later hired him as an adviser.

· · ·

Light's Golden Jubilee, the 1929 celebration of the fiftieth anniversary of Thomas A. Edison's invention of the electric light, is widely regarded as Bernays's shining triumph and one of the brightest public relations performances ever. But close inspection casts his role in a dimmer light, raising doubts about the PR maestro and his profession.

The jubilee came at a busy time for Bernays, who was urging women to reach for Luckies instead of sweets, pushing Cartier's jewels, Dodge's Victory Six car, Knox's gelatin, and New Jersey Bell's new phone services. Yet, as he wrote later, "to many we were still sensation mongers and ballyhoo artists—a menace to the integrity of press and business alike. I hoped for a dramatic event that would make others see us as we saw ourselves."[12]

The Golden Jubilee was that event. Bernays had a true hero in Edison, a truly significant invention in the incandescent light, and a nation that, in the heady days before the stock market crash, believed the boom would last forever and was forever ready to celebrate. All that remained was to decide who would plan the bash—General Electric, which had been invited in by a collection of Edison's friends and colleagues called the Edison Pioneers, or Henry Ford, who idolized Edison and volunteered to step in when the aging inventor said he was worried that GE would commercialize the celebration. Ford won out, getting the event moved from GE's headquarters in Schenectady to Ford's own backyard—Dearborn, Michigan—with GE invited along as a junior partner.

General Electric, meanwhile, asked Bernays to handle its end of the publicity, and soon after he came onboard things started happening. Newspapers reprinted issues from fifty years before announcing Edison's discovery. Letters of tribute poured in from luminaries like Albert Einstein and General John J. Pershing. George M. Cohan wrote a song called "Edison—Miracle Man," and Admiral Richard Byrd named a beacon in the Arctic after the inventor. Proclamations were issued from New Hampshire to New Mexico and by leaders of countries as diverse as China and Canada. And the post office issued a commemorative two-cent stamp printed in red, which depicted Edison's lamp with rays emanating outward.

The jubilee itself, on October 21, 1929, drew one of the most impressive lineups ever. The greats included President Herbert Hoover, Marie Curie, Orville Wright, Will Rogers, and J. P. Morgan. Bernays managed to land in the center of things, as he recalled later: "The president stood outside the [train] station, flanked by a crowd of guests, his aide, and his personal physician. Nobody seemed to be in charge, so I pushed into the crowd and yelled for the 'gentlemen please to move back, form a line, and meet the president in orderly fashion.' I stood opposite Mr. Hoover. As the line moved slowly between us, I asked the name of each approaching man and repeated it to the president."[13]

Activities reached a climax when Edison appeared on the second floor of his laboratory, which Ford had moved from New Jersey to Michigan, and demonstrated, for millions of radio listeners worldwide, how he first lit a light. "Will it light? Will it burn?" NBC Radio's Graham McNamee asked, fanning the anticipation. "Or will it flicker and die, as so many previous lamps had died? Oh, you could hear a pin drop in this long room. Now the group is once more about the old vacuum pump. Mr. Edison has the two wires in his hand; now he is reaching up to the old lamp; now he is making the connection. It lights!"[14]

No matter that, as the celebration was dying down, Edison slumped in his chair and turned a deathly white. He was helped into a nearby room, laid on a sofa, and given medication, then taken to the Ford home and put to bed for several days. That did little to diminish the elation, as the jubilee was universally judged a triumph.

In one account after another, credit was lavished on a certain public relations man. "The high point in promotion work for 1929—which should certainly win a Harvard advertising prize—was the feat of persuading the post office to get out a special two-cent stamp advertising Mr. Edison's electric light," wrote *The Nation*. "But a close runner-up has been the publicity given, free of charge, to the advertising stunt of bringing bright boys from forty-eight states to Mr. Edison's New Jersey laboratory. Every day for a week these lads—aided by the forethought of the publicity man in arranging for the simultaneous presence of Messrs. Edison, Eastman, Ford, and Lindbergh—made the front pages. Every day the thought was subtly instilled into impressionable young minds that the electric-light companies yearned to help bright boys and to achieve more inventions, all for the benefit of the dear old Ultimate Consumer. . . . Credit for this super-advertising, we understand, belongs to Mr. Edward L. Bernays, 'counsel on public relations.' If Mr. Ivy Lee is to maintain his reputation, he will have to do some tall thinking."[15]

The New Yorker agreed: "Bernays works well with multimillionaires, as the success of the great celebration shows. Under Ford's aegis he got into touch with governors, other countries, syndicates, etc. Under his direction committees were formed from Maine to Honolulu, holidays declared, lights turned on and off, speeches made, and a special stamp issued by the Post Office Department. Of course, the real greatness of Edison deserved all these things, and the people from the President down were sincerely desirous of honoring him in a big way, but it took a public-relations counsellor [*sic*] to put it over."[16]

The *Atlantic Monthly*, meanwhile, said that "Henry Ford was supposed to be the manager of the show, but the man who set the stage and pulled the strings attached to all the dignified marionettes was Edward L. Bernays."[17] And Yale University psychologist Leonard Doob called what Bernays did in Dearborn "one of the most astonishing pieces of propaganda ever engineered in this country during peace time."[18]

Edison himself wrote Bernays to offer his "sincere thanks and appreciation" for the "immense amount of thought and work [that] was expended." The note's tone, however, suggests that it was a form letter.[19]

In the best tradition of his young profession, Bernays didn't merely bask in the publicity, he used it to his own advantage. "Will any of your clients celebrate important anniversaries in 1930?" asked a circular distributed by the Bernays office. "The remarkable tide of goodwill created by the Light's Golden Jubilee celebration of the 50th anniversary of the incandescent lamp proves that occasions of this kind can be made to capitalize on the past and to focus public attention on the present and the future. If our experience in handling the public relations aspects in the Light's Golden Jubilee and other clients interests you, we should be glad to discuss with you the anniversary possibilities of your clients."[20]

Yet some historians view the jubilee as a tribute not to Bernays's brilliance but to his propensity for puffery, especially where his own role in history is concerned—and to a penchant for secrecy that was tantamount to duplicity.

In a 1976 book historian David L. Lewis writes, "In later years many writers, in discussing the jubilee (which has become a 'public relations classic'), have greatly magnified Bernays's role. . . . Actually Bernays only helped to handle the press, and, in fact, he would have had nothing to do with the Dearborn celebration had not Ford, who had obtained Edison's promise to attend the dedication of the village on October 21, permitted General Electric to tie in the jubilee with the Ford ceremony. It was Ford's show, and it was he who issued the invitations to the prominent guests. As for the reconstruction of the Edison buildings, that project was begun before anyone in Dearborn had ever heard of Bernays."[21]

Ten years later Lewis, a professor of business history at the University of Michigan, read an interview in the *Detroit Free Press* where Bernays boasted about his role in the jubilee, calling it his "greatest triumph." Having gotten a decidedly different version from those close to Ford, Lewis started to write a rebuttal titled "Bernays Bragging Again" but decided against it, as he explains, because Bernays "was an old fellow and I didn't want to hurt his feelings."[22]

Bernays's name is only rarely associated with the jubilee in official histories at the Henry Ford Museum or in Edison's papers. And even before the event occurred in 1929, *Editor and Publisher* caught him doing a bit of exaggerating, implying he was handling press not only for the jubilee but also for President Hoover—a suggestion that was greeted by surprise at the White House and backpedaling by Bernays, who publicly expressed hope that he had not "embarrassed Mr. Hoover."[23]

Did he deserve the credit others lavished on him and that he had heaped upon himself? Yes and no. Five boxes of Library of Congress papers on the celebration make clear that he was more than merely a press agent, that he helped dream up promotions which made the event an international extravaganza, and that he was involved in the sort of detailed orchestration that Ford's staff probably didn't want to be troubled with. The fact that Ford confidants remembered things differently isn't surprising. They and their boss resented from the start the involvement of GE and its hyperactive publicity man. Also, they may not have been aware of all that Bernays did behind the scenes or why it mattered, next to the $3 million Ford spent and the yeomanlike work his architects and builders did. And Ford's well-documented anti-Semitism likely soured his and his staff's perception of Bernays.

Bernays's papers and his many recollections of the jubilee over the years make clear, however, that he did embellish his role, which becomes a bit more vital to the celebrations with each retelling. By 1977 the journal *Dun's Review* was crediting him with having orchestrated the relocation to Dearborn of the New Jersey building where Edison invented the lightbulb. As Lewis suggests, as more and more principals who might have contradicted him passed away, Bernays's version became the official version.

Bernays also upset his PR colleagues and others by perpetually taking center stage during the jubilee. He "incurred Ford's wrath after the dedicatory party arrived in Dearborn because he tried repeatedly to inject himself into a group picture with Hoover, Edison, and the host," Lewis wrote. "Ford took [newspaperman and Ford adviser] Fred Black aside and told him to 'get Bernays the hell out of here or I'll have [Ford bodyguard] Harry Bennett's men throw him over the fence.' Black told Bernays of Ford's threat, and the publicist moved out of camera range."[24] Scott M. Cutlip, a prominent PR historian, said such behavior "was characteristic of Bernays. He always confused who the client was. It's a basic principle of PR that the public relations man stays in the background."[25]

But it was Bernays's secrecy that elicited the loudest outcry. As *Editor and Publisher* noted shortly before the celebration, "it is known that Bernays has been at work upon the Jubilee since last spring. . . . Just who his employers are is not known."[26] Five days after the bash the journal still was in the dark: "No one knew who was employing him, but Bernays freely admitted he was being paid. He told one newspaper man that he was acting for the 'Edison Pioneers.' His copy frequently mentioned the electric light and power industry. He may have been employed by Ford interests, or General Electric, or Westinghouse or Edison Lamp or all of them cooperatively."[27]

Bernays made a conscious effort to get people to believe the celebration was unfolding spontaneously rather than being stage-managed by GE or anyone else. He wrote early in 1929 to a GE sales promotion executive, "Did you see the enclosed [article] in the *Times* of this morning? . . . The slant in this article, from the standpoint of propaganda, is all wrong to our mind. It gives the emphasis to the technique of how interest will be brought about rather than to create the impression that this will be an event that has developed naturally."[28]

His defense then, as always, was the age-old principle of client confidentiality. "We would no more violate our confidence," he said, "than would a doctor or a lawyer." But while doctors and lawyers don't identify clients, they also don't seek to mislead the way the GE team did. And Bernays's argument is disingenuous since, as far back as 1930, he was naming clients for reporters writing sympathetic stories.

· · ·

Questions raised about Light's Golden Jubilee also can be asked about other Bernays campaigns and other claims he made over the years.

Did his ingenious soap sculpture initiative, for instance, really revolutionize the way Procter and Gamble sold Ivory? No, says Oliver Gale, the longtime P&G public relations boss: "I don't think Eddie Bernays had any idea how we sold soap. The real world of selling soap was not of interest to him. . . . His ideas were conceptual and creative and magical, but they had very little effect on our business. That's where I think he came up short." Robert G. Eagen, a later P&G public relations chief, agrees. The soap sculpture project, he explains, was "a worthwhile thing, sort of a low-cost project. Did it help us sell soap? I doubt it. We had much more efficient ways of selling soap."[29] Official histories of the sculpture contest make clear that Bernays's claim that 21 million children took part the first year can't be substantiated and probably is a gross exaggeration.

It could be that other PR executives at Procter and Gamble didn't recognize the long-term consequences of what Bernays was doing, that they were concerned with day-to-day sales while he cared about Ivory's long-term reputation with consumers. The full-time PR men also might have resented the intrusion of a part-time consultant, especially one who started at $12,000 a year in 1923 and almost certainly got raises over the next three decades. And it's possible that the bolder claims in the stream of profiles on him were pumped up by reporters who knew it made a stronger story to credit him with everything from orchestrating a presidential visit to relocating an inventor's lab, and by columnists like Walter Winchell who Bernays says started the rumor that he, rather than the post office, was behind the Edison stamp.

What about the brash claims in his autobiography and in scores of articles he wrote which maintained, among other things, that his work for Dodge was responsible for "keeping the auto industry rolling," that his work for General Motors helped convince that company and corporate America at large of the primacy of PR, that his efforts in Massachusetts "pretty single-handedly" got a law passed making it illegal to fire workers based on age, that he got Franklin Roosevelt to name Henry Wallace secretary of agriculture, and that he was the man behind the "mental hygiene" movement reinventing itself as "mental health"?

Many of these claims are difficult to confirm or deny. The companies involved say they don't have the records, and Bernays's files don't make clear whether his machinations were effective. Most of his co-workers are dead or don't remember. Press accounts often simply repeat his version of what happened, which is to be expected when you outlive your contemporaries, are more skilled at getting across your viewpoint, and write an 849-page autobiography that, while too cumbersome for most readers to plow through, has been used repeatedly by historians writing about such varied topics as cigarette sales and the U.S.-backed defeat of Guatemala's socialist regime.

But some of his claims clearly come up short. That happened with the Green Ball and the Committee on Public Information. It happens again with his often-repeated assertion that he was the one who got United Parcel Service to paint its trucks brown to blend in with residential neighborhoods. UPS officials can't find any record of his involvement and say brown was chosen simply to match the popular Pullman railroad cars. Mental health historians agree that Bernays may well have suggested the switch from mental hygiene, but so did many others. No one remembers his participation when the national associations actually changed their titles in the mid-1940s. He did battle age discrimination in Massachusetts, but the law he claimed credit for was approved more than twenty years before he moved to the Bay State.

Even stranger circumstances surround Bernays's insistence, in his memoirs and in stories over the years, that *Time* magazine founder Henry Luce wanted to cut him in at the beginning as an investor and

PR adviser. "I declined their offer of $125 a week for public relations counsel because I thought their evaluation of the market was incorrect and I didn't want to take their money for a project I felt would not succeed," Bernays wrote forty-two years later. "Besides, our fees were higher than they could afford to pay."[30]

His Library of Congress papers tell a decidedly different story, however. On April 9, 1923, Bernays sent Luce a four-page letter expressing his conviction that "the appeal of *Time* is potentially an appeal to the entire American public," outlining his ideas for promoting the magazine, and offering to do that promotional work for $100 a week. Luce wrote back on April 27, "We are not yet ready to undertake any considerable obligations for public counsel relations," but he left the door open for the future. Bernays answered on April 30, saying, "I should be happy at any time to co-operate with you because I really believe in the future of your magazine."[31] He ultimately did help out with press releases on the opening of the magazine, "as a *beau geste*," and years later he did PR work for *Time*.

It's unclear why he amended the story for his memoirs, especially since the actual account was available in his personal papers, which were due to be made public upon his death. Perhaps he enjoyed the opportunity for self-deprecation by pointing out how wrong he'd been in misjudging *Time*'s potential, although his letters make clear he was right in predicting its rosy future. Perhaps, looking back more than four decades later, he couldn't find the right papers to jog his memory and simply got it wrong. Most likely he was embarrassed that Luce declined his offer of help and decided to leave that detail out of his memoirs.

And his contention that he carried clout at General Motors? Paul Garrett, GM's longtime PR guru, says he was the one who pushed GM to hire Bernays, but only because his boss insisted that the company get all the advice it could during the depression. Garrett had faith that Bernays would quickly wear out his welcome, and he wasn't disappointed, as he made clear in a 1963 letter to a graduate student chronicling his career. "You can do what you want about Bernays," Garrett wrote. "To me the kindest thing all around would be not to mention him at all . . . Eddy [*sic*] had no 'impact' on me in the development of my public relations philosophy for General Motors. If I were to compile a list of twenty-five men inside and outside General Motors who had an impact on my development during the early General Motors years, it would not even occur to me to put Eddy on that list. . . . This whole Bernays thing has assumed a dimension that is ridiculous as I think it would be clear from the fact that we dismissed him at the end of his first year. But I would very much prefer professionally not to do anything on my part to hurt him, who is after all a much older man in the profession than I."[32]

That wasn't the first time Bernays was fired, or the last. His short tenure with client after client suggests he didn't always make the impact he claimed, and even a thirty-year relationship like the one he had with Procter and Gamble ended with his dismissal. "I had the unhappy task of telling him," Gale recalled. "His whole approach was indirect, and that just kind of fell by the wayside as far as we were concerned. It no longer was pertinent."[33]

Bernays admitted that his clients often let him go sooner than he'd have liked, but he had an explanation for every firing, usually involving personalities rather than performance. With General Motors, he told a different story than Garrett, attributing the company's refusal to extend his one-year contract to an article in a Detroit newspaper that credited him, rather than two GM vice presidents, with delivering a GM loan to two failing Detroit banks during the depression. "That line of type in the *Detroit Free Press* about Bernays, the $12,500,000 personal representative of Alfred P. Sloan, Jr., who had saved Detroit from economic collapse, had a greater force in the situation than any other thing I had done or might do," Bernays wrote in his memoirs. "The line had rankled in the minds and hearts of the two vice presidents, who were deeply frustrated by missing their great opportunity for glory. When the termination date arrived, the contract was not renewed." As for Garrett, Bernays said he was "as green about public relations as I was about motor mechanics," adding that Garrett and the other GM publicity men "were to make decisions on the public relations program I was presenting to them, but none had the requisite knowledge or experience on which to base such decisions."[34]

Similarly, he said that Procter and Gamble dismissed him because he insisted on keeping his PR organization small even though P&G wanted a big firm able to handle everything from writing and printing to mailing, polling, and press-agentry. "I had decided long ago," he wrote, "that I wanted to be an independent adviser, not head of a public relations factory, where my time would be spent as an executive. I preferred problem solving to drill majoring."[35]

"People ask me why clients discontinued our services," he wrote on another occasion. "There are almost as many causes as there were clients. A change of policy with no ascertainable reason for it was one case. . . . Sometimes a client's unrealizable expectations are not met. Sometimes his realizable hopes have not been met, due to no circumstances the public relations counsel can possibly control. Sometimes the relationship is severed because the counsel on public relations has been so successful that the client feels he can proceed on his own. Sometimes a man in the organization, after a year's experience with counsel on public relations, convinces the client he doesn't need outside help, hoping to profit thereby."[36]

Never, judging from his writings, was he fired for anything that was his fault.

Yet if his short tenures reflect his shortcomings, the fact that he continually landed new, bigger clients attests to his reputation for producing results, to his resiliency, which let him bounce back from falls that would have kept down less resourceful men, and most of all to his ability to persuade prospective clients that his troubles with earlier clients weren't his fault. And if some of his claims clearly were exaggerated, others were quite accurate and often even understated. Consider his taking credit for shortening multiple sclerosis to its familiar initials, MS. Sylvia Lawry, founder and director of the National Multiple Sclerosis Society, recalls that "when we were first organized there was a lot of conjecture about whether we should change our name to one that could more easily be dealt with by the public.

Bernays said we shouldn't change the name but should use the initials MS. He was the first to suggest that. Whenever other problems came up over the years," she added, "I'd ask myself, How would Eddie Bernays have reacted? Usually I knew the answer, and I'd follow the advice."[37]

The American Heart Association tells a similar story about his claim that he helped take the group "from its unimportance and made it a large, effective organization." It was the $1.5 million that the association got from Procter and Gamble's radio show *Truth or Consequences* that let the organization go national, officials say, and Bernays apparently was the one who picked the association out of all the charities seeking such support. What about his insistence that he helped shape the Columbia Broadcasting System and, through it, the wider worlds of radio and TV? Sally Bedell Smith, biographer of longtime CBS boss William S. Paley, tells a similar story, saying "Bernays gave Paley advice not only about publicity but about organizational structure, sales techniques, and scouting talent." And she credits the PR man with scripting Paley's promise to Congress that the networks would aggressively promote public affairs and news programming. The fact that he wrote that bold pledge, Smith adds, means that Bernays shares with Paley the blame for CBS's failure to deliver on its high-minded proposal.[38]

Bernays's stories almost always began with a factual account, then were puffed up as he recounted his own role or insisted that whatever happened was a "first of its kind." As his granddaughter Hester Kaplan says, "I never doubted his stories; I just doubted their magnitude."[39]

It was tough to get mad at Bernays, though, because he was such a good storyteller and brought such energy to each tale, especially in his later years. And it was tough to separate fact from fiction because, like Woody Allen's character Leonard Zelig, Bernays was present at so many key moments in history and, unlike Zelig, he often did markedly influence the outcome.

So why did he embellish?

Doris Held, Eddie's older daughter who is a psychotherapist, looks to her profession for insight. Having grown up in the shadow of Freud, his overachieving uncle, and Ely Bernays, his domineering father, Eddie overcompensated by making his big achievements even bigger, she says. "He couldn't let it be, he had to keep on constructing it and defining it and embellishing it."[40]

People who live as long as he did often magnify their accomplishments, remembering vividly their triumphs and barely recalling their failures. "He reminds me of the war veteran whose exploits grow in stature with the passage of years and the deaths of his comrades," writes David Lewis, the University of Michigan historian. "He was a public relations pioneer and had a great career. Why not leave it at that instead of making exaggerated claims?"[41]

Leaving it at that, however, would have denied who Eddie truly was—the consummate PR man—and what he did for his clients, which was meticulously massage the facts, then filter them through letters, speeches, and front groups until even he could not say for sure what was truth and what spin. This, after all, was the man who got kids to carve bars of soap into works of art and persuaded their parents to serve bacon and eggs for breakfast. Ballyhooing like that for a living and believing in it so ardently, he found it tough to turn off the rhetoric even when he was telling his own story.

The irony, as Lewis notes, is that Eddie's actual accomplishments were so momentous that he didn't need to bend the truth. And embellishing the way he did with Light's Golden Jubilee raised unfair doubts about whether he deserved credit for all the precedent-setting campaigns he really had carried out.

Eddie knew about the whispering; he knew colleagues and historians bought most of what he was selling but doubted some of his stories. He resolutely denied that he exaggerated, and when questioned, even into his late nineties, he would jump up from his desk and begin pulling papers from his files, eager to prove he'd done precisely what he said. But he also conceded in his autobiography, and again and again in conversations, that "in an era of mass communication, modesty is a private virtue and a public fault."

Setting the SPIN

4

BIG THINK WORKED SO WELL IN SELLING EVERYTHING FROM BEER TO ballet dancers that politicians couldn't resist seeing whether it could sell them, too. And Eddie Bernays, America's number one salesman, was anxious to oblige.

The first to call on him were supporters of President Calvin Coolidge who, in 1924, were trying to elect their man to his first full term. Vice President Coolidge had moved into the White House and dropped the "vice" from his title when President Warren G. Harding died a year earlier. But his new prominence did nothing to sweeten a personality so sour that Alice Roosevelt Longworth, Teddy Roosevelt's daughter, surmised that Coolidge was "weaned on a pickle."

The public was equally wary of the new president, which was worrisome to Rhinelander Waldo, the ex–police commissioner of New York City. Even though Waldo was a Democrat, he admired Coolidge, who was a Republican. More to the point, Waldo, a lanky Connecticut Yankee, realized that if he helped elect Coolidge, Coolidge might help him become governor of New York. Or maybe governor of the Philippines. To promote the president's cause and his own, Waldo created the Coolidge Non-Partisan League, but he realized he'd need the help of a specialist like Bernays to sell voters on the league and on the dour president.

Today it's standard procedure for Democrats to show off the Republicans who have rallied to their candidacy, and vice versa, but back then it was more of an oddity and, as Bernays understood, more likely to draw press attention. So, as he'd done for front groups he set up for corporate clients, Bernays set out to spread the word on the Non-Partisan League. He had a poster delivered to a thousand newspapers that told the league's story; to ensure that everyone got the point about nonpartisanship, it featured a picture of Waldo sandwiched between an elephant and a donkey.

Bernays also searched for prominent Democrats who would back Coolidge. He found several who were willing to say nice things about the president's positions on issues ranging from welfare to low-cost transportation to protective tariffs—mainly because, like Waldo, they had an interest they hoped could be advanced by extending the White House stay of the Republican president. Every newspaper story mentioned Waldo's name along with Coolidge's.

The campaign was going fine, but Bernays and Waldo worried that too few voters were being swayed by such partisan appeals, even when couched in nonpartisanship. And they knew such serious-minded stories only reinforced the president's serious-minded image. Something else was needed, a masterstroke like the one Bernays had struck with Caruso and the Ballet Russe, which would, at least for a moment, transform the president from a cold introvert into the homespun figure people wanted in the White House. The PR man contemplated bringing to Washington a collection of female novelists or a special delegation of mothers.

Even better, he decided, would be leading figures from the stage, people like troubadour Al Jolson and fellow entertainers John Drew, Raymond Hitchcock, and the Dolly Sisters, whose every performance rang out with humanity and energy. One night, after the curtains fell on Broadway, a troupe of forty performers boarded the midnight train to the nation's capital. A caravan of Cadillacs met them at Union Station and shuttled them to the White House, where Mr. and Mrs.

Coolidge were waiting at the entrance. One by one the stars and star-lets shook hands with the president, with Bernays acting as intermediary and the president maintaining his trademark deadpan expression. Then they all adjourned to the state dining room for coffee, fruit, toast, griddle cakes, and sausages.

After breakfast the president led his guests onto the White House lawn, where Jolson serenaded him with a song entitled "Keep Coolidge." "The race is now begun, and Coolidge is the one, the one to fill the presidential chair. Without a lot of fuss he did a lot for us, so let's reciprocate and keep him there," he sang. Mrs. Coolidge and the rest of the Broadway delegation joined in the refrain: "Keep Coolidge! Keep Coolidge! And have no fears for four more years!"

The newspapers loved it. The *New York Times* headlined its story, "Actors Eat Cakes with the Coolidges . . . President Nearly Laughs."[1] The *New York Review* went a step further, topping its story with the headline "Jolson Makes President Laugh for the First Time in Public."[2] And the *New York World* wrote, "It took a group of New York actors three minutes to accomplish with Calvin Coolidge what society leaders of Washington had attempted and failed, what traditionally was impossible, at least in public, and what even the Senate during his two years and a half as presiding officer could not make him do. They forced him to show his teeth, open his mouth and laugh."[3]

Years afterward, Bernays reflected on what he'd done: "To the country at large the headlines and the stories reflected surprise and undoubtedly changed the reputation of Coolidge as intended."[4] Whether or not he had single-handedly transformed Coolidge's image, he did give the press and the nation an event so surprising and irresistible that it touched a nerve. Three weeks later Coolidge won a landslide victory. And, of perhaps greater significance, Bernays proved that the skills he had used to craft public attitudes toward cigarettes and cigars could be employed to reshape the image of elected officials.

That lesson wasn't lost on another president seeking reelection eight years later. Herbert Hoover summoned Bernays to the White House a month before the 1932 election, eager to hear his ideas on how to overcome the seemingly endless depression and, even more pressing, what to do about his formidable Democratic opponent, Franklin Delano Roosevelt. A strategy paper in Bernays's files lays out his last-minute plan.[5] First he would enlist his cadre of "disinterested experts" from business, labor, and academia. Only this time he was out to win over the entire nation, which meant signing up as many as 25,000 "group leaders" to his Non-partisan Fact-Finding Committee for Hoover. They would get out the word that the economy was about to turn around. And they would help "puncture the inferior personality" of Roosevelt by convincing voters that the Democratic candidate was "not the progressive" people thought he was and that he "has been subject to Tammany and political jobbery."

Dividing the opposition was key to conquering it, Bernays believed. In this case that meant persuading the 15 million Americans who had voted four years before for Democrat Alfred E. Smith to switch to Hoover, write in Smith's name, or simply stay home on election day. One publicity campaign would spotlight leading Democrats who thought it had been a mistake to nominate Roosevelt instead of Smith. Another would show Hoover to be a courageous, humane leader who'd brought the nation peace if not prosperity. And, in the biggest reach of all in a nation where 12 million people were unemployed, Bernays's experts would make the case that Hoover's plan for deliberate recovery was more prudent than Roosevelt's promise of a quick end to the Great Depression.

Bernays also made clear, as he had in his corporate campaigns, that the best way to win over the public was by appealing to instinct rather than reason. "Always keep in mind the tendency of human beings to symbolize their leaders as Achilles' heel proof," his strategy paper advised. "Also that the inferiority complex of individuals will respond to feeling superior to a fool. . . . Create issues that appeal to pugnacious instincts of human beings."

Even the savviest campaign couldn't paper over the bleak economic picture, however: Hoover captured just 59 electoral votes to Roosevelt's 472.

. . .

the Spin

Building on his early experiences to benefit later clients—and himself—had become a maxim for Bernays. He was perpetually sifting out and writing down new ways of doing everything from filing contacts to marketing clients, in the process offering direction to his young staff and transforming his novel field of press-agentry into the profession of public relations. The same rules that had let him sell Caruso to an American public wary of Europeans, and of opera, helped him peddle cigarettes to an entire generation of American women.

So it was in politics. What began with Coolidge and Hoover as ad hoc responses had become, by 1940, sophisticated campaign strategies. That new scientific approach was on full display in the work Bernays did that year for William O'Dwyer, who was trying to unseat two-term New York mayor Fiorello H. La Guardia.

"I can only give advice if I first know what people's attitudes are," Bernays told O'Dwyer, who had approached the PR man just two months before the election.[6] Bernays's caution appears eminently reasonable today, when survey researchers and spin doctors are even firmer fixtures in campaigns than poll watchers and leafleteers. Back then the notion of measuring public sentiment seemed quixotic, but Bernays set out to prove otherwise. He scattered members of his staff across the five boroughs to interview a thousand voters, then began analyzing previous citywide election results and gathering all available data on New Yorkers' educational, economic, and political affiliations. He even undertook a "psychological survey" of voters of various religious and ethnic backgrounds "to discover the emotional or logical basis for attitude and action in the campaign."

The result was forty-six pages of recommendations that may have been the first voter portrait of its kind, and was almost certainly the most sophisticated.[7] The public relations adviser broke voters down by religion, ethnicity, issues, and ideology, and suggested detailed appeals for each group. O'Dwyer should approach fellow Irish Catholics, Bernays said, by pointing out that when he was the district attorney in Brooklyn he'd helped break up a band of mob hit men known as Murder, Incorporated, and by highlighting his Democratic Party credentials. When he made his pitch to Italians, however, he should play up the need to reform the police department, stress his political independence, and show that the man he was trying to unseat, La Guardia, had failed to appoint fellow Italians to city jobs. With union members the theme should be his "pro labor and pro union attitude," while with big business it should be his "fairness in labor disputes, fair hearing of employers' side."

Those messages would be carried by conventional media like newspapers and radio, but also by new ones like motion pictures and newsreels, with their ability to present symbols as well as substance. A Non-Partisan Committee for O'Dwyer would keep the candidate at arm's length from the tainted political machinery of Tammany Hall and the Democratic Party. And, much as fifty years later Bill Clinton's presidential campaign would insist on one overriding campaign message—"it's the economy, stupid"—so Bernays told the O'Dwyer campaign that "every event, every speech, every release, every action, should fit into the broad pattern of the six points" he'd spelled out in an earlier manifesto.

Bernays also grasped the importance of language in political discourse, and he knew how much more appealing an active candidate was than a passive one. So he made a list of verbs that should guide the campaign's actions: express (confidence), assail, deny, predict, hail, ask, promise, appeal, urge, hope, advocate, see, say, tell, declare, deplore, request, remark, reveal, propose, condemn, exhort, praise, forecast, demand, thank.

One group and one message mattered more than all the others, however: Jews and the insecurity they were feeling at that time in New York and around the world. Jews were important, Bernays said, because they made up one-third of the city's population and were the biggest block of swing voters, and because his surveys had revealed that an overwhelming 84 percent of them favored La Guardia, whose mother was Jewish. To win, O'Dwyer had to win over those Jews. And the key to doing that, Bernays wrote, was to convince Jewish voters "that the candidate is not anti-Semitic."

His plan for doing that could be a casebook in ethnic politics, one

Eddie, at age 7, poses in Central Park
with his younger sisters Hella and Martha
and his mother, Anna Freud Bernays.

Eddie handled publicity for the first U.S. tour of Daighilev's Ballet Russe, which was sponsored by the Metropolitan Opera Company, pictured here in 1916.

Members of the U.S. Committee on Public Information are set to sail from New York to Paris on November 19, 1918, eight days after the Armistice. They were supposed to handle press relations for the U.S. mission to the Paris Peace Conference but ended up generating their own headlines as Congress accused the committee of muzzling the press. Bernays, with mustache, is the next to last on the right.

OPPOSITE: *Enrico Caruso welcomed by the army brass band in Toledo in 1917 with a doughboy who was a Caruso look-alike opening the car door for the famous tenor. Eddie, who helped arrange this tour, is at the far right with his press kit.*

*Eddie and Doris in Paris in 1925
for a meeting of the International
Exposition of Modern Decorative
and Industrial Arts. He helped
convince Secretary of Commerce
Herbert Hoover to name an official
U.S. delegation to the exposition,
and to name him an "associate
commissioner." The post let him
promote the interests of long-time
client Cheney Brothers, a silk
manufacturer.*

*As they prepare to leave for Europe,
Eddie holds Doris's U.S. passport,
issued in the name Doris E.
Fleischman. It was the first time the
government allowed a married
woman to use her maiden name on
a passport.*

Eddie and Doris stand before the famous Lalique glass fountain in Paris at the 1925 International Exposition of Modern Decorative and Industrial Arts.

Eddie and, to his left, Doris, with their public relations office staff in 1926, seven years after he set up his pioneering practice. His clients at the time included soap-maker Procter & Gamble and Cartier's, the Fifth Avenue jeweler. While he insisted that he and Doris were equal partners, the office was called "Edward L. Bernays, Counsel on Public Relations."

The four-story Georgian brownstone in Washington Square that Eddie and Doris leased in 1929 from diplomat and businessman William Averell Harriman. It had two bronze roosters standing watch on the stoop, a drawing room with high ceilings and a white marble mantle, and sliding doors of mahogany opening onto music and dining rooms.

Eddie and Doris with other family members.

Eddie and his older daughter, Doris, when she was two or three. It was the only time his children remember seeing Eddie without a mustache, which he temporarily shaved because young Doris told him the facial hair tickled when he kissed her.

A birthday party for Eddie's older daughter, Doris, at the Bernays home at Eight Washington Square North, in Greenwich Village, in the thirties. Standing next to Eddie are his nephew Peter Bernays, Eddie's wife Doris, and Doris's mother, sister, and brother-in-law. The children include, from left to right, Eddie's children Anne and Doris, his nephew Martin, and young Doris's friend Jack Lemann.

the Spin

that would be as relevant today as it was back then. O'Dwyer not only had to endorse anti-Nazi and anti-Fascist groups, he had to be there at their meetings, deliver a memorable address, and have his picture taken. He had to align himself squarely with President Roosevelt and his efforts in behalf of the Allies, appear before the Jewish War Veterans, and, of course, have his picture taken with both. He had to speak out forcefully in favor of civil rights and civil liberties. And he had to take on anti-Semitic groups like the Christian Front, although to ensure that wouldn't alienate Catholic supporters Bernays advised that "the attack should be carried out by utilizing names of individuals with the same national or other background as the group being attacked."

O'Dwyer lost the election, although by the narrowest margin in a mayoral race since 1905. Four years later he ran again and won.

The same year he worked for O'Dwyer Bernays compiled an analysis of the New York State electorate for Democratic Lieutenant Governor Charles Poletti, who was considering a run for governor.[8] The news this time, based on interviews with political, labor, civic, and other leaders, wasn't encouraging. Poletti's Italian nationality worked against him, Bernays reported. So did his record of interventionism. His "change of religion costs him the Catholic vote without winning him the Protestant vote," and he was unpopular with farmers, business-men, and political organizations. "He lacks color," Bernays wrote, and "he lacks strength." Former governor Al Smith didn't like Poletti, nor did the Democratic establishment. And "he is irritating to many of his political associates." There were favorable findings, too, but they took up just ten lines as compared to the twenty-seven unfavorable ones.

Poletti apparently took the analysis to heart and chose to run for reelection as lieutenant governor. And while others might have bridled at Bernays's blunt analysis of his unpopularity, Poletti remained grate-ful. "Now it [public relations] has become a profession but in those days it wasn't as well organized as it is now," Poletti recalled in a 1978 interview. Bernays, he added, "was a very intelligent fellow in the field of public relations. He had a good roster of clients; and he took a liking to me, and he studied my career, and I remember [he] prepared several analyses of it with suggestions as to what I might do or not do to improve what is now called the image, the political image. And he never charged me anything for it; he just did it as a friend."[9]

. . .

Bernays offered comparable counsel to an assortment of other prominent political figures, from First Lady Eleanor Roosevelt to President Dwight D. Eisenhower. Sometimes, as with Eisenhower, he lobbied for programs he respected, like the U.S. Information Agency; with Eleanor Roosevelt, he primarily promoted her memoirs. And he briefly advised Al Smith when Smith was governor of New York and contemplating the run he later made for president. Smith was a "natural-born" leader, Bernays said, the kind who "understand intuitively what other people learned the hard way through books."[10]

The U.S. government called on Bernays repeatedly. After World War I he worked for the War Department, mapping out a national campaign to find jobs for veterans and concocting slogans like "He's not a dead one, so after you've put his name on the honor roll don't forget to put it on the payroll, too," and "A job inside is worth a hundred Welcome Home signs in the window." Just before World War II he went back to work for Uncle Sam, advising a presidential authority that had been set up to battle the depression. "They were going to call it the Committee for Unemployment," Bernays recalled later. "I suggested to them that they change that over to 'the President's'—the president being a godhead symbol—to 'Emergency,' which made it an impermanent committee to take care of the emergency, and 'for Employment,' which set affirmative goals instead of negative ones."[11] So the group became the President's Emergency Committee for Employment.

Bernays advised the U.S. Information Agency on how to do a better job of disseminating U.S. propaganda, told the army and navy how to handle public relations during World War II, and was called in to counsel the Departments of State and the Interior. In 1925 Secretary of Commerce Herbert Hoover named him associate commissioner of commerce to the Paris Exposition of Decorative Arts, and in the 1940s he was named chairman of the National Advisory Committee of the Third U.S. War Loan, cochairman of the Victory Book campaign, and a member of the New York State Defense Council.

Sometimes his work for the government let him in on state secrets, although, as his wedding antics had shown, he had a tough time keeping a secret. In unpublished notes for his autobiography he recounted how Leslie Richard Groves, the all-powerful U.S. Army general who oversaw production of the first atomic bomb, left the army in 1949 and "took with him a lot of secret papers of the project he had no right to take. Those papers covered the dossiers and background of many atomic scientists. Some went back to their earliest childhood. In order to keep the project in the hands of the army, Groves took whatever information was derogatory, or could be distorted to be derogatory to the civilian control of atomic power, and turned it over to the [U.S. House] Un-American [Activities] Committee. The committee has studied it carefully and will use it to smear the idea of civilian control of atomic energy."[12]

Other times the information he picked up wasn't secret, but it did offer an inside look at his era's most powerful political figures. And Bernays's comments on these people, as on so much else in his world, were delivered with a crispness and a cutting edge he knew would be irresistible to journalists and historians.

He got to know Henry A. Wallace before Franklin D. Roosevelt named him secretary of agriculture, and Bernays claims credit for helping smooth the way for that appointment. Much later, after Wallace had served as vice president, Bernays handled publicity for his appointment as editor of the *New Republic*. Wallace, Bernays said, was "a man whose mind was full of dreams, daydreams, aspirations and hopes, with a fuzziness or muzziness about delineating them in terms of Act 1, step 1, step 2, Act 2."[13]

Years later he offered an equally ambivalent appraisal of another former vice president, Hubert Humphrey of Minnesota, who was the Democratic presidential nominee in 1968: "If Hubert Humphrey had been able to delimit his activity, he might have been a good president.

But he spread himself so thin and had what we used to call verbal diarrhea, that would practically set him off at the drop of an agate line to just go on [and] ad lib."[14]

While politicians often left Bernays cold, the men behind the scenes intrigued him, as they might any student of public relations. James A. Farley, chairman of the Democratic National Committee, was especially alluring because of his critical role in electing Franklin Roosevelt to the first of his four terms and because he was willing to tell Bernays just how he did it. FDR's success was, Farley claimed, first and foremost a result of Teddy Roosevelt's cousin having inherited a great name and of having a great voice and great smile.

Once he recognized Roosevelt's potential, Farley went to work selling him to America in just the way Bernays might have done. He got a check-writing machine, the crude forebear of today's automated autographer, and used it to write "personal" letters to each of the nation's three thousand Democratic county chairmen. Such mass mailings were highly unusual then, and Farley told Bernays that "by the time I got through [with] this correspondence his nomination was in the bag."

Lots of things about Farley impressed Bernays, starting with his height of 6 feet 2 inches, which to the short PR man seemed "overpoweringly tall." Then there was "a warmth that came out through his fingertips. His handshake was the kind of handshake you read about in your civics books. The handshake that elects presidents." Most of all, Bernays was captivated by Farley's instinctiveness, by his understanding of what made people think and how, with so little effort, they could be made to think differently. Farley, he wrote, "had such practical wisdom, with no theories. . . . His attitude toward you depended on his quick intuitive grasp of what he had to do to win your friendship and to influence you."[15]

His relationship was more intimate with Clare Boothe Luce, a congresswoman from Connecticut and wife of *Time* magazine owner Henry Luce. "When Harry asked me to advise Mrs. Luce," Bernays remembered in his autobiography, "the three of us met in the Luce apartment, high up in the Waldorf Towers, to discuss ways and means to speed her on her new career. I was, as other men must have been,

before and afterward, fascinated by her provocative presence. I understood why Harry had fallen in love with her. Her lively ebullience, her
beauty, sparkling eyes, blond hair and warm personality were combined with a mind as sharp as the new stainless-steel razor blades. . . .
Clare Boothe Luce's actions demonstrated a principle Thomas
Jefferson had first enunciated: No one in our society is as powerful as
the individual American."[16]

The two worked together to battle racism, push for profit sharing,
and ensure the welfare of American children. And judging from their
correspondence, Mrs. Luce was as captivated by the PR man as he
with her. "Don't let us have a professional arrangement," he wrote in
February 1946. "My conscience would not allow me to accept a fee for
any advice you might ask of me on the causes in which I am as greatly
interested as you are. . . . Please call on me whenever there is anything
you want to discuss on these matters." She wrote back that August,
"We have rented [a] farmhouse for the summer. Some day when you
feel like a drive to the country, come up and sit under her old apple
trees with me, and I will tell you lots of things that I have been thinking about the state of the Union's public relations with Maestro
Bernays."[17]

Not everyone wanted Bernays's help, of course. Supreme Court
Justice Robert H. Jackson at one point had contemplated making a bid
for governor of New York, and as he recalled, "Bernays wanted to take
up my case. He wanted to manage the publicity for this Young
Democrats dinner, the buildup and all that went into the making of a
candidate. I just couldn't agree to it. The program sounded to me just
like the kind of a buildup that [Wendell] Willkie got in 1940, when
they all turned in a high-pressure publicity campaign."[18]

Despite Jackson's reservations, word of Bernays's skills spread so far
that political figures from other nations came to him seeking counsel.
In 1918, when he was working for America's World War I propaganda
agency, Bernays had lunch with Tomáš Garrigue Masaryk, the Czech
nationalist leader who'd fled his country at the start of the war.
Masaryk "told me he intended to declare the freedom of Czecho-
slovakia 'tomorrow afternoon,' Saturday, October 18," Bernays

recalled. But the PR man warned that the announcement would be lost among the fashion advice and funnies of the Sunday papers, whereas if he waited until Sunday, generally a slow time for news, the story would be prominently displayed on Monday in papers world-wide. "He was startled," Bernays said, and protested that "'that would be making history for the [wire service] cables.' I assured him the cables make history. Masaryk accepted my recommendation and waited a day. He declared the independence of Czechoslovakia on Sunday, October 19, 1918. . . . That is why the people of Czecho-slovakia celebrated their 'Fourth of July' annually one day later than they might otherwise."[19]

The Masaryk story, one of Bernays's favorites, turned up in several newspaper and magazine interviews as well as in his autobiography. But like many of his tales of corporate accomplishment, it contains inconsistencies that make it, in the words of George Kovtun, a Czech and Slovak specialist at the Library of Congress, "rather doubtful." Bernays himself frequently switched his dates around, writing in his memoirs that his lunch with Masaryk was in 1914, but in notes for the memoirs giving the more likely year of 1918. Sometimes he dates the declaration of freedom as October 19, other times October 28. Another problem, explains Kovtun, who has written extensively about Masaryk's relations with America, is that the Czech leader issued his Declaration of Independence on a Friday (October 18), and newspapers reported it on Saturday, which makes clear that Bernays got his days and dates wrong. The official Czech national holiday is October 28, but Kovtun says that's not directly connected with events in America or with Masaryk. Perhaps most telling, according to Kovtun, "Masaryk wrote detailed memoirs about his activities in the First World War. He writes about many of his American supporters, but Edward L. Bernays's name is never mentioned in his book."[20]

· · ·

Just as Bernays anticipated the tactics of today's spinmeisters, he also anticipated the ethical dilemmas created by their craft. And as he watched presidents like Richard Nixon and Lyndon Johnson use public relations strategies in their attempts to paper over their troubles with Watergate and Vietnam, he realized he had to distance himself from at least the excesses of the enterprise.

That's why, in his later years, Bernays spent almost as much time telling stories about clients he had turned down as those he had accepted. He says, for instance, that in the 1930s he was asked to handle publicity for the Leipzig Fair, an offer that "was undoubtedly a ruse by the Nazis to have me work with them. I turned it down because what the Nazi stood for was not my social objective."[21]

He declined again when representatives of Nicaragua's right-wing government sought his help. "The reason I turned them down was not because Nicaragua isn't accepted by the United Nations," he explained. "If I'd been a doctor I might have an obligation to take them—but as a counsel on public relations, I can turn down something that I object to as an individual." There also was a call from "some Spanish Jews and they wanted me to take Franco, and told me how kind Franco was to Jews. Well, I wouldn't work for Franco. Now, I confess that supposing I'd had five children and I needed to feed them, I don't know at what point I would have taken Franco. I don't think I would have taken him if I could have gotten something else."[22]

The call was somewhat less clear-cut when Vice President Richard Nixon came looking for help in the 1950s. Nixon apparently wanted to polish his image as he prepared for a run at the White House, but Bernays was wary and his wife even warier. "Unless we're in the poorhouse," a friend recalls Doris Fleischman Bernays saying, "we can't go in this direction." So Bernays once again declined.[23]

But while some distancing was advisable and inevitable, Bernays was not one to back away from the basic PR principles to which he had devoted his life. So when those principles were brought into disrepute by figures ranging from Nixon to Franco, the PR master insisted it was the way his concepts were interpreted that was the problem, not the concepts themselves.

"[P]ublic relations in politics . . . as in any other professional field, can be used constructively or abused," he said. "The same thing is true of any human function. You have honest lawyers and shyster lawyers.

You can use the law to bring justice or you can use the law to abuse the principles of justice on which the society rests."[24]

An honest public relations practitioner, Bernays reasoned, could use all the wiles of the profession to measure public opinion and try to sway it, to see how people perceived politicians and repackage them more to the public's liking—provided it was all done "to lead the people to where they want to go. Leadership in a democracy is solving the problems they believe need solving."[25]

What about the demagogue? What was the PR man to do when a client, like Nixon, was willing to cover up a break-in at the opposition party's headquarters and, until the very end, to deny his culpability and blame his downfall on his enemies?

Bernays had an easy answer here as elsewhere: a reputable public relations counselor should simply say no, just as he had with Hitler and Franco. Beyond that, he said it was up to the public to ensure that it was not manipulated by unscrupulous politicians or their unscrupulous consultants.

"Just as Consumers Union has made women more aware of what to look for in a given commodity they buy, so the voter, as a result of more education, as a result of more discussion of this subject, will be more sophisticated in protecting his own interests, and the public interest," Bernays said. Education, he added, increasingly is creating American voters who are "able to penetrate the words, the pictures, and the actions they are exposed to and to look behind them and act accordingly."[26]

Rationale for a PROFESSION

5

AN ART APPLIED TO A SCIENCE. THAT'S HOW EDWARD L. BERNAYS saw his evolving profession of public relations. And while he knew others would invent their own art forms the same way he'd dreamed up Big Think, he felt it was his calling to spell out the precepts of the science.

Bernays's first rule: Public relations is a two-way street. On one side the PR man interprets his client to the public, presenting as upbeat an image as he can. It is equally important to interpret the public to the client, telling company executives what people want and need, and altering the behavior of those executives just as he did that of the public.

To do the job right, Bernays believed, the PR man not only needs to be smart and intuitive, he needs to understand psychology, sociology, and enough other social sciences to get under the skin of the public and the client, to know what makes them act the way they do and how they can be enticed to act differently. Realizing this second goal, he added, requires poring over books and journals, interviewing experts, and doing all the other research a social scientist would do.

Precept three: America will be a much better place as a result of the public relations counselor's efforts. In fact, a society this complex needs someone like him to sort through the ideas and options competing for our attention.

His first two "scientific" principles were novel, maybe even revolutionary, in the world of public relations, but the rest of the world didn't pay much attention. His third notion hit a nerve because it seemed so preposterous: the public relations man as prophet and savior? Yet it was this idea that catapulted Bernays into the forefront of a cadre of social engineers that emerged at the turn of the century. If it seemed to contradict his own notion of everyone being free to determine their own future, he had a ready explanation: freedom is an admirable ideal, but it's impractical in a nation this big, with a population that isn't equal in talent or training.

"In almost every act of our daily lives, whether in the sphere of politics or business, in our social conduct or our ethical thinking, we are dominated by the relatively small number of persons—a trifling fraction of our hundred and twenty million—who understand the mental processes and social patterns of the masses," Bernays wrote in his 1928 book *Propaganda*. That "trifling fraction" was composed of PR professionals like him, who "pull the wires which control the public mind, who harness old forces and contrive new ways to bind and guide the world."[1]

Such hidden propagandists might alarm others, but Bernays saw them as tamers of the wild crowd and guardians of a civil society. "It is not usually realized how necessary these invisible governors are to the orderly functioning of our group life," he explained. "Intelligent men must realize that propaganda is the modern instrument by which they can fight for productive ends and help to bring order out of chaos."[2]

But who was to blame when that science of propaganda was applied to evil ends, as it was when a Nazi propagandist consulted Bernays's works in plotting his campaign to exterminate the Jews? Or when Bernays's lofty standards for the PR man conflicted with his own lofty salary for helping tobacco companies push their deadly products? In the first case he pleaded that he was powerless to stop his ideas from being misused, and that if the bad guys were using propaganda, the good guys had to use it to fight back—the same defense used by the inventors of the atom bomb. As for his own alleged hypocrisy, he was adept at reshaping his professional history to make it fit his professed ideals.

Perhaps no one would have noticed those inconsistencies if Bernays had quietly formulated his theories, as most social scientists did, and been content for them to be discussed within a closed community of scholars. That, however, was not the Bernays way. He was too impatient, too much the publicity man. He understood that his theories had to be known if they were to be debated, and they had to be debated if they were to change people's thinking and behavior. So he delivered a nonstop series of speeches, artfully guiding reporters who wrote up most of what he fed them. He wrote or edited 15 books, 300 articles, and more than 125 letters to the editor—all at the same time he was representing hundreds of clients. He had a lot to say about his fledgling profession, about its strategies and the philosophy behind it. And he made sure it was all there in black and white, in edition after edition and translation after translation, to the point where it was difficult for people not to notice.

The topics changed as quickly as the times he was living in, from war and peace, to depression and recovery, to why America and England weren't getting along. But underlying everything were the singular precepts about the science of public relations and the role of the PR man, precepts that became Bernays's mantra over a career that spanned four generations.

. . .

Bernays was an original thinker, but his theories weren't conceived in a vacuum. To understand his ideas it's essential to understand his times. America in the 1920s seemed blessed with limitless horizons. The economy was soaring. Lindbergh had shown how far man could fly, and RCA was showing how loud a man's voice and ideas could resonate. Ford was turning out a Model T every ten seconds, and the average American could finally afford a car, the ultimate sign of modernity in a decade that celebrated things modern. Bernays, meanwhile, was learning that the technological and psychological forces that helped him shape public opinion for Caruso and rally America against the German kaiser could be tapped to do much, much more.

All that economic growth and technological change brought with it new public attitudes and social norms. Americans were beginning to view the captains of capitalism in a less flattering light. Muckraking journalists dug up proof of just how venal John D. Rockefeller and his robber baron pals were, of how William Henry Vanderbilt hadn't been kidding when he'd scoffed "the public be damned," and of how corrupt politicians had condoned their actions. At the same time the social fabric was fraying as people migrated from farms to cities, abandoning old ties of community, looking for new associations to bind them, and demanding an unprecedented accountability from leaders in business and government.

Change added an unsettling volatility to American life. Victorian ideals of an ordered society no longer held much sway, nor did the religious principles of delayed gratification and presumed hierarchies. It was unclear what would take their place. Anarchy? The rule of the unbridled crowd, or such new and untested groups as labor unions? And how would all this be affected by the new technologies of radio, long-distance telephone lines, and the printing presses proliferating everywhere—technologies that had proved so effective in rallying the nation to war?

The great social theorists of the day were struggling for answers, and trying to construct new modes of behavior. One of the first to outline his ideas was Gustave Le Bon, a French social psychologist who in 1895 published *The Crowd—A Study of the Popular Mind*. Le Bon raised the specter of a frightening new era dominated by the masses, by a crowd unbound by the rules of reason that governed the middle class. The conscious personality of the individual is submerged once he joins the crowd, Le Bon argued, to be replaced by a mass mind whose behavior is unanimous, emotional, and ultimately dangerous.

Another French social scientist, Gabriel Tarde, began to respond to fears raised by his friend Le Bon. Yes, the crowd could be worrisome,

Tarde said, but the mass media, and particularly newspapers, could help tame that crowd into a public bound and ordered by shared, constructive goals. British surgeon and sociologist Wilfred Trotter, in his 1916 book *The Instincts of the Herd in Peace and War,* offered a different prescription. He saw the crowd as governed by the same Freudian instincts that drove individuals, and the way to rein it in, he said, was to master and manipulate those instincts. That, Trotter believed, could best be done not by the press, as Tarde proposed, but by an elite group of intellectuals able to exploit the same sorts of psychological symbols Freud was using with his patients.

Trotter and his compatriots wanted to use their understanding of sociology and psychology to make sense of a world that seemed out of control, particularly in light of the brutal war raging around them. But their writings and observations begged as many questions as they answered: Just what sorts of symbols did they have in mind? And who would constitute this elite group exercising the symbols?

Many scholars had theories, but no one more clearly tied together the threads of his forebears than author and journalist Walter Lippmann. Leaders, Lippmann said, couldn't be expected to have a rational dialogue with their constituents about essential ideals like justice, or law and order. That would be too unwieldy, would take too long, and wouldn't ensure the desired outcome. Instead, they should find just the right word or image to capture the popular imagination, the way they had in rallying the nation to war. The ideal medium through which to exercise such symbols, he added, was the cinema, where Hollywood could make clear in an instant who were the good guys and who the bad, which ideas were worthy of loyalty and which should inspire anger.

Bernays had been experimenting with such symbols for a decade, and he'd been keeping up with the writings of Lippmann, Le Bon, and the others. He too was smart enough to sense the ferment, the search for new ways to control a society that seemed increasingly out of control. He was self-assured enough to believe that while others speculated about symbols and signs, about ways to manipulate the media and the cinema, he knew just how to do it. And he was competitive enough to know that, if he was the first in his field to weigh in with a book, he could shape that field and promote himself in the process.

He also happened to have as a client one of the leading publishers of the day, Horace Liveright.

In 1923, a year after Lippmann came out with his widely read *Public Opinion*, Bernays published his first book, *Crystallizing Public Opinion.* "I suggested to Horace Liveright that he publish a book on public relations," he recalled. "I believed it would be a sound public relations move for what we were doing. He told me it was a 'swell idea.'"[3]

. . .

That swell idea turned out to be ahead of its time. *Crystallizing* was greeted with lukewarm sales back then, when few knew or cared much about this unusual profession, but it eventually became the landmark work Bernays hoped it would. Reissued in 1961, it remains a classic in public relations studies.

The book defined the new "public relations counsel," distinguishing him from the crude press agent whose main motivation was "getting something for nothing from publishers," and the equally crude "circus advance-man" and "semi-journalist promoter of small-time actresses." The role of the counsel on public relations, Bernays wrote, was "to advise his clients how positive results can be accomplished in the field of public relations and to keep them from drifting into unfortunate or harmful situations."[4]

When it came to the wider society, Bernays's PR man could play a hero's part, just the sort Lippmann and the others sought to transform the angry masses into a calmer, more docile public. He could be objective enough to "step out of his own group to look at a particular problem with the eyes of an impartial observer," sagacious enough to pick out solutions that were good for his client and the public, and skillful enough to get the press to take up his cause. "It is his capacity for crystallizing the obscure tendencies of the public mind before they have reached definite expression," Bernays wrote, "which makes him so valuable."[5]

Bernays's ideas, here as elsewhere, reflected the profound influence of his uncle Sigmund. He talked about the use of symbols, as Freud did, and of the centrality of "stereotypes, individual and community, that will bring favorable responses." He was as driven as his uncle to know what subconscious forces motivated people, and he used Freud's writings to help him understand. But while the esteemed analyst tried to use psychology to free his patients from emotional crutches, Bernays used it to rob consumers of their free will, helping his clients predict, then manipulate, the very way their customers thought and acted—all of which he openly acknowledged in his writings.

He also made clear that his PR man was no democrat. Bernays, like Lippmann and Le Bon, was wary of the common man, especially when he got together with other common men. The social theorists were all for doing good, but felt that was best accomplished by socially enlightened leaders—drawn together, in Bernays's case, by the enlightened public relations counsel—who would replace princes, priests, and other benevolent rulers of bygone days. "The reader will recall from his own experience," Bernays wrote, "an almost infinite number of instances in which the amateur has been fully prepared to deliver expert advice and to give final judgment in matters upon which his ignorance is patent to every one except himself."[6] If you can't trust the "amateur" to get things done, he added in later works, try the experts, the men already in leadership posts in business, politics, and the arts, who can carry the message to the masses.

In getting that message across, Bernays was not afraid to defend his passion for propaganda. He wrote that "the only difference between 'propaganda' and 'education,' really, is in the point of view. The advocacy of what we believe in is education. The advocacy of what we don't believe in is propaganda."[7] He didn't mind being called a manipulator, either, for that was precisely what he envisioned his public relations counsel doing—blending the private interests of his clients with the public interests of society.

"What Lippmann set out in grand, overview terms, Bernays is running through in how-to-do-it terms," says Stuart Ewen, who writes and teaches about the social history of public relations. "He was engaged in it, he was reading it, and he was translating it into the finger knowledge of his trade."[8] But Bernays was "more than simply a public relations practitioner," Ewen adds in his book about public relations. "He would soon situate himself as the most important theorist of American public relations."[9]

PR historian Scott M. Cutlip was similarly impressed, calling *Crystallizing* a landmark work in the way it laid a philosophical foundation and, at least as important, an ethical base for the PR profession. "Bernays emphasized in this path-breaking work that the public relations man's ability to influence public opinion placed upon him an ethical duty above that of his clients to the larger society," wrote Cutlip. "Though these seem like platitudes today, they were revolutionary thoughts in the adolescent vocation."[10]

To really grasp Bernays's outlook on his profession, adds journalism professor Marvin N. Olasky, it's essential to understand his outlook on religion. "Bernays's fundamental faith has been his lack of belief in God," explains Olasky, who interviewed Bernays on this topic. He "saw what he called in our interview 'a world without God' rapidly descending into social chaos. Therefore, he contended that social manipulation by public relations counselors was justified by the end of creating man-made gods who could assert subtle social control and prevent disaster. . . . Pulling strings behind the scenes was necessary not only for personal advantage but for social salvation."[11]

It was radical enough for Bernays to reject religion and God, but he fervently believed that he and other PR counselors could do the job at least as well.

Critics of his day weren't sure what to make of Bernays's ideas or his seminal work *Crystallizing.* H. L. Mencken referred to it as a "pioneer book" in a 1923 article in *American Mercury* magazine. But thirteen years later, in *The American Language,* he dismissed "public relations counsel" as a fancy name for press agent, writing that "practically all American press-agents are now 'public relations counsel,' *for a Profession*

'contact-managers,' or 'publicists,' all tree-trimmers are 'tree sur-geons'. . . and the corn-doctors, after a generation as 'chiropodists,' have burst forth as 'podiatrists.'"[12] Ernest Gruening, later a U.S. sena-tor, applauded the fact that business had outgrown its "public be damned" approach, but wondered whether "the final result [would] be greatly different for the public which, while it no longer tolerates being 'damned,' guilelessly permits itself to be 'bunked'? Is seduction preferable to ravishment?"[13]

The *New York Times* reviewer was somewhat kinder, compliment-ing Bernays's work as "the first book to be devoted exclusively to the occupation which is gradually becoming of overwhelming national importance," but adding in its April 6, 1924, story that "if, with the change of name, there is to come a change in the ethics and manners of the press agent, people will be delighted to call him a public rela-tions counsel or sweet little buttercup or anything he wishes."

Because Bernays wished to be noticed, even the bad reviews were strangely satisfying to him and encouraged him to keep writing. In his 1928 book *Propaganda* he presented a code of ethics for the profes-sion, starting with the precept that a PR man "refuses a client whom he believes dishonest, a product which he believes to be fraudulent, or a cause which he believes to be antisocial." Similarly, a PR campaign should "not attempt to stampede the public with exaggerated claims and false pretenses, but to interpret the individual business vividly and truly through every avenue that leads to public opinion."[14]

His critics were less interested in what his book and essays on pro-paganda said about ethics than what they preached about social con-trol. While Bernays saw himself setting constructive limits on the control he felt was inevitable in a large modern democracy, others saw him crafting a how-to for governments or corporations that were eager to amass power. And they let him have it. "Who are you to decide for the public, and for a fee, what is social or anti-social, what true or false, what is reason or prejudice, what is good or bad?" *Editor and Publisher* asked on September 15, 1928. "To whom are you accountable, in the event of misjudgment?"

Part of Bernays's problem was timing. *Propaganda* was published just as disillusionment over America's failure to achieve its high-minded aims in World War I was reaching its peak, and Americans were blaming British and U.S. propagandists for having dragged them into battle. Hearings also were being held in Washington that unmasked an unprecedented propaganda campaign by the big power and light companies to get across their viewpoint and stifle that of their opponents. Against that backdrop, the very title of Bernays's book "handed the infant field's critics a club with which to bludgeon it," as Cutlip notes. "Creditable propaganda for public relations *Propaganda* wasn't!"[15]

Bernays, of course, saw the furor as sheer opportunity. *The Engineering of Consent*, which appeared in 1955, included an essay of the same title that he had written twenty years earlier, along with seven articles by "social scientists." In his chapter, Bernays laid out what would become a famous eight-part formula for a PR campaign: define your objectives; conduct research; modify your objectives based on that research; set a strategy; establish themes, symbols, and appeals; create an organization to execute your strategy; decide on timing and tactics; and carry out your plans. Individually each element sounded obvious enough, but putting them together the way Bernays did set him apart from his contemporaries, and the essay rings as true today as it did forty years ago.

But *Engineering*, like many of his later works, was more a matter of organizing other people's writings than doing his own, and more recycling of stale ideas than laying out fresh ones. As one reviewer noted, "the disturbing fact is that the contents of the eight chapters vary widely in consideration of the level of understanding" and "add little to the knowledge possessed by a practicing member of the profession."[16]

In *Public Relations*, which had come out three years earlier, Bernays traced the history of the field "from the Dark Ages to the modern world," then illustrated themes he'd talked about before, this time in the context of thirty-five years of personal case histories. "Business should make it clear that it is concerned not only with production, markets, and profits, but also with human rights and aspirations," he wrote. "It is only by the extension of this process in the broadest possible ways, by the voluntary action of all American business, that we shall achieve the goal of a stable advancing economy, with liberty and security for all within the framework of the American way of life."[17]

Books weren't his only way of weighing in on the debate and reaching out to the public. He also wrote magazine stories and essays, hundreds of them, and outlined his ideas in 1971 for an oral historian at Columbia University. One theme he returned to repeatedly, at Columbia and elsewhere, was the distinction between public relations and advertising. The PR person, he explained, is responsible for "every impingement of his principal's or client's action on every phase of public opinion." The adman, by contrast, is narrowly focused on "the selling of a product to the public through paid space."[18] That outlook, which saw advertising as one of many small tools available to the Big Think PR master, might be a tough sell today, when the nation's biggest public relations firms are owned by ad agencies.

Bernays also weighed in early on the controversial topic of public opinion polls, writing an article in 1945 that would have been just as timely in 1995. Real leaders "truly lead," he wrote. "But the polls encourage pseudo-leaders, who in most cases are really followers, to keep on playing follow the leader. They help maintain the status quo—which often needs changing."[19]

· · ·

Not all of Bernays's writing was that high-minded, although much of it was equally prophetic. Often he zeroed in on practical issues, sharing lessons he'd learned during his many years on the job. He broke his advice down into easy-to-swallow maxims, many of which have become part of the American lexicon.

There was this on politics: In most elections you can count on 40 percent of voters siding with you and 40 against; what counts is the 20 percent in the middle. Winning over the undecided 20 percent is what public relations is all about. And, to Tip O'Neill's contention that all politics is local, Bernays added that all PR is, too.

He said any PR strategy must address the four *M*'s: mind power, manpower, mechanics, and money.

He had a theory on stubbornness: "It is sometimes possible to change the attitudes of millions but impossible to change the attitude of one man."

On how to justify high fees: "On the basis of a Latin phrase, *quantum meruit* [as much as one deserves], the man or the corporation is much more likely to do what you suggest if you charge a high fee than if you charge very little."

On a person's age: There are, he'd read and believed, five of them—chronological, mental, societal, physiological, and emotional. And they don't always match. When he was ninety-two, for instance, Bernays insisted that his physiological functions worked as well as those of a sixty-three-year-old, and he said he had a report from his doctor to prove it.

On why thank-you notes still are a good idea: The fact that most people no longer write them is all the more reason to write them. Doing so makes you special and makes the recipient remember you.

On the effectiveness of telegrams: "Everyone over thirty remembers the telegram was a message of some big or important news, and a great many of us are still under its tyranny."

On why he read *Playboy:* "For the same reason I read *National Geographic,* I like to see places that I will never visit."

On the best way to win someone over: It's easier to gain acceptance for your viewpoint by quoting respected authorities, outlining the reasons for your outlook, and referring to tradition than by telling someone he's wrong.

The best way to land a job: Analyze the field, narrow your choice to one or two firms, draft a blueprint for increasing their business, present the plan to a top executive, and write enough letters to make that person remember you, but not enough to make him want to forget you. Ask for the salary you think you're worth, and remember, you're not just looking for a job, you're looking for a career.

The best press releases: Each sentence should have no more than sixteen words and just one idea.

The best place to find things: the public library.

The best defense against propaganda: more propaganda.

for a Profession

On the finesse needed to practice PR: It's like shooting billiards, where you bounce the ball off cushions, as opposed to pool, where you aim directly for the pockets

Bernays's last book, a collection of essays entitled *The Later Years: Public Relations Insights, 1956–1986*, shows how he kept thinking and writing into his nineties, long after he gave up active practice. It also shows how wide-ranging his interests were, with essays ranging from "Down With Image, Up With Reality" to "Plan Your Future—Don't Gamble on It."

Any good PR man understood that the spoken word—spoken with the right modulation in the right forum—could be at least as effective as the written one. Bernays drew on that knowledge as he lectured before one professional group after another as well as in classrooms from Boston to Honolulu, sometimes with great success. "This was the most intense learning experience that I have encountered," Suzanne A. Poliquin wrote after he spoke to her PR seminar in 1983. "Just his continued interest in public relations is an inspiration."[20] But Melvin N. Poretz, who had taken Bernays's course at New York University more than thirty years earlier, wrote, "I recall him as a small man, shaped somewhat like the then well-known Little King character. He wore drab clothing and sat behind his desk reading from notes on large index cards. . . . Every once in a while he would venture up the aisle, all the while carrying on his discourse which allowed barely any time for comments from the gallery. He doted on two things: his connection with Sigmund Freud and his experiences in 'inventing' the field of war propaganda during WW I.

"He was, to my mind, the most boring teacher of my four years at NYU."[21]

· · ·

What does all that writing and speechifying tell us about Bernays's philosophy and politics?

First, he not only didn't fear controversy, he often sought it out. He seemed most comfortable in the center of a firestorm, as the titles of his writings suggest. The pattern was set with his first two books,

Crystallizing Public Opinion and *Propaganda*, which even in the 1920s had some people wondering who this grand orchestrator was and whether he was undermining the public's freedom to make up its own mind. The questions mounted in the wake of his 1928 article "Manipulating Public Opinion: The Why and How" in the *American Journal of Sociology*. In 1935 another academic journal ran his "Molding Public Opinion," in 1949 *Household* published "Why We Behave Like Inhuman Beings," and in 1955 he edited *The Engineering of Consent*, which then, as now, was a troubling notion to many.

J. Carroll Bateman, who reviewed the third edition of *Engineering* in 1970 for *Public Relations Journal*, echoed others within the profession when he worried that Bernays's choice of title "seemed to confirm the worst suspicions of our detractors: we in public relations are 'manipulators' of mass man. It implied that we bend him to our wills, for some good ends and bad, regardless of his self-interest and by means that are sometimes something less than scrupulous. Worst still, the content of the book bears out the unhappy implications of the title."[22]

Backed into a corner, Bernays responded as he always did—by coming out snarling, standing up to his detractors and taking umbrage at having his motives questioned. Yet he managed to mix in enough sense of history, and of his own innocence, to make the indefensible suddenly sound convincing. "Now, the concept of consent came from the Declaration of Independence, 'the consent of the governed,'" he told an interviewer. "Nobody is led anywhere unless he wants to be led." He chose the word "engineering," he added, because in America "the only way to approach a problem of millions—200 millions today—is to look at it as an engineering problem. Some people thought the use of the word 'engineering' was cynical to use in connection with consent, but I didn't mean it as that. I think I found the words in a book on politics."[23]

Bernays considered himself a liberal, but he wasn't always the classic kind. He did trumpet the importance of civil liberties and democracy. He spoke out against Nazism and on behalf of Henry Wallace and other liberal politicians, and he offered his PR services to causes like the NAACP, the ACLU, and labor unions. He supported feminist causes at a time when few men did and, with his wife, spoke up for such radical notions as requiring husbands to pay their wives for housework, child care, cooking, and other household duties. And although he tried to help President Hoover stave off a challenge by Franklin D. Roosevelt, he endorsed the direction, if not all the specifics, of Roosevelt's New Deal, defending it to clients like Mack Truck president E. L. Bransome, who saw Roosevelt as a traitor to his class.

But he was an avowed elitist, too, distrusting the masses to the point where he was willing to manipulate them for what he insisted was a just end but which often turned out to be a business interest. He was a virulent anti-Communist, but at times he used precisely the same propaganda techniques as the Soviets. And he recognized the excesses of McCarthyism, but at times employed Red-baiting tactics identical to those of Senator Joseph McCarthy.

Equally discomforting to liberals was how, whatever the problem, Bernays's solution always centered on public relations and, in many cases, on hiring him. Consider "Plain Talk to Liberals," a series of full-page advertisements he took out in 1944 in *The Nation* and *The New Republic*, two leading liberal journals. In the ads, which were later turned into a book, Bernays offers advice to fellow liberals on pressing "problems" of the day—things like the shortage of household servants and the elitism of voluntary welfare organizations that made it difficult for them to raise money. His solution, in each case, was to use the public relations approach, and his firm's name and address appeared in large print at the bottom of each ad. The messages were such a shameless solicitation of business that they failed to endear him to liberals or anyone else.

Other writings generated a warmer reception among liberals and almost everyone else. A 1940 essay, "Speak Up for Democracy," was dedicated to "Doris and Anne and all other American children who, if we will it now, shall inherit democracy and freedom." It laid out a detailed plan whereby average Americans could write letters, appear on radio, and hold forums to show their support for democracy and their opposition to the totalitarianism that was sweeping Europe. A

1943 address, "Democratic Leadership in Total War," outlined a similar plan for America to maintain its will to fight during World War II. Two years later he released a longer work called *Take Your Place at the Peace Table*, urging a national outpouring on behalf of "a just and enduring United Nations peace."

"In the last war, America failed to play her proper peace role because the people had so little voice in preliminary discussions," Bernays wrote, still miffed because President Wilson had disbanded the U.S. press-propaganda mission just before the Paris talks that followed World War I. "In the present war, unless men and women outside of government discuss peace plans openly and intelligently, and then step forward to take their place at the peace table, the future will bring new failures."[24]

Commentators praised his broad objectives, but ridiculed him for trying to enlist millions of Americans in what seemed like a mammoth propaganda campaign. *Take Your Place* is "a mixture of honest liberalism and incipient cynical fascism. There is much talk of the individual common man and open discussion and truth and accuracy, but much more of molding public opinion by various tools and weapons and plans and strategies," Pitman B. Potter wrote in 1945 in *The American Political Science Review*. "The author presumably intends only welfare and happiness for humanity, but his methods are largely identical with those portrayed in Chapters VI and XI of *Mein Kampf*."[25]

Marvin N. Olasky, writing forty-two years later, says Potter missed the point. Such a blending of liberalism and fascism, Olasky says, "was exactly what Bernays believed to be essential, given his understanding of the failure of nineteenth-century liberalism, and the twentieth-century 'necessity' of uniting liberalism with social control to avoid chaos." As for Bernays's endorsement of propaganda, Olasky adds, "if Hitler had hit upon the techniques and used them for evil purposes, then that would be all the more reason—given the inevitability of these techniques being put into use and the inability of men to resist them—for liberals such as Bernays to use them before fascists had the chance." While it may be hard to grasp today, Olasky writes, "Bernays believed we must be manipulative in order to save democracy, that we have to burn the village in order to save it."[26]

The popular press of his day was less concerned with criticizing Bernays than with celebrating him and his revolutionary profession. He "has reduced the once jovial craft of press agent to a science," Henry F. Pringle wrote in "The Mass Psychologist," a 1930 profile in the *American Mercury*. "Only poets delude themselves with the notion that love, that is to say sex, causes the world to revolve. Mr. Bernays, whose rank as public relations counsel is at least the equal of Ivy Ledbetter Lee's, knows that it is really money that furnishes the motive power. The mass psychologist, moreover, goes much further than the psychoanalyst who, as I understand it, can do no more than explain what has already taken place. Eddie can foretell the future. . . . His science, once understood, is really very simple. What he does is to create a demand by molding the public mind. He creates a desire for specified goods or ideas."[27]

John T. Flynn, writing two years later in the *Atlantic Monthly*, was equally enamored of "The Science of Ballyhoo": "Bernays is a philosopher, not a mere businessman. He is a nephew of that other great philosopher, Dr. Sigmund Freud. Unlike his distinguished uncle, he is not known as a practicing psychoanalyst, but he is a psychoanalyst just the same, for he deals with the science of unconscious mental processes. His business is to treat unconscious mental acts by conscious ones. The great Viennese doctor is interested in releasing the pent-up libido of the individual; his American nephew is engaged in releasing (and directing) the suppressed desires of the crowd."[28]

· · ·

Bernays loved to be written about in such sweeping terms. He loved to be thought of as an esteemed theorist in the mold of his revered uncle, a practitioner of the social sciences as well as of PR. And he loved spending time with scholars and editors of academic journals. All that, he hoped, would help extinguish the image of public relations men as crude or smarmy and would put him at the center of a new field that, as he said, was a tasteful blend of art and science.

But practicing public relations at the same time he was preaching about it created a conundrum: his words would be compared with his actions—which could be embarrassing.

Take his admonition, in *Propaganda*, that the PR man "should be candid in his dealings. It must be repeated that his business is not to fool or hoodwink the public. . . . When he is sending out propaganda material, it is clearly labeled as to source. The editor knows from whom it comes and what its purpose is, and accepts it on its merits as news."[29]

Was that merely more PR, or did Bernays mean what he wrote? If he did, he'd have had a tough time squaring his lofty ideal of candor with his "front groups." The Radio Institute of the Audible Arts, for instance, appeared to be promoting a public cause, but Bernays's whole reason for proposing it was to advance the private interests of its founder, the Philco Radio and Television Corporation. Other times Bernays worked through legitimate charities but failed to point out that his corporate client was paying the bills and benefiting from the link. That's what happened when the National Foundation for Infantile Paralysis agreed to help the United Fruit Company refute a damaging rumor that bananas were causing polio. "No one would believe a direct refutation by the company," Bernays recounted in his memoirs. So he placed ads nationwide making clear that "meat, fruit, vegetables, and other foods do not cause paralysis." The ads, he added, "stated that funds had been provided by friends of the National Foundation as a contribution to the educational activities of that organization. The friends were the Fruit Company."[30]

Bernays repeatedly disparaged so-called experts, writing that they "are effective in evaluating the past, but I would rather have poets evaluate the future. Experts are circumscribed by the limitations their own work has imposed on them, poets by their imagination."[31] Yet those were the very experts he and Lippmann hoped would steer society through the twentieth century. And while he was publicly berating them, he was privately putting many of them to work. He apparently considered economics expert Warren Persons trustworthy enough to hire him for PR campaigns in behalf of the *Ladies' Home Journal,* then Kelvinator, then the United Brewers Industrial Foundation.

While Bernays was imploring his fellow PR professionals not to sign on with unsavory clients, he was simultaneously representing the American Tobacco Company and reading reports linking tobacco to heart attacks and cancer. He advised other PR men to operate in the background, but Bernays himself couldn't help moving to center stage. Although he proclaimed the importance of civil liberties, he wasn't sure they included the right to remain free from manipulation. And while he wanted desperately to be taken seriously as a scholar, he promoted PR in a way that made a mockery of academic objectivity.

His refusal to openly debate ideas was starkly apparent in attacks Bernays launched in 1951 against J. A. R. Pimlott, a twenty-eight-year-old writer who was about to release a book, *Public Relations and American Democracy,* that Bernays thought would scoop one he was finishing. He attacked Pimlott's book in a review, reprinted and distributed "ten thousand reprints of the attack," and wrote but didn't have the courage to sign letters to Pimlott condemning his work, according to Joseph Freeman, a former member of Bernays's staff. "All that was wrong with this young man," Freeman wrote of Pimlott, "was that he had the gall to publish a book on public relations before Mr. B. had his own book ready."[32]

Freeman also accused Bernays of being "a professional liberal." The PR maestro had a "love affair" with General Douglas MacArthur, Freeman wrote, but hid his admiration from his liberal friends who despised MacArthur. And Bernays cynically "told Business that its best bet was to make money with a veneer of idealism, to make it appear that while they were after Profit—the God of Things as They Are— their activities at the same time served the public welfare," said Freeman. "Sure, Beech Nut makes money selling bacon, but you can hire doctors to tell the public that big breakfasts are good for the health; thus Beech Nut is more than a commercial firm selling bacon; it is a public benefactor aiding us to eat heavy breakfasts for the good of our health."[33]

On other occasions, however, Bernays's motives were beyond reproach and he acted like the liberal he said he was. That was the case with his work for better race relations. In 1920, for example, he helped ensure the success of the NAACP's first national conference in the South, and over the years he pushed clients like Procter and Gamble to reform what he said were racist and anti-Semitic hiring policies. He was even more outspoken, and further ahead of his time, in promoting health reforms. In 1932 he orchestrated a campaign in behalf of a national commission that was proposing group medical practices, group payment through private and public insurers, and more emphasis on training midwives and nursing attendants. Bernays was determined that the commission's good work be recognized, so he convened hearings across the country, encouraged newspapers to print stories with local angles on the national themes, mailed thousands of letters, and spoke on shows like *The National Farm Hour* and *The Home Radio Hour.*

But he was outmaneuvered by the American Medical Association, which borrowed his tactics to convince the public that the commission's proposals were dangerous. "The alignment is clear," argued a two-and-a-half-page AMA editorial. "On the one side the forces representing the great foundations, public health officialdom, social theory—even Socialism and Communism—inciting to revolution; on the other side, the organized medical profession of this country urging an evolution guided by controlled experimentation which will observe the principles that have been found through the centuries to be necessary to the sound practice of medicine." Being beaten at his own game was so unsettling that Bernays was still steaming forty-five years later. "As a result of this effort," he told an interviewer, the AMA "was able to stop medical progress in this country until [President Lyndon] Johnson came along some thirty years after."

If it was sometimes tough to make his actions consistent with his words, Bernays found it even tougher to get his fellow PR practitioners to adhere to the high moral standards he set. That, he explained, was why he was consumed, during his last fifty years, with requiring that PR professionals be licensed and trained in ethics. "Such procedure," he said in 1986, "is followed by medical doctors, architects, engineers, and other professions. It safeguards the public against quacks, know-nothings, or the antisocial in behavior. . . . When I wrote *Crystallizing Public Opinion*, published in 1923, I tried to lay down the principles, practices, and ethics of a new profession. I was unaware then that words, unless defined by law, are in the public domain and have the stability of soap bubbles."[34]

How must he have felt, then, when he learned in 1933 that Nazi propaganda chief Joseph Goebbels was using *Crystallizing Public Opinion* "as a basis for his destructive campaign against the Jews of Germany"? Bernays heard about it from Karl von Wiegand, foreign correspondent for the Hearst papers, who had visited with Goebbels in Germany and been given a tour of his library. While scholars still debate the extent to which the Nazis used Bernays's works, Goebbels did employ techniques nearly identical to those used by Bernays—skillfully exploiting symbols by making Jews into scapegoats and Hitler into the embodiment of righteousness; manipulating the media by trumpeting Nazi triumphs on the battlefield and hiding their exter-mination campaigns; and vesting unheard-of power in state propagan-dists just as Bernays had advised in *Crystallizing.*

Bernays was savvy enough not to retell the Goebbels tale in the 1930s and 1940s, when it could have tarnished his image, and to dwell instead on how his propaganda techniques had aided America in the two world wars. But he couldn't resist recounting von Wiegand's story in his autobiography, published in 1965. News that his book was on Goebbels's shelf "shocked me," Bernays wrote. "But I knew any human activity can be used for social purposes or misused for antisocial ones. Obviously the attack on the Jews of Germany was no emotional out-burst of the Nazis, but a deliberate, planned campaign."[35] In which Eddie Bernays may unwittingly have had a hand.

Getting

PERSONAL

6

THE FATHER OF PUBLIC RELATIONS MAY HAVE BEEN A PATERNAL powerhouse at the office, ever coddling and nurturing his fledgling child, but at the Washington Square town house he shared with his wife and two daughters Eddie was regarded as something less than the perfect parent. Part of the problem was that he simply wasn't around much. When he was at home his behavior could be as infuriating as it was endearing.

Especially troubling to his daughters was the way Eddie treated his wife, Doris. He perpetually described her as his twenty-four-hour-a-day partner, his equal at home and at work. But while Doris shared the burden at the office, Eddie did nothing to help her manage the household even though her chronic back pain became so intense that she eventually needed a motorized chair to carry her upstairs. "He wanted to maintain the fiction that [the household] worked by itself," says his older daughter, also named Doris. "Mother waited until he left the house before she did any housewifely stuff."[1]

He also related to his children on his own terms. Anne, his younger daughter, was confused about her Jewishness and asked when she was five, "What am I?" Eddie, she wrote years later, "answered with admirable simplicity that I was 'nothing,' adding, 'You can choose when you grow up.' Squirming at being removed from the possibility of an identity, I took another tack: 'What is a Jew?' His reply, something complex about races and how I must never confuse race with religion and since our family was not 'religious,' I was (again) 'nothing,' left me even squirmier. I said to him that even if he and I could agree I was nothing, why did other people think I was Jewish? 'Because,' said he, grinning at the opportunity to deliver such an all-purpose punch line, 'they are wrong.'"[2] All of which was confounding to a little girl who simply wanted to know how she fit in.

There were good times, too, of course. Like the nights when Eddie would appear at the foot of their beds with news about the swash-buckling "Captain Merriwell," choosing the ideal intonation for the captain's comrades, the freewheeling Frenchman and the gruff German, and vesting the tales with such vitality that his daughters knew they were the most important people in his world at that moment. Or when he walked with them down Fifth Avenue, in a three-piece suit and work shoes, and suddenly began to skip. It was his way of defying convention, explains his older daughter, Doris. "He was saying, 'The hell with it, I'm not going to play that game.'"

Those were sides of Eddie that both daughters adored but saw too seldom.

"He defined himself entirely by his work," Doris says. It was partly that Eddie came to fatherhood in an era when few fathers actively participated in raising their kids. His age also was a factor; by the time Doris was born he was almost thirty-seven and was deeply invested in his career. Most of all, it was Eddie himself.

Like Doris, Anne remembers her father always being at work or at after-work gatherings. When he was home he couldn't sit still for long. Family dinners often evolved into discussions about the office—discussions the girls weren't invited to join and didn't want to. And after a whole weekend with the children Eddie would be ready to burst, the remedy for which was inviting a houseful of guests on Sunday night. He did relish his special time with his daughters, but he felt that raising them was their mother's responsibility.

"The word 'workaholic' was invented for him. I hate that word," says Anne, a novelist and writing instructor. "I don't think he was meant to be a father, really."[3]

· · ·

Eddie might have said the same of his own father. Ely Bernays, a moody and strident man, had to work endless hours to get ahead as a new arrival in America in the 1890s. He wasn't home much, and when he was, his children often cowered before his temperamental outbursts. As a child, Eddie told himself and others that he would never marry, have children, or repeat the mistakes of his father. And yet, in a way, that is precisely what he did.

Ely didn't have the luxury of musing about his future when he was young. His father died in Vienna of a heart attack in 1879, and Ely, at nineteen, had to sacrifice his dream of college and become family provider by taking his father's place as secretary to a well-known economist. He eventually met, fell in love with, and married Anna Freud, Sigmund's younger sister. And, having heard the U.S. consul describe America as the promised land, the young administrator resolved to relocate his family there, hoping he could earn enough money to support his three children and help his sisters and mother.

Ely may have had another incentive to leave Austria, one his son apparently never suspected: He had "several" illegitimate children he "was secretly paying for," according to Freud biographer Ernest Jones. Hoping to spare Eddie and his sisters, Jones never mentioned his suspicions in his books, but he did outline them in a 1952 letter to Freud's daughter, also named Anna.[4]

The Bernayses' move to America wasn't easy or quick. First Ely had to borrow money from his brother-in-law, Sigmund Freud, which was embarrassing, given recent strains in their relations. Then he temporarily left his two daughters behind with the Freuds, taking only his wife and Eddie, who celebrated his first birthday on the steamer. The three lived in boardinghouses until Ely established himself as a grain exporter on the Manhattan Produce Exchange and could afford nicer quarters, at which point he brought over his other children.

For much of Eddie's youth Ely and his family prospered, buying their first home on 139th Street, then moving more than a mile downtown to a spacious, three-story brownstone at Madison Avenue and 121st Street. It faced lush Mount Morris Park (now called Marcus Garvey Park), where the children watched Theodore Roosevelt's Rough Riders parade by. From there it was another step up, to a brownstone at 121 West 119th Street in Harlem, which was then a thriving, self-assured neighborhood. Summers meant a three-month escape to the spas of Sharon Springs, New York; to the Adirondack Mountains; or, on one special occasion, to Ossiacher Lake in Austria, where Uncle Sigmund paid a visit.

Eddie now had two younger sisters to go with his two older ones. With four girls milling about, along with three maids and a cook, he stole away as often as possible to play stickball in the streets. Even better, he would retreat to his bedroom and disappear into a book by Kipling or Dickens or into one of Gilbert Patten's dime novels about Frank Merriwell, the inspiration for the tales he later told his kids and grandkids.

His youthful recollections were more sobering than serene, however, and focused disproportionately on his inability to please his father. "The household during the day centered around Mother," he remembered decades later. But "in the evenings and on holidays and Sundays my father dominated everything and everyone, intimidating all of us with his unpredictable temperament. My earliest recollection of him is that of a heavyset man leaving the house every weekday and Saturday morning for a place called 'downtown' to make money.

"My mother was constantly on the alert to prevent explosions of Father's temper. Cooking odors were anathema. He would sniff the air like a lion when he stepped into the vestibule of the house each evening. If someone had forgotten to close the dumbwaiter and odors sifted up from the kitchen through the house, he would call out in a loud, stern voice, 'Open the windows!' My mother would rush to the windows and throw them open regardless of outside weather. I never knew why my father was so obsessed with details.

"My sisters and I stood in awe of our father. We observed silence in his presence until we were addressed. When he left the house in the morning he called good-bye to us from the hall. We then ran from wherever we were and pecked a farewell on his bearded cheek. After dark he returned. I saw him for a few moments after supper, before I was sent to bed. . . . He occasionally raised his voice to us in commanding tones, which had the shock effect of a New York traffic cop on a timid motorist. His awesome personality made corporal punishment unnecessary."[5]

Eddie's wife, Doris, offered an even more telling glimpse of life in Ely Bernays's home. "Eddie's father was a famous disciplinarian," she wrote. "Every evening one of his children stood sentry duty to warn the rest that they saw his jaunty figure coming up the avenue, swinging a cane. 'Papa's here,' the lookout yelled and all the children ducked. They seemed to fear him long after they were grown."[6]

Ely's letters to his young son suggest that he genuinely tried to communicate. Yet their interaction was curiously indirect, even formal. If its tenor was standard for father-son relationships of the time, it also reflected a coolness between the two that intensified over the years. When Eddie was thirteen and at summer camp, Ely wrote, "Horseback riding will do you a world of good. It will make you strong and tall, and when the boy who left us early in July comes back, I expect to see a man. All the other diversions are of a far more pleasant character than those you could have at Lake Placid, and therefore, whilst I don't want to banish you, or put you in exile, I would very much like to have you stay for the whole season." He ended by saying, "I embrace you as I love you, and am, your affectionate father," then asked the boy "how much money [do] you have left so I can send you some more?"[7]

Money, however, soon became another source of tension between the two. Ely's business, which was vulnerable to the vagaries of international grain markets, suffered setbacks, and during his last year in grammar school Eddie had to transfer from private to public school. "Here, for the first time," he wrote later, "I came into close contact with a cross-section of cosmopolitan New York. I now recognized that the society I was living in was much more complicated than I had thought. I was surprised and confused when I found that the boys in my 8B class didn't talk, think and act as I did. Their home backgrounds were unlike mine. I recognized I had a much more protected life than they, the underprivileged children of poor Irish, Italian, Russian and Polish immigrants. They were rougher, hardier, tougher, more aggressive and belligerent than the children I had known. The fist was the instrument of survival, a right swing to the jaw the arbiter of discussions. I had never been aware that people like these existed."[8]

Eddie had even less contact with blacks. In fact, during his entire youth he knew only two. One was Freeman, the butler, who walked him to school when he was ten. The other was Matilde Wilson, his mother's companion for forty years.

Despite his unfamiliarity with his surroundings, and the fact he attended Public School 184 for only one year, Eddie was class valedictorian. From there he enrolled in De Witt Clinton High School, which back then was in Manhattan and was known for its setting in the slums of the old San Juan Hill as well as its dedicated faculty. Eddie thrived, sinking into school activities like the *Magpie* newspaper, the Biological Field Club, and the City History Club. He headed downtown whenever he could to catch a vaudeville act or a Broadway opening.

But those carefree enthusiasms were ever tempered by his father's ambitions for him. "He wanted me to be a farmer because he believed that America's future rested on the development of its rural areas; on the other hand, I don't think he expected me to farm but hoped I would follow in his footsteps on the Produce Exchange," Eddie remembered in his memoirs. "On a black night in September 1908 I bade good-bye to my parents and left for the dreary Jersey City station, a bare wood platform covered by a tin roof, and boarded the overnight train to Ithaca."[9]

Their correspondence while Eddie was at Cornell makes it clear that Ely cared deeply about his son but didn't know or care how much Eddie detested farming, and that Eddie couldn't bring himself to confront his father. "My Dear Son Edward," Ely wrote in 1909 from a train heading to Chicago. "I was very glad to hear that in your farm-work you have attained that feeling of safety and surety which is after all the basis of every successful achievement, and what pleased me most of the remarks, which you have made about this farm-work, is the one point which you mentioned, viz., that if anyone would put you on a farm today, you would be able to know where to start when the beginning of the work were left to you. . . . I want you to keep me posted, on the current, about everything that you are doing because you must naturally know what an interest I take in the plans and welfare of my only son. Lovingly your father."[10]

In a letter to Ely on the eve of his graduation, Eddie explained that, while he wanted to briefly test the wider world, "I believe that as I grow older I shall feel more and more attracted to enter your business, with the advantages and chances I have there. . . . I am glad you left the decision of the degree in my hands, for it shows that you have at least a certain degree of confidence in me."[11]

But Eddie had no intention of ever again having anything to do with horses or hogs, or with raising or trading in grain. He may have loved his father deeply, but he was determined not to follow in his footsteps. That he could not articulate that, that he was forced to dwell in the shadow of his father's disapproval, rankled throughout his life and made him feel that whatever heights he reached were never quite enough.

When he landed a job with the *Medical Review of Reviews* in 1913 he was eager to share his joy with his family, but as he recalled fifty-two years later, "My mother, of course, acquiesced. She would have agreed with any decision I made. My father looked disapproving. He said deliberately, 'How can you be a competent editor of a medical journal when Cornell University prepared you for an agricultural career and not medicine?'"[12]

The relationship between father and son didn't improve as Eddie's career in publicity blossomed. "My father's attitude toward my activities remained less than lukewarm," he remembered. "He was disappointed that his son had turned press agent. He enjoyed good theater and concerts. To occupy an orchestra seat at a performance was one thing, but for his only son to make a career of the theater, in daily contact with actors and managers, was something else. The influences of his Edwardian background put Broadway life outside the pale of respectability. Theater people were vagabond troupers in his mind; they were amoral or, worse, immoral; they had little family life, background or culture."[13]

Eddie and Ely were men who had sprung from vastly different soil. The father was rooted in yesterday, defined by the precise manners and rigid rituals of turn-of-the-century Europe. The son, having been nourished by the raw American earth, was brash and direct and ever striving for the new. Both regretted that they could never find greater common ground.

Yet Eddie told the story of his father the way he told about his public relations triumphs, often skewing the facts to make a point. He repeatedly portrayed Ely as insensitive and self-absorbed, discounting contradictory evidence in his own autobiography: that his father had served as trustee of a settlement house on East Broadway and was dispatched by Governor Theodore Roosevelt to report on orphan asylums in Europe; that Ely provided for his mother and sisters back in Europe as well as for his wife's family; and, perhaps most important, that he knew his son well enough to be the only one who guessed his plan to marry Doris Fleischman even as Eddie insisted he would never marry.

Ely's life in his last years, as in his first, was hard. World War I blocked U.S. grain exports to the point where he had to retire. In 1922 he and Anna bought a large Georgian-style home in the Quaker Ridge section of Scarsdale, an affluent village north of the city, and settled down to what they hoped would be a quiet life. But several months later, at the age of sixty-three, he developed appendicitis, and when his doctors failed to diagnose the ailment, he went into shock, his appendix burst, and he developed peritonitis. "After a week in which the doctors could do little to alleviate his suffering, I visited him for the last time," Eddie recalled. "He couldn't speak, but his eyes recognized me and they appeared to be saying good-bye out of an almost unconscious state."[14]

· · ·

The young man who awaited his turn at the marriage chapel that Saturday in 1922, giddily dispensing twenty-dollar bills to every clerk within arm's reach since there were no friends present to share his joy, was certain his marriage would be free from his parents' uncompromising, gender-prescribed patterns. That, after all, was a big part of what had drawn him to the freethinking Doris Fleischman.

Doris was equally determined to resist repeating what she saw as the mistakes of her parents. Her father, Samuel Fleischman, was a distinguished New York attorney who ruled his household nearly as rigidly as Ely Bernays. "My father," she explained years later, "kept us in an uneasy subjection by lowering the temperature of his blue eyes. . . . My mother's attitude showed the futility of any struggle. She was completely docile, never argued with Pop, always followed his wishes. . . . I was dominated, and still am, by Pop's value judgments."[15]

Such qualms about their parents' marriages may explain why their courtship was so prolonged and tentative. They met during family vacations at Far Rockaway Beach, on Long Island, when Eddie was seventeen, Doris sixteen, and became fast friends. She shared with him the fiction she wrote in high school and college, and he arranged a surprise beach party for her seventeenth birthday. She sang for him and played the piano when he visited her at Barnard College and after Eddie left Cornell, he helped his parents relocate to an apartment off Riverside Drive, "not unmindful of the fact that my good friend Doris lived around the corner with her family." But having moved next door, "I did not immediately 'rush her'; I knew she was there and that was good, I saw her from time to time and we became close friends."[16] Doris was also preoccupied with other passions, as she good-naturedly recalled: "When I think of the boys I might have married if they had proposed to me—a moron, a genius, an athlete, an esthete [*sic*] and a soul-torn introvert! Luckily they were still in school or fresh out of college. I was sure of only one thing and that was that I would marry an athlete. (Eddie thinks fresh air is unwholesome, and the sun is poisonous.)"[17]

Their friendship evolved into a business relationship when she joined his newly opened publicity firm in 1919, and after work they began spending more time together, attending balls in Greenwich Village and strolling along Fifth Avenue. "I did not realize our relationship was growing closer, nor did she," he remembered afterward. "Actually I don't recall what happened in the last few months before our marriage—it was all so exciting. When our friendship grew so intense that we didn't want to leave each other, we decided to marry."[18]

It took a full thirteen years from meeting on the beach to marrying, and while they'd succumbed to an institution about which both had doubts, they signaled from the start that it would be a different kind of union by not inviting, or even informing, their parents.

The signals didn't stop there. A year before marriage both joined the Lucy Stone League, a feminist group dedicated to ensuring a woman the right to retain her maiden name after marriage. Doris used the name Fleischman when she signed in at the Waldorf on her wedding night, leading editorial writers to fret about a national wave of immorality. Several months later she requested a passport in her maiden name, then agreed to take one reading "Doris Fleischman Bernays (professionally known as Doris E. Fleischman)." Two years later the State Department simplified things by making her the first married woman ever to get a passport in her maiden name. And when young Doris was born, health officials at first refused to accept her mother's maiden name on the birth certificate, then backed down in the same precedent-setting way the State Department had.

An even clearer sign of their intention to do things differently was the business union Eddie and Doris formed alongside the personal one. "Twenty-four-hour-a-day partnership" is the way Eddie described it over the years, which was a radical notion back then. They even signed papers promising to split fully and equally the firm's profits and losses. "In 1922 a woman entering any profession other than nursing, teaching or social work was a novelty," he wrote later, "and treating her as an equal in a profession was a source of even more wonderment."[19]

Taken together, the symbols amounted to a Big Think–like campaign, this time on behalf of his novel profession and his pathbreaking way of practicing it. He'd already transformed his wedding rites into a magnificent stunt that generated worldwide publicity, and now the marriage itself was becoming absorbed into his world of public relations. It was increasingly difficult to separate his personal from his professional life.

But the gestures themselves were not as clear-cut as they seemed. Doris was a pioneer in the world of work, but she was a forerunner with a guide. She was talented enough to seek a career in the flourishing world of opera or as a painter or a psychiatrist. Instead, she took Eddie's advice and, in 1914, accepted an offer, which he'd help secure, to write for the women's pages of the *New York Tribune*. She immersed herself in her new occupation, interviewing luminaries like Colonel Teddy Roosevelt, settlement house pioneer Jane Addams, and Lewis E. Lawes, the warden of Sing Sing. She became the first woman to cover a prizefight, and she rose to assistant women's page editor, then assistant Sunday editor. Again at Eddie's urgings, but with some trepidation, she gave up working for newspapers and magazines to become the first employee at the "publicity direction" office he opened in the summer of 1919.

Doris also was a pioneer for women's rights, but winning the right to use her maiden name wasn't one of her proudest achievements. Eddie admitted it was he who'd insisted on their joining the Lucy Stone League, "bringing a reluctant Doris with me." And it was he who pushed her to use her maiden name on their wedding night, because "I had an inner fear that marriage (though I wanted it fiercely with Doris) would take away some of my liberties as an individual if there were a Mrs. added to my name."[20] Doris took greater satisfaction in having marched in the first Women's Peace Parade in 1917 and in having written books and articles urging women to assert themselves at home and work. As for her battle to keep her maiden name, she reflected in 1949 that "a Lucy Stoner is mistaken in thinking that keeping her father's name is more significant than taking her husband's name. We were guilty of belief in magic. We thought a name itself had power to confer a separate identity.

"Miss," she added good-naturedly, "will now endeavor to turn herself into Mrs. She will secure a new passport, a new checkbook, a new letterhead. Some of her professional acquaintances and a few of her friends will deplore the defection. But basically, since a word at best can reflect only a truth, there will be no change in the inner life or external motions of an ex-miss."[21] True to her word, Doris six years later officially traded in her father's Fleischman for her husband's Bernays.

Once she resolved to enter her husband's world of public relations, Doris did play a central role in building the Bernays empire, and when the press dubbed him the prince of publicity she could rightfully claim to be the princess. She made her mark first as a wordsmith, churning out press releases and polished stories on clients ranging from the U.S. War Department to the American Tobacco Company. She also conceived of, wrote, and edited a four-page newsletter called *Contact*, which reprinted parts of speeches and articles on public relations, sorted through new ideas in the field, and promoted the activities of the Bernays office. And she ghost-wrote scores of speeches and strategy papers that were delivered under her husband's name. It's easy to pick out her writings from among the many papers that Eddie Bernays left behind: they're the ones with rich vocabulary and poetic flourish, free from the more formal style that was his trademark. They reflected the same careful crafting and subtle insight we see in her 1955 book, where she writes, "Men are commonly thought to be frightened at the responsibility of marriage. But like most traditional ideas about the two sexes, this belief is somewhat misleading. It is the bride who ought to faint at the altar. She is about to assume domestic omnipotence as if it were a superwedding gown. And she is agreeing to split her personality into two parts, although most people believe that her two personalities are the same, that woman is synonymous with housewife."[22]

Doris consulted on clients, too, usually behind the scenes, acting as a sounding board for Eddie's strategic and tactical decisions, reinforcing what she liked and suggesting revisions for what she didn't. While most of that counseling is difficult to reconstruct, because it happened at home in the evening, her soft-spoken but hard-hitting approach is clear in her handling of the NAACP national convention in 1920.

A Jewish woman from New York wasn't the delegate most publicity offices would have dispatched to argue on behalf of blacks before the governor of Georgia, but Eddie and Doris liked to surprise people. And Doris could be just as persuasive as her husband. She convinced the governor to put the militia on standby, made a personal pitch to the Atlanta mayor to attend the convention, then advised the city editor at the *Constitution* to print the story on the front page. As she recounted later, she was so busy that she never noticed the four bodyguards that the NAACP organizers had assigned to protect her, or the white men at her hotel who tossed pennies at her feet, implying she was a prostitute who could be had cheaply.

Doris's most valuable contribution to the practice was in the brilliant way she compensated for Eddie's shortcomings. It was she who provided precision and organization when he was overcommitted and behind schedule. It was her unerring eye that astutely sized up would-be clients and associates where he was easily hoodwinked. And it was she who tempered his lofty, and often exaggerated, rhetoric.

"Eddie could get a client totally mad, but in ten minutes Doris could get them back. She was totally gracious," recalls Pat Jackson, a PR pro who worked with them in their later years.[23] Camille Roman, who was close to both Bernayses, says that Doris "was the one who I felt was grounded in the practical, what would really work. Eddie was always dealing in the great potential." In their later years, Roman added, "they'd gotten that partnership really worked out. It was almost seamless."[24]

Seamless, except that one partner was invisible—an odd way for a 50-50 partnership to work.

For all her contributions, Doris never worked face-to-face with the firm's clients. She never outlined in person the recommendations she'd spent hours drawing up, never made the contacts she described in her newsletter, *Contact*. Most clients never knew she was involved at all, and Eddie and Doris's co-workers never knew precisely what she did, although they were aware she had a huge influence on her husband.

Eddie offered gender as the reason for her silent presence. "She recognized immediately that her ideas might be treated as 'a woman's' rather than judged on their merits," he explained in his memoirs, "so she decided early to withdraw from personal relations with clients. I conferred with her after the client had left. All in all, I think Doris was right to avoid the day-to-day ups and downs of interpersonal relationships with clients."[25]

Doris had offered an almost identical explanation a decade earlier: "If ideas were considered first in terms of my sex, they might never get around to being judged on their merits." Yet she went on to ask, "Have I been a coward to withdraw from such active company? Perhaps I have."[26]

Her role in the shadows may have been a sign of the times, and that may be why the only name clients generally saw when they hired the firm was that of Edward L. Bernays, Counsel on Public Relations. Hers sometimes appeared, in smaller type, making clear that the firm consisted of "A Partnership of Edward L. Bernays and Doris Fleischman."

"A joint decision seems to have been made that Bernays would command the foreground and Fleischman would stay in the background in most matters," reports historian Susan Henry, who has studied Doris's life and works. When she asked Eddie about that, Henry adds, "he also admitted that her partnership was downplayed deliberately in order to 'make the "Bernays" stand for advice on public relations.' And he acknowledged that his own reputation might have suffered if Fleischman's involvement had been common knowledge, since 'if a woman partner had been publicized who wasn't already well known, it could deprecate the man because it would have been strange and unusual.'"[27]

It would also have been strange and unusual for Eddie to have shared the spotlight with anyone, even his beloved wife. He relished the publicity his unusual partnership produced, especially later, when feminism became the rage and he was regarded as an early prophet.

Personal

He had encouraged Doris to pursue a career at a time when that was highly controversial, but he also had set the limits. Her contributions notwithstanding, it is Eddie, not Doris, who today is widely viewed as the founder of the profession they pioneered together.

Anne Bernays says she's disturbed that her father didn't push the limits of convention with his own wife the way he did with other feminist causes. "He wanted her to be a feminist outside the house," she concludes, "but inside he wanted her to be a Victorian wife."[28]

· · ·

The Bernays household was anything but Victorian.

Eddie and Doris's approach to child-rearing was founded on two simple principles: learning from the mistakes of their parents, especially their fathers; and applying the most modern thinking from psychology, sociology, and the rest of the social sciences.

That meant hiring separate nannies for Anne and young Doris to ensure that neither was favored, a tendency their parents felt was inevitable with a single caretaker. The Bernays approach also meant being as permissive as possible—spanking the girls just once, "for running into the street," letting them raise in a spare bathroom a chicken Anne had hatched in a school experiment, and asking whether they'd "like to" pick up their toys rather than ordering them to do so. It meant accepting nudity as natural but steering clear of comic books, hiring a psychology student as a nurse, and scheduling everything from feedings to playtime by the clock rather than by the child.

From the time they could talk, the girls called their father Eddie. Not Daddy, Dad, Pop, or Father. "He said, 'If you call me Father,'" Doris recalls, "'I'll call you daughter.'"[29]

"Eddie and I became parents when our babies and the squalling sciences of child care and child psychology were new," Doris Fleischman wrote years later. "We opened our arms wide to each new theory, believing that each latest one would solve all problems of bringing up children, and with equal enthusiasm we discarded old theories, believing they were quite wrong."[30] How did they find out about the latest theories? From books, the same place they got so many ideas at work.

"Whenever a new problem has come up in my job as wife, house-keeper, and mother, I have found it helpful to read a few books, spend a few days in special libraries, talk to authorities, or make a fairly broad survey," Doris explained.[31] Eddie, too, was concerned that each stage of development happen on time and in the right direction. "Little Doris's routine was carefully researched and adoringly watched," he remembered. "We felt we were really the first parents in the world."[32]

His burgeoning public relations practice let Eddie meet all his family's material needs, ensuring they lived in even greater comfort than he had enjoyed during the best times of his own childhood, and liberating them from the downturns that had perpetually plagued his father.

Their first real home at 8 Washington Square North was around the corner from 44 Washington Mews, the meticulously converted stables where Eddie and Doris had spent the first seven years of their marriage. The Washington Square town house offered the space they needed for a family while letting them stay in the Greenwich Village neighborhood they loved. The four-story brick-front Colonial, which they leased in 1929 from diplomat and businessman William Averell Harriman, had two bronze roosters standing watch on the stoop, a drawing room with high ceilings and a white marble mantel, and sliding doors of mahogany opening onto the music room and dining room. A staircase with a smooth railing led up to three floors of bedrooms. Across the street was magnificently maintained Washington Square Park, the perfect place to push a pair of baby strollers.

The view was even better, and the appointments finer, at the Sherry Netherland Hotel, where in 1932 they took over the twenty-seventh floor. Directly across the street was Central Park, where the children came to cherish the duck pond and stone bridge. The Bernayses stayed in that neighborhood for thirty years, later moving to a spacious apartment at 817 Fifth Avenue where the children bumped into Gloria Swanson in the elevator and had a glorious view of the park. Still later they moved back to the Sherry Netherland, then to a private home at 163 East Sixty-third Street, which was the first they owned rather than rented. Built by architect Frederick Sterner, it was actually a double house with 40 feet of frontage and a dining room that looked onto a backyard of trees and bushes. The living room was 18 feet high and 40 feet across, with a balcony at one end and a fireplace big enough to stand in.

Summers were spent in suburban Irvington, Mount Kisco, Port Chester, and Purchase, New York, in rented mansions with as many as thirty rooms. Eddie eventually bought a farm in the Berkshire Hills near Litchfield, Connecticut, with "a pastoral view of green rolling landscape that Doris painted and that I could admire from my bed when I woke up."

It's unclear why they moved so often, except that motion and change were defining metaphors for Eddie. They were part of what it meant to be prosperous in the new America, to be unbound by conventions of religion, profession, or even household roots. That energy was a big part of what made him so appealing to clients and acquaintances, and it was something to which his wife and children simply had to adjust.

A 1937 insurance appraisal offers a glimpse of the lifestyle the Bernayses maintained. A Steinway grand piano stood ready to entertain in the drawing room, where listeners could sink into a Hepplewhite sofa covered with mulberry silk velour or sit straight-backed on mahogany Chippendale chairs draped in early-seventeenth-century Flemish tapestry. If the music didn't move them, they could inspect a twenty-one-inch portrait of Doris, an oil painting by Jules Pascin, a drawing by André Derain, or an unsigned watercolor by Paul Cézanne titled "Study of One Colored and Four Black and White Apples." The room also featured a small menagerie—a pair of modern Chinese turquoise pottery parrots on tree stumps, an eight-inch heavy brass cat, and a seven-inch Royal Doulton red-and-black glazed China penguin. The drawing room furnishings were valued at $14,828.50, while those in the whole house were appraised at $32,327, the equivalent of more than $300,000 today.[33]

Eddie liked to show off his homes, so much so that a big factor in choosing them was how they'd accommodate the salons for which he was becoming famous. Screen star Edward G. Robinson might drop by to talk, along with hotel magnate Prince Serge Obolensky, former Rusian prime minister Aleksandr Kerenski, dancers from the American Ballet Theatre, professors from Columbia and Princeton, business leaders and journalists. Eddie often decided to play host at the last minute, making twenty to thirty calls on Sunday morning for an affair that evening. Doris, overcoming her natural shyness, managed to assemble just the right ingredients for a splendid feast. "Parties," he wrote afterward, "never served any purpose except that of enjoying our guests."

Which wasn't quite true. For Eddie, parties were a form of sustenance. He couldn't stand being alone. That would have required self-sufficiency and even introspection—anathema to a man whose whole definition of himself revolved around his work in the public arena. And to him, parties were the most marvelous public arena of all.

Not surprisingly, Eddie was the ideal host. He would greet his guests as they arrived, taking them by the elbow and steering them around the room, remembering everyone's name and occupation and presenting the latest arrivals in a way that made them seem twice as fascinating as they were. He also understood how to generate just enough tension to keep things interesting without offending anyone. "We found people emerged most," he observed years later, "when they were in contrast with one another and had divergent backgrounds and points of view. Conformity is a sin, even at parties."[34]

In the summer, when the celebrations moved to the estates he rented in the suburbs, he would insist that his guests take a dip in the pool or stay for a game of croquet. New Year's was even more festive. In 1929 Eddie and Doris threw a bash to which 250 were invited and 300 turned out. The next year they did it again, and they put out a press release trumpeting their best-known guests. The numbers were getting so big that, as Eddie recalled, "in 1932 we invited no one and went to bed early." Expectations had been set, however, and "the doorbell rang seventeen times between 10:00 P.M. and 1:00 A.M."[35]

Homes that big and a lifestyle that active required lots of maintenance, which meant a huge household staff. On Washington Square they had a butler, laundress, cook, kitchen maid, houseman, waitress, upstairs girl, and nurse. "I was waited on hand and foot," remembers Anne, who knew what she was talking about when she wrote her 1975 novel *Growing Up Rich*, about another wealthy family. "I was awoken by a maid climbing three flights of stairs and saying, 'Time to get up, Miss Anne.' I'd come home and my bed was made, everything was picked up. I remember asking my mother if I could do some work, I felt literally helpless because there was so much help, and she said, 'No, that's Celia's job, or that's Catherine's job.'"[36]

Celia, Catherine, and the other servants knew their place. If they didn't, they were quickly told that it was in the kitchen, their bedrooms, or the cramped servants' dining area, but not the family rooms when the family was there and not in the swimming pool at any time. Bernays treated his household help fairly, but he was exceedingly class-conscious and wasn't above referring to the chauffeur as "Jack Dot Dope."

The girls also got the best, and the most costly, schooling. First it was the City & Country School, which Eddie describes as "a progressive school in the Village run by Caroline Pratt, who loved children and hated parents." Then he decided on a more formal and fashionable approach, opting for the Brearley School, which came strongly recommended by his client and friend Orlando Weber, president of Allied Chemical and Dye Corporation. Young Doris graduated from Radcliffe. Anne started at Wellesley and finished at Barnard, where her mother had gone.

If his daughters were grateful for those advantages, they were confused by their father's inconsistent spending habits. Eddie was almost monastic when it came to clothes, owning a single pair of shoes, which he wore even after they had holes, along with several plain suits he had Doris pick out. He didn't mind when the stuffing came out of couches, and during the war he gave up his car and couldn't abide friends who bought steaks on the black market. Yet he owned lavish homes, had more servants than most people had rooms, and was carted around in Renault and Lincoln town cars or Cadillacs. "My parents would have the chauffeur drive us to school," Doris recalls, "and I was so deeply ashamed that I made him stop before the school so no one would realize I was driven by a chauffeur."[37]

Even more confusing was his attitude toward religion. He came from a distinguished Jewish family that had been driven out of Spain when Jews were expelled in the fifteenth century. His great-grandfather Isaac ben Jacob Bernays was chief rabbi of Hamburg and a pioneer of modern Orthodox Judaism. His father Ely founded a neighborhood temple on 139th Street in New York in the 1890s and later was vice president of Stephen Wise's esteemed Free Synagogue, while Doris's father was legal counsel to B'Nai B'Rith. And Eddie proudly pointed to his Jewish roots when it served him in business, as when American Tobacco asked him to kill rumors that the company was anti-Semitic.

But he didn't believe in religion or God, as he would tell anyone who asked. He disdained religion and in 1978 proudly proclaimed that "I've never been to a temple for a service. Never." Like many prosperous German Jews of that era, he was keenly aware of the social hierarchies that defined old-line German Jews as several notches above the more recently arrived, poorer Russian Jews.[38] He also believed the wisest course for Jews was to mute their differences with Gentiles. "The Jews," he wrote in 1932, "must educate themselves to accept an attitude of tolerance toward the non-Jewish world in which they live. The pushing and climbing of many over-eager Jews to achieve leadership as a compensation for what they believe is a social inferiority, is unnecessary and unwise."[39]

Such stereotyping and arguments for assimilation were an understandable, if not admirable, response to an anti-Semitism in 1930s New York that limited the number of clients that upwardly mobile Jews like Eddie could secure, the clubs they could join, and the apartment houses where they could live. They even had to make sure that fashionable resorts would accept Jews as guests; those that wouldn't often signaled it in ads noting they were "convenient to churches." While much of this prejudice persisted after World War II, the Holocaust inspired many Jews for the first time to stand up for their heritage and take pride in their thriving community of Jewish artists, writers, and intellectuals.

Yet Eddie's notion that being Jewish was a matter of elective association was a deeply held belief rather than a matter of convenience, which is why he held on to it even after the Nazis. He was pleading for people to determine their own destiny, free from the influence of any group. And it wasn't just in his writings that he made clear his ambivalence about religion. Naming his daughter Doris after his wife—a clear violation of the tradition among Eastern European Jews of not naming children after living relatives—was one more way to tell the world he wouldn't be bound by what he regarded as archaic conventions.

That approach left Anne uncertain about who she was and what it meant to be a Jew. Her sister, Doris, meanwhile, couldn't understand why Eddie wouldn't acknowledge the anti-Semitism the girls encountered at their private school. "It was a very Waspy atmosphere," Doris says, "and I mean he was literally blind to that. It wasn't that he saw it and ignored it. It would have assaulted his basic belief that one can be what one wants to be. . . . This was a man who invented himself and figured everybody else had a chance to invent themselves [and to become] what they wanted to be. Religion was an impediment because it wasn't something you chose for yourself."[40]

What maddened the girls even more, as children and later as adults, was Eddie's approach to gender roles. He preached feminism and pushed his wife to break symbolic barriers, but he made all the decisions that counted, including when they would move, where the children would attend school, and what their lifestyle would be. Doris, meanwhile, was expected to handle household matters, managing the staff, rushing home to have lunch with the girls and again to tuck them in at night, and running their summer homes in the country, where Eddie came only on weekends—all the while serving as "full and equal partner" at the office.

And there was more: Eddie flirted with women at work and at parties, arousing suspicion in his daughters and others that he was doing more than flirting. He carried on a lively correspondence with bright, attractive women who called him "Eddie darling" and "sweet Bernaysy," while at the same time worrying, to the point of calling the police, if his wife Doris stayed out late at a movie without telling him. Some Sundays he even refused to say where he'd been, teasing the kids, when they persisted, that he'd been to see "Dottie Jelly Roll."

It may be, as Doris insisted in her writings, that being married to Eddie gave her a full and satisfied life, even if it didn't always live up to her feminist ideals. She realized how hard Eddie worked. She knew he was helping the family back in Europe as well as providing so well for his immediate family, and she knew that it was unusual for a woman of her era to be so deeply involved in her husband's career. She also believed she was "conventional looking," or worse, and, as historian Susan Henry suggests, "that she married so late indicates she may not have believed she would find a compatible husband at all."[41] This could explain why, as Anne recalls, "when I got married my mother said, 'I want you to remember something, Anne. When you get in a fight with your husband, he is always right.'"[42]

Doris made her position even clearer in her 1955 book: "Eddie's word is final and he casts the deciding vote in our partnership. I have elected him Chairman of the Board and Executive President in our personal life, where he decides where we shall live and when we shall diet, and in our public relations office where he was boss even before we were married."[43]

Yet there are hints Doris was not as contented as she wanted everyone to believe. In a 1949 article she wrote, "Once at a cocktail party, a beautiful woman attached herself to my husband and after a few minutes of intense pre-symbolic conversation looked indignantly at me as if to say, 'I saw him first—why don't you scram?' I did, of course, to my husband's delight, since he didn't want to be saddled with a Mrs."[44] The tone was light, part of her explaining how tough it was to keep things straight when she kept her maiden name, but she wasn't amused by Eddie's perpetual flirting. And it may not have been a joke when she warned Anne that "men always sleep with their secretaries."

"I think at some point she wanted to leave him, but felt she couldn't get another man. Given the times, it was very important not to be manless," says Anne, who is intrigued and disturbed enough about her parents' relationship that she's using it as the basis of a novel "exploring the nature of a marriage in which the woman is completely outwardly submissive to a very domineering husband, but not necessarily inwardly submissive."[45]

Anne's older sister recalls a period in the late 1940s when her mother "sat at a card table hour after hour playing solitaire. I knew something was wrong because ordinarily she and Eddie spent evenings together. It was later that I suspected he was having some kind of affair."[46]

A family friend tells a similar tale: "I asked Doris if she ever thought of leaving him. She said one time she did, shortly after their marriage. She came home and saw something she didn't want to see and promptly left. Eddie came after her, and that was the end of that."[47]

Doris was surely thinking of her own life and of her children when, in her later years, she approached Mary Ann Pires at a party the young PR woman was hosting. "She was very taken with our daughter, who was just two or three at the time," Pires recalls. "Afterward she said to me, 'Be certain to keep a balance where that little girl is concerned. Be sure not to let her get lost in your busy life.' I've thought about that over and over again."[48]

Eddie did dominate his wife in so many ways, much as he did everyone in his life. She submitted, at least superficially, to keep her marriage and family intact. But whatever her reservations, Doris surely meant it when she told an interviewer in 1980 that "love has been the big thing in my life."[49] Eddie surely meant it, too, when he repeatedly professed his admiration and love for his wife, whom he lovingly called Da.

But did he believe he'd done all he could have, and should have, at home? "There is no dichotomy, as in the usual marriage, with the husband the economic provider; the wife, the homebody," Eddie wrote in 1975. "To us marriage has been and is a total living experience in symbiosis."[50]

Privately, however, he conceded that he hadn't given Doris much help raising the girls or running the house. In a 1948 letter to his sister

Judith he referred to the milestones he was missing in his children's lives by remaining behind at work while they vacationed in Nantucket: "Little Doris is learning to ride a bicycle, and I gather that in her excitement of learning, she gets blisters on her hands from holding on to the handle bars so tightly. Anne, I understand, is learning how to play tennis. Big Doris is so bored that, I gather, she works three or four hours a day writing a piece on why feminism and a Lucy Stone name haven't worked out after twenty-five years."[51] In his autobiography he devotes just thirteen of 849 pages to family matters, worrying that any more would bore readers. Anne and Doris, he added, "were victims of a father who had the current attitude of the male parent in the thirties. He loved his children, but wasn't around much to show his love."[52] Which, as he acknowledged, was just how things had been with his own parents.

. . .

How could Doris handle all those responsibilities at home and work, and how could Eddie, who in many ways was deeply solicitous of his wife, let her do it all? "I don't think he had a clue as to what it entailed to run a household," his daughter Doris surmises. "Mother didn't do any cleaning or cooking or that sort of stuff, but she did have to oversee the staff. . . . She did it by being extremely well organized, very self-disciplined. She'd write out schedules for all the help that they were supposed to follow at fifteen-minute intervals. She had a very organized mind. She should have been a scientist."[53]

Doris Fleischman Bernays offered a similar answer in her 1955 book. "'How do you find time to work at your office, take care of your children and your home, and entertain so much?' people ask me frequently. It is a simple problem in temporal mathematics," she wrote with her trademark light touch. "The great trick is to weed out unnecessary activities, and then to divide essentials into two categories. The first group can be characterized as expendable necessities. The second group or residue can be defined as reducible necessities. These can be shrunken by the application of systems, shortcuts and other technical devices. . . . If the making of a house were elevated to the status of a science, where it properly belongs, our houses would be homes instead of careers and we should have more time for the pleasant intangibles of family and community life."[54]

Doris's address book offers a further glimpse into how organized the Bernays household was—and how privileged. There were entries for Bowring Arundel and Company, their favorite source for men's shirts, and for Margaret Koehler Gowns, the best place to buy dresses. There were addresses and numbers for a linen and underwear shop, for Mrs. Herbst's Pastries and Scandinavian Delicacies, and for Frank Ondra, a furniture refinisher in Long Island City. There were people to sweep the chimney, tune the piano, deliver ice or logs, build cabinets, repair the stove, air conditioner, and refrigerator, and replace lost or damaged silver or lace. There were even listings—five of them—under "waitresses," presumably to make entertaining a bit easier.

There was no entry, however, for the one thing Anne and her sister most wanted while they were growing up: to have their father around more and to make him more approachable—which was the same thing Eddie had craved. Eddie tried, taking young Doris to an American Home Economics Association convention in Pittsburgh and Anne on a trip to Washington and a visit to FBI headquarters. He brought Anne to the office one day after school and let her try carving a bar of Ivory soap, as thousands of other children were doing at his prompting. But, as she recalls, "I immediately cut my finger very badly. I was six years old and not used to cutting. He took me right home, and the doctor came. [The cut] was really deep, and my mother was outraged."[55]

It was bad enough that their father was totally occupied with his work, but it was even worse that he could not accept the choices the girls made. "When I was in college, a senior, I joined a poetry club. There were six of us; we met with a senior faculty member once a week and learned how to write poetry and turned out a tiny little book," recalls Anne, who went on to publish eight works of fiction and to coauthor two of nonfiction. "My father said people would just as soon sit on a tack as read poetry. Yes, it was horrible, but I was twenty-one then, so I shouldn't have minded so much."[56]

It became even clearer how little Eddie understood his younger daughter when, several years after Anne graduated from Barnard, he and Doris offered to turn over to her their PR business. They truly hoped she'd come to understand and respect what they did. But Anne didn't even have to mull the offer over before turning it down.

If Eddie had spent more time listening to her as she was growing up, he might have seen her decision coming. But that never happened, she says. "He couldn't sit down and say, 'What are your ideas, Anne?' If I questioned anything, he would lose his temper, so I learned to keep my mouth shut. Mother said, 'Your father is always right.' It was a united front against the kids."[57]

Young Doris agrees that her parents never disagreed in front of her or Anne, and that Eddie got defensive during "ideological disagreements" with his daughters. But she also recalls that he maintained a childlike fascination with life, once even buying "dreck candy" from a mom-and-pop store on Third Avenue, eating some himself, and giving the rest to the kids.[58] What seemed like paradoxes to others were to him the joys of remaining unpredictable: he sometimes served his dinner guests spaghetti and meatballs and at other times invited them to feast on stuffed squab, avocado, and crabmeat at a table set with Steuben glass and Cartier silver.

The one thing he never joked about was his profession. And the older his daughters got, the more Eddie brought his Big Think strategies and tactics to bear on them and their families.

When Anne got married, Eddie dispatched telegrams to the Associated Press and United Press, the *Daily News* and the *New York Times*. Which wasn't surprising, since word of her engagement had been circulated everywhere from *Advertising Age* to *Variety* and *Publishers Weekly*. And when she was retained on the waiting list at Swarthmore College, Eddie wrote the dean of admissions to thank her, adding, "May I say in passing, as a technician in public relations, that your letter was an extremely difficult one to write, and a most effective one. Possibly you have seen the book 'How to Use Letters in College Public Relations.'. . . I have carefully studied this book but no letter in it quite gets over its points the way yours did."[59]

Personal

Young Doris received the same treatment, with Eddie writing to her a year after her marriage with detailed advice on how to organize her tax records and bank statements. This wasn't simply a father tutoring his daughter in life's practicalities; it was a man applying to his offspring his own obsessions and drives, his meticulousness and perpetual search for an edge over his opponents. He did all of this with the best of intentions, but with no insight into whether she or her new husband cared, which was just the way Ely had advised Eddie. "And this reminds me, too, about making a will," Eddie went on in a letter to Doris. "If you don't want to go to a lawyer, you can go to any stationery store and buy one of the blanks for five cents and fill it out just as you would like to. But it is highly inadvisable to let matters just go by the board, particularly since it means that everything reverts to the state, and your estate may get into the hands of a person who is incompetent and, in addition, doesn't care."[60]

He also advised Doris on how she and her husband should invest their money, whether and what to build on their lot of land, and how to attract patients to her new practice as a therapist. "He couldn't imagine that I did my work without giving advice," she says. "He was absolutely sure what I did was sit there and tell people how to live their lives, even though I told him, I don't know how many times, that's not what I did. He couldn't believe it because that's how he felt valued—giving his advice. And if we didn't take his advice he felt hurt because that's what he had to give."[61]

What she and her sister really wanted growing up, Anne says, "was for our father to do what other fathers did. I wanted him to be a doctor or a college president or something like that."[62]

At the OFFICE

7

TO HIS CLIENTS EDDIE SEEMED THE EPITOME OF PROPRIETY. HIS uniform was a three-piece suit, a soft-collared white shirt, and black shoes. The style may have been a decade out of date, the sleeves a bit longer than a tailor would have tolerated, the waist too tight, and the necktie skewed a few degrees to the right. But the image was always one of decorum, just what one expected from a proper public relations man.

If they had walked into his office unannounced, however, they would have seen a decidedly different Eddie—sitting behind a cluttered desk with his tie loosened, his jacket out of sight, and his shoes off. Four or five young staff members, their chairs pulled close, would have been listening to him spew forth a stream of thoughts about peddling Ivory or keeping Luckies number one. With each new idea he'd scratch out a note, wad it up, and toss it on the floor.

This image wasn't one of propriety, but it was every bit as calculated as the one he presented to clients. "By the end there was so much paper it looked like the floor had snow on it," recalls one of those young employees, James Parton. "It was a trick to demonstrate all the ideas he was generating."[1]

Eddie was also demonstrating that *he* was the idea man, the star. Staff members were limited to supporting roles, listening but seldom responding, all chairs, eyes, and ears zeroed in on Eddie. After all, he was the one who'd landed the clients, and he was responsible for keeping them satisfied. He'd concocted the strategies and mapped out tactics. He alone knew what it took to get things done and to pay the bills. As in many offices that revolve around a charismatic personality, he gave the orders and surrounded himself with people who were willing to carry them out. And like others who had launched their own empires, he ruled with an imperial air that sometimes crossed over into meanness.

There was a time, in 1921, when Eddie tried taking on a partner, a former magazine advertising man named J. Mitchel Thorsen. He got equal billing on the masthead, and Eddie assumed his contacts and drive would draw clients to the upstart agency. But Thorsen lasted only about three years, and their parting wasn't especially amicable. Only two references to Thorsen appear in Eddie's autobiography. One is a line calling him "the prototype of the manic, euphoric salesman," and the other is a kinder word in the Acknowledgments referring to Thorsen as one of "the many gifted men and women who have worked with us."

After Thorsen, Eddie hired mainly young staff people, often fresh from college. There could be as many as thirty when several campaigns were gearing up at once, but the number would drop to ten or twelve when the big campaigns ended. Most were bright enough to handle any task he tossed their way, even if it was beyond their expertise, and hungry enough not to complain about the long hours, the modest salary of about $30 a week, and Eddie's occasional torrents of temper. Most also were impressionable, and their impressions of Eddie remain vivid.

One impression was of Eddie as charismatic personality, the kind who, soon after he entered a room, any room, took center stage. It wasn't his physical presence. He was short and plain, with a paunch that increased over time and that he accentuated by patting. He also had disconcerting habits like biting his nails and jiggling his leg. But it didn't take long for his audience to realize how much he knew about almost everything and to understand that he was worth listening to. It was the same magic that had captivated industrial tycoons, that had landed him new clients to replace those who left after an economic setback or too big a dose of Eddie's boasting, and that had, one special day years later, made such an impression on his younger daughter.

Eddie, Anne, and her husband, Justin Kaplan, had planned to spend that sticky summer afternoon lounging on a Long Island beach. Instead they found themselves in a cramped garage off Rockaway Boulevard, in a section of Queens half a step up from a slum, with no assurance from the mechanic how long it would take him to repair "Cornelia," their 1954 green Ford convertible. To Anne and Justin the experience was a misery to be endured; to Eddie it was a chance to make a friend. "Within five minutes my father was sitting on one of those little folding chairs next to an elderly woman working at a vegetable stand, having the most animated conversation I had ever seen," Anne recalled forty years later. "If he had said to this old woman, 'Come with me, Bertha,' she would have come right in the car and left her whole family and the vegetable stand."[2]

Walter Wiener, Eddie's nephew and unofficial chief of staff, has similar recollections: "If you were in a room with him you'd never say, 'Who was that? Eddie who?' You'd say it was Eddie Bernays, because he dominated the conversation."[3] Part of his charm was drawing others in, making them feel important, says Luther Conant, who worked for Eddie in the early 1950s. "He could meet a roomful of forty people and be introduced to them, to strangers," Conant explains. "Then he'd introduce them right back to someone else."[4] Stanley Silverman, another young recruit from that era, says Eddie still had that knack at his one-hundredth-birthday bash in Cambridge: "I hadn't seen him in forty or fifty years, and he remembered me. I was very impressed with that. It wasn't a PR stunt."[5]

Eddie also had a showman's side, of course, drawing attention to what he said with inflated introductions like "In the interests of truth, accuracy, and fair play," or proclaiming, when he was in a fix, "I'm the victim rather than the beneficiary of my own propaganda." It was this flair for histrionics that prompted him to drive around New York in a sleek gray Renault, with the chauffeur sitting out in the cold and Eddie lounging inside, soaking in the envious gazes of passersby.

And there was Eddie as taskmaster—a side of him that his young protégés endured almost every day. Sometimes he demonstrated a thoroughness that bordered on obsessiveness, demanding that each of the scores of letters and memos that left the office be reviewed by someone other than the author, insisting on being filled in on every development, and signing off on every idea. A staff member was home recovering from pneumonia? He found take-home work to justify keeping her on the payroll—no matter that she was his younger sister, Hella. Another associate was off getting married? Make sure the three days were deducted from his vacation.

Eddie demanded excellence and obeisance. When they were forthcoming he seldom gave his staff credit, but when they weren't he could be unforgiving. A secretary was fired for typing "pubic" instead of "public" in one of his speeches, though it was the speechwriter who mistakenly penciled in "pubic." Jim Caldwell, who later became a Catholic priest, was fired for falling asleep in the file room. Victor Schiff, who became a star in the Carl Byoir public relations agency, was fired and told he wouldn't get dismissal pay because he'd been incompetent and disloyal. Wiener's secretary was dismissed for refusing to ride out to Eddie's new apartment and take measurements for rugs and curtains.

"Eddie had a tough ending with everybody," says Robert Hutchings, who spent two years with the Bernays office in the late 1930s. "I was the only person who ever left moderately happy with him; he kind of liked me. His other relationships were very sour, and I never did figure out why."[6] Parton, who later founded *American Heritage* magazine, was glad he was fired, because "there was no future there for anybody but Bernays."[7]

Wiener experienced firsthand his uncle's unyielding side when, after serving with the Office of Strategic Services during World War II, he turned down Eddie's offer to return to the Bernays agency. Eddie's response was to end all contact with his nephew for nearly forty years, refusing even to acknowledge him when he bumped into him in Grand Central. He did the same to Conant when he resigned after three years. "Eddie told me if I left he'd never talk to me again, and he never did," Conant recalls. "He took my leaving as almost a personal thing. I remember him saying, 'You were going to inherit this business.' But he just would not pay what seemed to me, even in those years, enough money. These accounts I was working on were paying him $1,000 a week, and I was getting $6,000 a year."[8]

The break was even more jarring with Edmund Whitman, publicity chief at United Fruit Company and one of Eddie's closest friends. Whitman had to pass on word that after years of faithful service, Eddie was being terminated by the fruit company's new boss. "Eddie never, ever spoke to Ed Whitman again," says Tom McCann, who worked closely with the two at United Fruit. "That hurt Whit a lot. Whit thought he had a relationship with Eddie."[9] Anne Bernays recalls that "when Eddie would come home from the office he'd be on the phone for at least an hour every single night with Ed Whitman. They spent vacations together. For years this was his very, very, very closest friend. But after that falling-out Whitman's name was never mentioned in the house. It was as if he'd never existed."

Marguerite Clark, medical editor at *Newsweek*, was yet another dear friend who was in Eddie's life every day for a while but then suddenly vanished. "There was one moral error. I don't know what it was, but he cut her off, too," says Anne. "With my father it was really all or nothing."[10]

· · ·

Eddie's boss man persona was easier to bear for younger employees passing through for a year or two. While he worked them hard, he worked even harder himself, staying at the office until late at night and coming in on weekends. Young staff members learned from a master how this new field of public relations worked, and some benefited personally from the Big Think advice he was making legendary.

"I was making about thirty dollars a week—standard in those days for a bright college graduate—and I was interested in getting another job somewhere," remembers Ralph Bugli, who worked for Eddie in 1937. "I had a lead and thought I'd be smart by putting together a four-page mini-newspaper that highlighted my capabilities. I was working in the office surreptitiously one Saturday afternoon after everyone had gone home, and I didn't realize Bernays was still around. He came in and said, 'What are you doing?' I said, 'I'm looking for a job. I want to get married and need another five dollars a week.'

"He said, 'You're doing the right thing, but this isn't the way to go about it. Don't do a single thing like this; do it on a multiple basis. And never ask a person for a job because you need the money; ask for a job because you deserve it.' He looked at it as if I was his client and he was trying to show me how to cope. And a couple weeks later I got a five-dollar raise.

"Bernays," Bugli adds, "was a formative influence in the lives of all of these young guys who worked for him."[11]

Molly Schuchat was hired just as she was graduating from college to help the Bernays office with Thomas Dewey's presidential campaign. "I was superfluous," she remembers, "and he was doing one of his usual good turns in hiring me. I said I couldn't start up right away [because] I was going to a Cornell football game, and he said, 'I think we can wait.'"[12] And Elizabeth di Sant'Agnese says that when she worked for Eddie in the mid-1940s, "he even paid my salary while I was home pregnant and did nothing."[13]

Not all have such fond memories, however.

"It was a very good experience for me," Hutchings says of his two years in the Bernays office, "because I never had a boss that bad the rest of my life." He concedes that Eddie was "brilliant," a "marvelous consultant," and "great salesman," but says the campaign he worked on for Kelvinator refrigerators involved "sitting there and thinking up 'news' releases. I put 'news' in quotes," he adds, "because there was no news there. I'd send out recipes, but they were terrible. Every so often I'd write a story somebody would print, but mostly they didn't print them. I was getting paid thirty bucks a week and was practically running the whole program."[14]

Others shared that sense that the Bernays office was run largely on smoke and mirrors. They felt that Bernays was like the unassuming little man behind the curtain in *The Wizard of Oz*, dazzling his clients not with the magic he promised but with ill-informed offerings from his underpaid young staff, all wrapped up in a fancy, high-priced package.

The only thing Peter Straus knew about labor issues when Eddie hired him in the mid-1940s came from two courses he'd taken in college. But that didn't stop Eddie from putting him to work rewriting the labor handbook for the huge Columbia Rope Company—or from charging Columbia $5,000 for the "collective advice" of his "labor staff." "He got a lot out of very junior, underpaid people and charged a lot for it. I sort of admired that," says Straus, who was paid $45 a week back then and is now chairman of the board of New York–based Straus Communications, which runs eight radio stations and five weekly newspapers.[15]

Cynthia Donnelly had just graduated Phi Beta Kappa from Vassar when she went to work for Eddie in 1939. In that depression climate she was glad to have a job, even as a secretary. Maybe that was why she stayed on despite Eddie's referring to her as "Little Miss Nitwit." "All his secretaries were Little Miss Nitwits," she recalls. "He'd say it not in a kindly way. That was his real evaluation.

"Little Miss Nitwit would get in the door, and before I'd have a chance to get my notebook open he'd be saying, 'Dear Bill.' He'd never tell you who Dear Bill was. I'd spend hours in the office after work figuring out who the hell the letters were supposed to go to, and if you asked a question you were likely to get canned. I think he was mean. That was my impression."[16]

A better description might be "mercurial," as he alternately revealed a generous side and a stingy one. Like many famous men he was insecure, a trait that manifested itself in various ways. Feeling he was too short, at 5 feet 4 inches, Eddie seemed determined to make everything else larger than life. He even inflated his name with an *L.*, a middle initial that was not on his birth record in Vienna. It apparently stood for Louis, although even his daughters aren't sure, since he didn't like to talk about it.

Whatever the reasons for his being difficult, so many ex-employees thought he was that they used to joke about organizing themselves into a club. If they had, it would have been one of the most distinguished public relations associations of the era. While most staff members didn't last long and many left angry, almost everyone he hired was smart and talented. Many, like Conant, used what they had learned in the Bernays office to launch successful careers in public relations. "I certainly recognized I was getting my Ph.D. in public relations," the retired PR man said. "Eddie was a brilliant man, very brilliant."[17]

None of the staff members who left the agency knew much about Eddie as a person or about what drove him professionally. Few lasted long enough to get a long-range look, most weren't wise enough to have formed a considered judgment even if they had lasted, and those who had known him first on a social basis found the party invitations stopped once the professional relationship began. They knew even less about Doris, who arrived at the office later in the day or worked from home, keeping to herself and never letting anyone but Eddie know about the vital tasks she was taking on.

"We were aware of her," says Bugli, expressing a consensus among the junior staff. "I don't recall seeing her more than once, although I was aware she was there. There was a feeling that Mr. Bernays paid a great deal of attention to what Mrs. Bernays thought and did."[18]

The frequent office moves almost certainly were Eddie's idea, much as the changes in homes had been. He began working from his parents' house on West 106th Street, then in 1919 opened his first office in three rented rooms on the fifth floor of a remodeled house at 19 East Forty-eighth Street. He made do then with three golden oak desk chairs, two wooden file cabinets, three typewriters, and a telephone, all purchased for $1,102. His rent was just $255 a month, and his weekly payroll was $192.50, of which $75 went to his brother-in-law Murray C. Bernays, a Harvard Law School graduate just back from World War I; $50 to his wife-to-be, Doris; $30 to a secretary; $25 to a mail clerk; and $12.50 to an office boy.

Two years later he moved into a corner suite in the new S. W. Straus Company building at Forty-sixth Street and Fifth Avenue. The striking white structure offered sufficient space for his growing staff, views of downtown and Fifth Avenue, and the prestige of being next to the elegant Ritz-Carlton Hotel. He pulled up stakes again in the 1930s, settling in at the Graybar Building next to Grand Central, then renting offices at One Wall Street, next to the venerable New York Stock Exchange. In 1942 he moved to 9 Rockefeller Center, and two years later he bought a four-story house, which he converted to offices, at 26 East Sixty-fourth Street. While some of the moves were a result of restlessness, others reflected practical considerations such as a decrease in business during the early years of World War II.

Each office offered its own touch of grace. The one he occupied in 1930 was a "chastely elegant suite," according to the *American Mercury.* "Costly etchings, and an occasional modernistic painting, adorn the walls. Beautiful secretaries glide over voluptuous rugs to ask visitors if they have an appointment with the master of mass psychology."[19] *Printer's Ink* described his East Sixty-fourth Street setting as "a chic black-and-white town house. . . . Bernays' book-lined office is on the front parlor floor, furnished with a large old cumbersome desk and a clutter of papers, mementos, awards and framed letters. Doris Fleischman's office, one floor above, has not quite as many books but still a great number. It is all pink but also comfortable."[20]

Eddie didn't spend that much time in the offices, however, as his appointment calendars make clear. He was too busy lunching with Helen Reid of the *New York Tribune* or Arthur Hays Sulzberger of the *New York Times,* hosting parties for big-name clients and people he was courting as clients, and hopping the train to Albany or Washington, Princeton, Detroit, or California. He'd been superstitious about flying ever since a close friend was killed in a plane crash, and his defective vision made him leery of driving. While he enjoyed riding the train, he was so busy that he sometimes had to spend part of the trip plotting strategies with a junior associate, who would disembark at the next stop and hop a train back to New York to put Eddie's plans into motion.

That was one of many tricks Eddie used to save time. He'd hold two telephone conversations at the same time, one phone to each ear. He'd have his driver clock every possible route from New York to the suburbs, where he spent weekends during the summer, and would carve into quarters books he'd agreed to review, handing each quarter to a junior staff member to read and report on. But he never found the time for golf, tennis, handball, or any of the other sports that executives used to release stress, keep fit, and bond with other men.

"I knew him from childhood, and I never knew of him doing any regular exercise," Wiener says. "Eddie was a workaholic. He worked in public relations all his waking hours, and his social life was work-related to a large extent. It was his weltanschauung, his whole view of the world."[21]

. . .

Most of his staff understood that worldview and, at least in hindsight, respected it. Yes, Eddie was self-absorbed and stingy, but he'd taught them a lot and, thanks in part to that tutelage, they'd gone on to build the careers they wanted.

But Joseph Freeman was older than the rest when he went to work for Eddie, and he suffered wrongs he believed were unforgivable.

Freeman joined the Bernays firm in 1948, when he was fifty or fifty-one. He wrote speeches, articles, and manuscripts; stood in for Eddie at social gatherings; and was a close friend. Freeman left in 1952, forced to retire, he says, because Eddie was afraid that clients would react adversely to publicity about Freeman's political past—a past that included pledging his fealty to socialism at age seventeen, publishing Marxist literary criticism, editing and writing for the leftist journals *New Masses* and the *Liberator,* serving as New York correspondent for Tass, the Soviet news agency, visiting and writing about Russia, and participating in the Communist movement here and overseas.

Freeman's frustration, which began while he was working for the Bernays agency and built into an abiding anger as he believed he was about to be fired, offer disturbing insights into how Eddie operated. Freeman outlined those grievances in a stream of letters from the summer of 1951 to the summer of 1952, to a friend identified only as "Floyd." Freeman died in 1965, but the letters as well as his other papers are preserved at Stanford University's Hoover Institution.

The letters portray Eddie, whom Freeman calls Mr. Barnes, as the most insensitive of bosses. In November 1951 Freeman was reeling from the death of his mother, and "when I returned to the office after a week's absence, the members of the staff, men and women, were particularly kind to me. Mr. Barnes did not even see me. He had not phoned or written or wired the week of my mother's death; now he ignored me completely. . . . It puzzled me that an adult, presumably civilized man (who is America's No. 1 expert on public and human relations) should act like this at a time like this. . . . What I most resented about Mr. Barnes' silence at this time was that he forced a place for himself by the side of my mother in the sorrow her passing had evoked." Freeman understood Eddie well enough, however, to know that his approach partly reflected his own "horror of death, not only the approaching death of his own mother, but his own death at some unknown point in the future; he never talked about death; the word was taboo in his presence."[22]

The letters also paint Eddie as deceptive and greedy. He refused to give his executives a Christmas bonus so he'd have more money for an expensive vacation to Europe, Freeman says. He fired five employees on Christmas Eve, wrote nasty letters to competitors under fictitious names, and failed to credit Freeman for his contributions to a 374-page book, *Public Relations*, of which Freeman says he wrote more than half. "Perhaps I should have been mad," Freeman writes, "but I wasn't; I felt more like a physician who has just found one more example of a disease he is studying. I am studying a disease known as envy—and an excessence on society known as the Robber Baron, the Dictator, or the Predatory Man."[23]

Freeman also portrayed Eddie as a hypocrite. In 1952 Harper's published a book by a British author containing a footnote saying Freeman still was a member of the Communist Party. Freeman and others pointed out that it wasn't true, and Harper's and the author apologized. But, as Freeman recounts, Eddie insisted the apologies weren't enough and that Freeman must sue. "It was clear to me that I would either have to sue Harper's or resign my job," Freeman writes. "It was also clear to me that if I did sue Harper's, [Eddie] could not possibly keep me; no public relations office can afford to have a writer involved in any kind of scandal, particularly one in which that horrible, obscene word 'communism' is the main issue. So I resigned."[24]

It wasn't just the forced resignation that upset Freeman; it was also the way he says Eddie handled it. First Eddie admitted he had secretly had Freeman investigated, apparently by the FBI, when Freeman started working for him. A week after the resignation Eddie signed an American Civil Liberties Union ad condemning blacklisting. Then, Freeman writes, Eddie "told Luther—the one remaining writer—that he loves me, that I have more character and integrity than anyone he has ever met, that it breaks his heart to let me go; but he sent me so little severance pay that Luther was shocked; and he has not called me or sent me a note or communicated with me—though I call the office every day for mail and messages, and have left word that I am not sore and would be glad to see him."[25]

Freeman concedes that Eddie was courageous for hiring him in the first place, given his controversial background, and for not bending earlier to the pressure to fire him. He also admits his critiques of Eddie are in part criticisms of the capitalist system Eddie represented. And it's impossible to get Eddie's side of the story, because he never offered it in his thousands of pages of writings, letters, and other records. The only mention of Freeman in Eddie's autobiography is a note that "Joe Freeman and [his wife] Charmion von Wiegand always enlivened a party. Charmion once brought in Mondrian, the painter, and we delighted in this simple, quiet man." Freeman is listed in the Acknowledgments, as one of "many gifted men and women who have worked with us."

Still, Freeman's portrayal rings true in part because it's so much like what so many others have said of the Bernays firm and of Eddie's way of running it. Even more troubling than his terminating Freeman, however, was the way he allegedly used PR tricks to put a positive spin on what he'd done.

"After I quit," Freeman writes, Eddie "sent word to me through his general manager that it would be better to give some other reason in public for my resignation. He got me out on a political issue, but wanted me to save his face, to say I had quit to do a book, or to make more money, so he could go on posing as a liberal. And the hell of it is that I am saving his face just that way, because in the current climate of opinion it will do me no good whatsoever to announce the real reasons for my resignation. . . . So for the time being I am compelled to keep silent. . . . It's as though a brick wall had fallen on me."[26]

· · ·

The Freeman letters suggest how strained Eddie's relations often were with his staff, and his breaks with old friends like Edmund Whitman and Marguerite Clark make clear how difficult it was for him to sustain friendships. So whom did he like and admire, want to see and be seen with?

Often it was his powerful clients, people he looked up to for having achieved the success he aspired to and whose idiosyncrasies he interpreted as brilliance. People like Amadeo Peter Giannini, known as A.P., a onetime vegetable peddler who assembled one of America's preeminent financial institutions, the San Francisco–based Bank of America.

Eddie went to work for Giannini in 1938, and he loved telling the tale of the bank chairman's rise to power. "He acted in banking like the aggressive pioneers who had built the West. He evaluated his actions by expedience, not by moral standards," Eddie wrote in his memoirs. "What pleased me was his willingness, his eagerness to reject the conventional and traditional. He had killed the idea that a banker had to wear a morning coat and top hat to be a banker, that stuffiness and banking were synonymous. He built his banking business by lending money to householders for the purchase of automobiles, vacuum cleaners, washing machines and other household appliances, previously an unheard-of activity."[27]

The banker's pioneer spirit and refusal to be bound by orthodoxy were appealing to Eddie because that was how he saw himself, as a PR pioneer smashing conventions as he shaped a new profession. Giannini's excesses—his "anger, egoism, and possessiveness"—were precisely the concerns that colleagues voiced about Eddie, and Eddie knew that by condemning them in Giannini he was suggesting that he himself couldn't be guilty of such excesses.

What Giannini was to banking, Orlando F. Weber was to chemicals, only more so, which made him even more attractive to Eddie. The president of Allied Chemical and Dye Corporation hired Eddie to help him keep his private business private, despite bids by stockholders and the New York Stock Exchange for him to open up. In the process Eddie got a rare look at this powerful, secretive man, and again he saw things he envied.

Weber, for instance, had a flair for the dramatic. His Rolls Royce had a "special body built high so that he could step in and out without stooping. He didn't want to stoop for anyone or anything." At work, Weber required that every memo be checked by the man who wrote it, his immediate superior, and his immediate subordinate, on the theory that "three company people know all about each letter. If two died, the third would maintain corporate continuity." Then there were the fears Weber and Eddie shared about communism, fears so deep-seated that Weber wanted stricken from Allied spreadsheets words like "profit," "interest," and "surplus," which were "associated with Karl Marx's [Das K]apital."[28]

One more thing appealed to Eddie about Weber and Giannini: they respected him. Both men were so egocentric they assumed they had the best answers to any question, but when it came to their public images both deferred to Eddie. They also liked him. And to Eddie, there was nothing better than being judged an equal by men of power and stature.

Going to WAR

8

IT WAS A WAR IN WHICH FEW SHOTS WOULD BE FIRED BUT UPON which the very safety of the free world was said to hang. It was a war where words and symbols were the primary weapons, and Eddie Bernays was the principal source of ammunition. And in 1954 Bernays's arsenal was as well stocked as it would ever be.

He had a plan for spying, one that involved putting in place a network of moles and flying in from Egypt a high-powered intelligence expert to survey enemy strengths and vulnerabilities.

He had a plan for waging psychological warfare, gathering for his side "authoritative information that will enable it to appraise the personality of the key men it has to deal with in order to survive." And another plan for wooing the press, acting as the eyes and ears of the *New York Times*, courting columnists like Drew Pearson, making life tough for critical journalists and rallying around friendly ones.

He even had a plan for contrasting his godless enemy's outlook with that of Christianity on twenty-two vital issues. Under the enemy, for instance, "the ideal ruler is the efficient, ruthless tyrant," whereas for the other side "the ideal ruler is Christ, the Good Shepherd, and those having authority from Him, who imitate Him."

All this for an undeclared war waged on behalf of United Fruit, one of America's richest companies—a war fought in quiet alliance with the U.S. government, on foreign soil, against the elected government of Guatemala. A war that, in the mid-1950s when the cold war seemed ready to boil over, was seen by those waging it as a crusade to keep Moscow from gaining a beachhead 1,000 miles south of New Orleans.

Bernays helped mastermind that war for his fruit company client, drawing on all of the public relations tactics and strategies he'd refined over forty years. It was the chance to go to war he'd been denied thirty-five years before, and he was readier than ever.

Historians have written extensively about that propaganda campaign, but they have always relied on the sketchy account Bernays provided in his autobiography and on the limited materials available from the American and Guatemalan governments, the fruit company, and others. Upon Bernays's death in 1995, however, the Library of Congress made public fifty-three boxes of his papers concerning United Fruit. Those documents paint in vivid detail his behind-the-scenes maneuvering and show how, in 1954, he helped topple Guatemala's left-leaning regime. The papers also offer insights into the foreign policies of U.S. corporations and the U.S. diplomatic corps during the turbulent 1950s. And they make clear how the United States viewed its Latin neighbors as ripe for economic exploitation and political manipulation—and how the propaganda war Bernays waged in Guatemala set the pattern for future U.S.-led campaigns in Cuba and, much later, Vietnam.

"This whole matter of effective counter-Communist propaganda is not one of improvising," Bernays noted in a 1952 memo to United Fruit's publicity chief. What was needed, he added, was "the same type of scientific approach that is applied, let us say, to a problem of fighting a certain plant disease through a scientific method of approach."[1]

. . .

Guatemala was not Bernays's first experiment with the science of foreign affairs.

That came just after the First World War when he was winding up his work with the Committee on Public Information, where he'd landed after being turned down for active duty. He was living at home and looking for a new adventure. Carl Byoir, a colleague at the CPI, made his search easier by offering him $150 a week to help the Lithuanian National Council of the United States win American recognition of Lithuania, which had detached itself from Russia and formed a republic.

"I said, 'Sure, I'd be glad to do it. What is it?' He said, 'Well, we'd like you to write stories justifying the validity of this little Baltic nation,'" Bernays recalled more than fifty years later. "I thought of a new idea at the time, getting out what we called fillers for the newspapers—stories about four inches long. They were the same width of column as a newspaper. They were sent to papers throughout the country, and if the newspaper editor, the makeup man, had to fill a gap, he could use them."[2] This was yet another Bernays innovation that became the standard way of doing business, helping editors around the world fill empty space and helping PR men promote their clients.

He also tapped his time-tested technique of coming up with stories that appealed to the special interests of certain groups of Americans. He wrote about Lithuanian music for American music lovers and about Lithuanian theater for American theater buffs. He sought similar links for fans of sports and business, food, clothes, and transportation. "Each story," he explained, "contained the message that Lithuania, the little republic on the Baltic, the bulwark against Bolshevism, was carrying on a fight for recognition in accord with the principle of self-determination laid down by President Wilson. This theme would appeal to Americans' identification with liberty and freedom."[3] It would also have appealed to Walter Lippmann and Sigmund Freud, Bernays's tutors in the use of symbols.

Bernays's strategy worked, albeit slowly. The Senate recognized Lithuania as an independent state in 1919; formal U.S. recognition came three years later.

He got involved with Israel, too. He pretended to have no special bond with those trying to start a Jewish state, just as he boasted about having severed his ties to Judaism. But just as he never truly divorced himself from Jewish culture, so he seemed drawn to the land whose heritage he shared. His relationship with Israel wasn't a formal client-counsel one; it grew out of his social relationship with Zionist leader Chaim Weizmann, who later helped found Israel and became its first president. On one visit to New York to raise money, Weizmann told Doris Fleischman, "I will make your husband first secretary of foreign affairs of our new country if he will help us." At least that was how Bernays remembered it decades afterward, adding that "Doris reported his offer to me. I expressed my appreciation to him at our next meeting and told him I did not believe in a religious state. 'But it will give status to Jews throughout the world,' he insisted, 'just as a free Ireland has given the Irish status.' I did not argue the point, and the nonexistent president of a nonexistent country accepted my firm refusal gracefully, passing over the issue to describe his unrelenting activities in pursuit of his objectives."[4]

More than thirty years later in New York, Bernays met with another famous Israeli, Golda Meir, then the foreign minister and later the prime minister. "She looked more like a pioneer from our western plains than a foreign minister of Israel," he recalled. "She told me of the difficult situation Israel was facing in the Gulf of Aqaba and the Gaza Strip. Secretary of State Dulles was always cordial to her, she said, when she visited him to talk about the dangers to Israel, but he always acted like a lawyer and was a dead wall when she tried to get support for Israel from him. He referred her to the United Nations."

That was where Bernays came in. Meir said she needed his help drafting a speech for the United Nations, one that called attention to the threat Arab states were posing in the late 1950s. "I urged her to abjure any wailing-wall techniques or emotional appeals to sympathy and to present her case by stressing a common denominator of interest between herself and her audience," he remembered. "She listened intently and thanked me. When a nonpaying client asks for advice I have found that since it has not been paid for it is usually not acted on, because it is not considered valuable. But to my surprise, from the papers the day after her speech, I found that Golda Meir had acted on my advice; she presented her case just as I outlined it. Her statement received a good reception from audience and press and advanced her cause."

And, like Weizmann, Meir supposedly offered him the position of foreign minister, which happened to be her job at the time. " 'Why not take it now, Mr. Bernays?' " he remembered her saying, " 'and I will go back to my old cabinet post, which was Labor.' " But, he added in his memoirs, "I had no desire for the post."[5] Meir, who died in 1978, made no mention of Bernays or of that offer in her memoirs.

His work with the government of India was more formal and longer-lasting, but like his interaction with Israel it began with dinner-party chitchat. And as he did with Israel, he cleared his plans with the State Department before agreeing to anything.

Tensions between India and the United States were running high when Bernays entered the picture in the early 1950s. America was upset that India hadn't joined the battle against North Korea and against communism in general. The people of India felt that America favored their archenemy, Pakistan, in the conflict over Kashmir and that Americans viewed India as a land of man-eating tigers and child brides, of cows roaming city streets, untouchables living in gutters, and cobras hypnotized by magic flutes. Bernays offered to help remake that image—for an annual retainer of $35,000 and another $175,000 in expenses.

His campaign was identical to the ones he'd run for Procter and Gamble, American Tobacco, and other industrial clients, only this time the front groups, letter-writing operations, and other propaganda tactics were employed in behalf of a country instead of a product. Instead of writing speeches and arranging barnstorming tours for the president of Mack Trucks, he was doing it for Benay Rayan Sen, Indian ambassador to the United States, and Vijayalakshmi Pandit, Sen's predecessor and Prime Minister Jawaharlal Nehru's sister. Bernays was characteristically direct in his advice. To assuage American fears about communism, for example, he advised Sen to remove from a speech "the two words 'dynamic futurism' and the word 'collective' as applied to aims, for the reason that they give a Communist connotation, which of course is not meant." He urged the head of the India Information Bureau to explain to U.S. newspapers that Socialists, not Communists, were India's second-biggest political party. He also recycled his Lithuania strategy, encouraging Indians to emphasize their Bill of Rights, their battles for public health and education, and other aspects of life in India that Americans could relate to.

Although Congress balked at the nearly $1 billion in aid India wanted, Bernays felt that after just a few months the "climate of opinion" had "greatly improved." He also was cementing relations with Ambassador Pandit, writing her flattering letters, and helping her negotiate a deal to publish her biography. His relations with Sen, her successor, were shakier and, as happened with so many clients, soon collapsed completely. The falling-out followed a May 1952 visit by the Indian consul general to Herbert Matthews of the *New York Times*, who'd written an editorial condemning India's stand on Kashmir. The consul, according to Bernays, "threatened war if the *Times* did not change its stand."[6] Bernays responded with an angry letter to his Indian employers. They were equally indignant. And on May 26 he wrote Sen saying he had no choice but to resign because of "a regrettable tendency on the part of the Embassy and Consular officials to underestimate American intelligence and integrity."[7]

Sen got the last word, writing on June 2, "It is, indeed, surprising to hear all this from a person like yourself who should be aware, perhaps more than any other American, of the intense desire both of my staff and myself to work for the betterment of relationships between India and the United States of America. If I may say so, your letter of May 26, 1952, reveals a complete misunderstanding of the attitude of the Indian Embassy and an equally complete misjudgment of our motives. However, it would be pointless to engage in what might be an endless controversial argument over these matters."[8]

. . .

Bernays's work for the United Fruit Company was less controversial, at least at first, when he was preoccupied with peddling bananas.

The fruit behemoth had been born over a bottle of rum and had grown into a classic entrepreneurial success story. In 1870 Lorenzo Dow Baker, skipper of the Boston schooner *Telegraph*, pulled into Jamaica for a cargo of bamboo and a taste of the island's famous distilled alcohol. While he was drinking, a local tradesman came by offering green bananas; Baker bought 160 bunches at 25 cents a bunch. Less than two weeks later he resold them in New York for up to $3.25 a bunch, a deal so sweet he couldn't resist doing it again. And again. By 1885, eleven ships were sailing under the banner of the new Boston Fruit Company, bringing to the United States 10 million bunches of bananas a year. United Fruit was formed in 1899, with assets that included more than 210,000 acres of land across the Caribbean and Central America, 112 miles of railroad, and so much political clout that Honduras, Costa Rica, and other countries in the region became known as banana republics. That term reflected North Americans' disdain for Latin Americans, whom they regarded as politically and socially backward and economically ripe for the picking.

The United Fruit Company soon had a kingpin worthy of its swashbuckling history: Samuel Zemurray, better known as Sam the Banana Man. Big and blunt, this Jewish immigrant from Russia used a blend of cleverness and cunning to buy up a bankrupt steamship company and plot the overthrow of the Honduran government, to acquire millions of dollars' worth of United Fruit stock, and then, convinced that the company was being mismanaged, to insert himself as head of the Boston-based firm, fully aware how uncomfortable that made its Brahmin overseers. By 1949 Zemurray had built United Fruit into one of America's biggest and best-run companies, with $54 million in earnings and an empire of railroads and ships, a reputation for fair treatment of its 83,000 workers in the Tropics, and control of more than half of the U.S. market in imported bananas.

But Zemurray was always looking to sell more fruit, especially during the winter, when frosts made shipment and storage more difficult. That was why, in the early 1940s, he hired Bernays as his public relations counsel.

Bernays showed him that one way to boost sales was to link bananas to good health. Dr. Sidney Haas, a New York pediatrician, had proved years before that the tropical fruit helped cure celiac disease, a chronic digestive disorder. The public relations man decided to use a celebration of Haas's fiftieth anniversary as a doctor to get out the word that bananas helped digestion. He printed 100,000 copies of a thin hardcover book on the topic and mailed them to editors, librarians, dieticians, home economists, pediatricians, and doctors specializing in digestive troubles. And he got United Fruit to sponsor Haas's research, although there was no mention of its sponsorship in such Haas publications as "The Value of the Banana in the Treatment of Celiac Disease."

Bernays also linked bananas to national defense, a connection less obtuse than it seems since United Fruit's "Great White Fleet" was used in both world wars to ferry supplies and troops. A 1942 memo outlined his three-part approach to demonstrating "that the maintenance of the banana import trade is basic to the United States (a) because it maintains the stability of the Central American republics, (b) because it provides an economic basis for taking defense material, vital to the United States, to the Panama Canal, [and] (c) because it is logical that the boats that take the material there should not come back unloaded, but that they should help to further hemispheric solidarity and the Good Neighbor Policy by bringing loads of bananas to this country." The strategy, he concluded, "is a political, economic, defense, and practical one."[9] In Big Think terms, it amounted to couching his client's private interests behind America's public interests.

On top of that he campaigned to get bananas into hotels, railroad dining cars, airplanes, and steamers; to feed them to professional and college football teams, summer campers, YMCA and YWCA members, Boy Scouts and Girl Scouts, and students of all ages; to promote them among cake, cookie, ice cream, and candy makers; and to secure a place for them in movie studio cafeterias and at top-of-the-line resorts in places like Palm Beach and Sun Valley.

But Bernays was farsighted enough to realize that if United Fruit wanted to cement its position in the North American economy, it had to teach North Americans about their neighbors to the south. The mission wasn't just to sell bananas, he told Zemurray, but to sell an entire region of the hemisphere. So he set up one of his trademark front groups, the Middle America Information Bureau, which churned out brochures and press releases with titles like "How about Tomato Lamburgers?" "Okra Is Decorative as well as Delicious," and "Middle America in Tomorrow's America: A Program of Activities for Men's Civic and Social Organizations." The bureau even renamed the region, explaining that "Middle America" was "a rational and timely expansion of the phrase 'Central America,' which by long usage includes only the republics of Guatemala, Honduras, Nicaragua, El Salvador, Costa Rica, Panama, and the colony of British Honduras." Middle America would include those countries, along with Mexico and the Caribbean island republics of Cuba, Haiti, and the Dominican Republic.[10]

The Middle America Information Bureau was in part an honest attempt to educate, providing scholars, journalists, and others with the latest information about a nearby place that most Americans knew almost nothing about. But Bernays noted in a memo to bureau writers and researchers that "all material released by this office must be approved by responsible executives of the United Fruit Company," and that "in view of the widely known constructive activities of the company, mention of United Fruit will enhance the value of the story to editor and readers and should be made."[11] Where did the bureau get its material on the region? From United Fruit, of course. "I wrote articles, one after another. I ground them out, and they were sent to newspapers throughout the country," recalled Samuel Rovner, who went to work for Bernays right after graduating from the Columbia University School of Journalism in 1943. "I didn't know much about Latin America. I did some research now and then, but for the most part [the articles were] based on material that came from the United Fruit Company."[12]

Even as he was trying to teach North America about Middle America, Bernays urged United Fruit to reform its Latin American operations as a way of proving it cared about the countries in which it was making money. He made sure everyone knew that Zemurray had restored an ancient Mayan ball court, and he got a stamp issued to commemorate the ruins. And when he returned from a monthlong company-sponsored trip to Guatemala and Honduras in September 1947, Bernays wrote his fruit company clients a long memo warning them about low worker morale and substandard living conditions.

"Good will of all groups towards fruit company is poor," he said. "Ignorance, conscious and unconscious distortion by politicos in power or seeking power, by fellow traveler[s] and Communist influences all contribute their part. Guatemala is in a state of transition. . . . All these situations complicate [the] issue and make the company vulnerable unless certain things happen. The American embassy might gain more power, or the government and people in authority as well as the literate [members] of the labor unions might recognize the real public interest and economic values of the Fruit Company."[13] He doubted such positive changes would happen on their own, however, and suggested a series of reforms.

His short visit had made him see clearly the simmering troubles that Zemurray had missed or chosen to ignore. Native workers had to remove their hats when Anglo managers rode by, for example, and employees felt they had no chance for advancement. Those were troubles he knew would negate Zemurray's good works in building housing, medical facilities, and schools. Yet, as always, Bernays believed most of United's problems could be resolved through aggressive public relations. As had happened when he tried to get Procter and Gamble to address racism within its ranks, however, even his modest bid for change was too drastic for his client. "A company does not break with tradition easily," Bernays wrote nearly twenty years later. "The people in the Tropics were remote from Boston; they produced their banana quotas, and that was what counted. Fruit Company executives in the Tropics were tough characters who had come up through the ranks; they were action-related men. What I proposed must have seemed like mollycoddling. I got no reaction to my voluminous report."[14]

What he did get, in 1948, was an edict to disband the Middle America Information Bureau. The order came from Thomas D. Cabot, who succeeded the aging Zemurray as president when Sam the Banana Man stepped up to chairman of the board. Cabot issued his directive "before he had had a chance to discuss the bureau or its func-tions," Bernays recalled. "He could see no relationship between the United Fruit Company and a four-eyed fish, a rare species found in a Columbian [*sic*] lake. We had used the strange fish in our story because those four eyes would lead the reader into a description of how citizen farmers of Columbia [*sic*] cultivated bananas. This fish ended a painstakingly developed and effective program. But fortu-nately for the company, the bureau's work had made a deep impres-sion on the country."[15]

United Fruit's shutdown of the information bureau and its refusal to redress what Bernays felt were deep-seated problems in its Latin American operations seemed like compelling reasons for Bernays to terminate his ties to the company. After all, he'd repeatedly admon-ished his PR colleagues not to represent unsavory clients and not to stick around when their advice was ignored. But leaving United Fruit would have meant giving up annual fees that reportedly reached $100,000. Instead, he resolved to stay on and work for change from the inside, however slowly that might come.

The company eventually did reconsider Bernays's blueprint for reform, although not until 1956, nine years after he issued it. As Diane K. Stanley wrote in 1994, the company, "which by then had experi-enced major difficulties with its Central American laborers, issued an eleven-page memorandum that incorporated several of the principles UFCO's counsel on public relations had initially advocated."[16]

· · ·

By the mid-1950s questions of reform, and even of selling bananas, were being subsumed by questions of politics for Bernays and his employers at the United Fruit Company.

Guatemala was a hot spot and had been since 1944, when a mass uprising ended the fourteen-year rule of military strongman General Jorge Ubico Castañeda. Juan José Arévalo, a professor living in exile in Argentina, returned home and was swept into office in 1945 with more than 85 percent of the vote. Arévalo faced overwhelming obsta-cles, from 70 percent illiteracy to more than 70 percent of the land being held by just 2 percent of the population. But he began to make changes, introducing a democratic political system, overseeing construction of new schools and hospitals, establishing a limited social security network, and giving workers the right to organize and strike. He also pursued limited land reform and distributed property confiscated from Germans and Nazi sympathizers. And he managed to survive more than two dozen plots to unseat him.

In March 1951 Arévalo was succeeded by his defense minister, Jacobo Arbenz Guzmán. Arbenz picked up the pace of change, enacting a modest income tax, upgrading roads and ports, and, most significantly, implementing a plan to redistribute uncultivated lands of large plantations, paying the old owners with government bonds. Between 1952 and 1954 the Arbenz government confiscated and turned over to 100,000 poor families 1.5 million acres—including, in March of 1953, some 210,000 acres of United Fruit Company holdings.

The fruit company had chosen Guatemala half a century earlier in large part because of its cooperative government. That choice had been reinforced over the years as Guatemalan leaders exempted the company from internal taxation, let it import goods duty-free, helped it maintain control of the country's only Atlantic seaport and virtually every mile of railroad, and guaranteed that workers would earn no more than fifty cents a day. It was a capitalist's dream. By the time Arévalo took over, United Fruit was Guatemala's number one landowner, employer, and exporter.

The Arévalo reign raised a red flag for the company. Workers went on strike at its banana plantation and seaport, forcing it for the first time to make concessions in a labor contract, and the fruit company was targeted as Guatemala's most glaring symbol of hated Yankee imperialism. If Arévalo was a portent, Arbenz was the realization of the dreaded prophecy. He wanted to build a highway to the Atlantic to break United Fruit's stranglehold on inland transport, a second port to compete with United's facilities at Puerto Barrios, and a hydroelectric plant to end the near-monopoly of U.S.-backed power suppliers. He also wanted to take another 177,000 acres of the fruit company's land, bringing the total to nearly 400,000 acres. The company would be reimbursed at about $3 an acre. That was what United Fruit said in its tax statements the fallow land was worth—far less than the $75 an acre it claimed once the land was expropriated.

All of this reinforced alarms Bernays had been sounding since he visited the region early in the Arévalo regime. He now warned that Guatemala was ripe for revolution and that the Communists were gaining increasing influence over Guatemala's leaders. And he counseled the company to scream so loud that the United States would step in to check this threat so near its border. Company officials were unconvinced at first but Bernays pushed ahead and, as the political situation in Guatemala heated up, he ratcheted up his counteroffensive.

In March 1951, two years before the Guatemalan land seizures, Bernays wrote United Fruit publicity chief Edmund Whitman warning that the Iranian government's recent seizure of British oil properties set an ominous precedent: "We recommend that immediate steps be undertaken to safeguard American business interests in Latin American countries against comparable action there. News knows no boundaries today. . . . To disregard the possibilities of the impact of events one upon another is to adopt a head-in-the-sand-ostrich policy." He urged the company to get a top Latin American official to condemn the expropriations, hire a top international attorney to outline "the moral, traditional and historical reasons that validate the necessity for outlawing expropriation," and convince a top university to convene a conference on how North America should respond to such hostility. Over time, he added, the company should launch a media blitz "to induce the President and State Department to issue a policy pronouncement comparable to the Monroe Doctrine concerning expropriation."[17]

In fact, he'd begun planning such a blitz months before, as he told Whitman in a November 1950 letter. He had picked out ten widely circulated magazines, including *Reader's Digest*, the *Saturday Evening Post*, and *Harper's*, and said each could be persuaded to run a slightly different story on the brewing Guatemalan crisis much the way they were covering the ongoing battle between the railroads and truckers. "In certain cases, stories would be written by staff men," Bernays wrote. "In certain other cases, the magazine might ask us to supply the story, and we, in turn, would engage a most suitable writer to handle the matter."[18]

While the United Fruit Company didn't move as quickly as Bernays wished, it did move, and articles began appearing in the *New York Times*, the *New York Herald Tribune*, the *Atlantic Monthly*, *Time*, *Newsweek*, the *New Leader*, and other publications, all discussing the growing influence of Guatemala's Communists. The fact that liberal journals like *The Nation* were also coming around was especially satisfying to Bernays, who believed that winning the liberals over was essential to winning America over.

He was pleased but not content. "As a result of many recent articles and editorials on this situation, a point of high visibility has now been temporarily achieved in this country as regards the deplorable pro-Communist conditions prevailing there and the potential dangers stemming therefrom, both to the United States and the United Fruit Company," Bernays wrote to Whitman. But "it is an axiom in government and politics that for publicity to be effective, it should be translated into an action program of platform planks. Words must lead to prompt action." What did he have in mind? The fruit company should think boldly, he wrote, considering, among other things, "(a) a change in present U.S. ambassadorial and consular representation, (b) the imposition of congressional sanctions in this country against government aid to pro-Communist regimes, (c) U.S. government subsidizing of research by disinterested groups like the Brookings Institute into various phases of the problem."[19]

He was also aware of the clout the *New York Times* carried with the public and the press, and he prodded the paper to publish more stories favorable to his client. He accomplished this by skillfully exploiting his ties to the publisher, Arthur Hays Sulzberger, who was a relative of Bernays's wife, Doris. He tried to influence the assignment of reporters, ensuring they were sympathetic to his cause and complaining when they weren't. He even weighed in on letters to the editor, writing Sulzberger in the summer of 1951 to complain about a letter the *Times* had run on "Guatemala Labor Democracy" written by the artist Rockwell Kent, who Bernays said "has been a fellow traveler over a period of years, which would appear to label the letter as covert propaganda of the Party."[20]

"Propaganda" was a word Bernays seldom used in a pejorative sense. And propaganda was precisely what he was promoting with the press here and abroad, pushing sympathetic publications to print sympathetic stories, then urging them to mail the stories to colleagues in the hope of getting even more such stories. He wrote, for example, to Whitman about his work with the *Havana Herald:* "We are taking the editorial submitted to us and rewriting it for submission to you. After your okay, we understand you will submit it to Mr. Schuyler in Havana. He will receive instructions from you on how to handle the situation, with a view of its insertion in the *HH.* He will also endeavor to make arrangements with the editor or publisher to send a reprint of the editorial after it has been completed, with a letter from the editor or publisher to editors and publishers in this country."[21]

A surprising number of respected reporters seemed not to know or care about that orchestration or about the fact that Bernays worked for a firm with huge economic interests at stake. What mattered was that his releases were filled with facts they could quickly transform into stories. Some journalists even forged personal bonds with him and began sharing information they'd collected. *New York Times* reporter Will Lissner offered Bernays this friendly advice: "I notice a somewhat unusual pre-occupation with the affairs of the United Fruit Co. in the Communist press. Note the two clippings enclosed. There were several other references in the period. I shall watch to see how the Moscow press handles these dispatches."[22] Bernays informed Whitman of an even friendlier talk he'd supposedly had with Lissner, saying, "Mr. Lissner pointed out that he believed it was only the strong and offensive strategy on the part of United Fruit that made the Guatemalans buckle down. He analyzed this strength as follows: First, the strength displayed in negotiation. Second, the strength manifested through the pitiless publicity focussed [*sic*] on the situation in the United States, which in turn had its reaction in the attitude displayed by the Guatemalan government of compromise."[23]

Columnist Walter Winchell was someone else the PR man felt he could count on. He cabled Winchell at Hollywood's Beverly Wilshire Hotel, telling him about a Manhattan rally that Paul Robeson, Florentine Luis, and other prominent leftists were planning "in defense of Guatemala." "You may care to deflate in your Sunday broadcast suggesting rally might discuss false accusations against United States made by Communists," the cable said.[24] Just how secure United Fruit was about Winchell's support became clear nine days later when Whitman wrote Bernays expressing doubts about columnist Drew Pearson and suggesting that "if we decided to try to straighten him out, perhaps Walter Winchell could do this job. What do you think?"[25]

Reporters and columnists weren't the only ones willing to see the Tropics through Bernays's lens. In January 1952 he took a group of journalists on a two-week tour of the region. With him were the publishers of *Newsweek*, the *Cincinnati Enquirer*, the *Nashville Banner*, and the *New Orleans Item*; a contributing editor from *Time*; the foreign editor of Scripps-Howard; and high-ranking officials from the United Press, the *San Francisco Chronicle*, the *Miami Herald*, and the *Christian Science Monitor*. Bernays insisted in his memoirs that the journalists were free "to go where they wanted, talk to whomever they wanted, and report their findings freely,"[26] and he reacted angrily to suggestions in later years that the trip was manipulative. But Thomas McCann, who in the 1950s was a young public relations official with United Fruit, wrote in his memoirs that that trip and others like it were "under the Company's careful guidance and, of course, at company expense. . . . The trips were ostensibly to gather information, but what the press would hear and see was carefully staged and regulated by the host. The plan represented a serious attempt to compromise objectivity. Moreover, it was a compromise implicit in the invitation—only underscored by Bernays' and the Company's repeated claims to the contrary."[27]

Both are right, at least in part. The editors involved were too sophisticated to be taken in by overt propaganda and too seasoned not to insist on seeing things for themselves, as Bernays suggested. Yet his own memos make clear that he used all of his PR wiles to make sure those editors came away concurring with United Fruit's stand on the conflict. Compromising objectivity, after all, was what he did for a living.

By whatever route he got there, the results of his trips to the Tropics were beyond dispute: more and more stories sounding an alarm about Guatemala. As Bernays recalled of the editors and publishers who traveled with him, "after their return, as I had anticipated, public interest in the Caribbean skyrocketed in this country. Ludwell Denny's stories in the Scripps-Howard newspapers told of efforts in Guatemala to 'engender hatred of Yankee monopoly capital and imperialism.' "[28]

Few of the reporters and editors who covered Guatemala are still alive, but those who are say Bernays won them over through a low-key presentation of the facts. "He did keep in touch with the foreign desk of the *Times* and with me during a good part of that period," remembers Morton Yarmon, an editor on the *New York Times* foreign desk from 1952 to 1960. "He was trying to find out what was happening. I'm sure he had his own agenda, but he never said, 'I want you to tell me what's happening because of such and such.' It was a subtle and kind of even-handed approach. . . . His name carried weight all by itself, Bernays was a name people in the field like myself would be impressed with. You might even say I was flattered to have Bernays calling up every so often to ask questions."[29]

Lissner says he's heard the claim that "Bernays exaggerated the situation, but there was no exaggeration. They say he was setting up trips to take reporters to Guatemala, and he did that, but he never actually attempted to tell them what they would find. . . . He felt if the press saw what was going on in Guatemala they would write about it. The notion that you can dupe reporters amuses me."[30]

Sidney Gruson, a *Times* writer who was more skeptical of Bernays's warnings about communism, says the public relations man "never tried to interfere with me. He sort of gave up on me before he started trying."[31] And Herbert Matthews, probably the most skeptical of *New York Times* reporters covering the Tropics, informed Bernays that "I did not admire United Fruit's previous record in Guatemala or some of the things they were doing in the 1950s, but they had legitimate grievances and a legitimate story and I could always get them honestly and straight from the Bernays office. A public relations representative, as Eddie Bernays always knew, had a value to others to the degree that he played straight. One deliberately false move and the connection becomes valueless to the person seeking information. Eddie Bernays never made one and never, so far as I could tell, presumed on the friendship that blossomed between our two families."[32]

Bernays must have delighted in those tributes. Subtlety was something he strove for but too seldom achieved, as his center-stage efforts in campaigns like Light's Golden Jubilee made clear. Playing it straight was also something he talked about, but it was tough to do, for a man who was so good at propagandizing. Here, in what may have been his boldest bid ever to orchestrate press coverage, he managed to win over the reporters while convincing them he was merely an honest broker of facts.

．．．

Bernays was gaining ground with the press, but like a relentless general, with each step forward he became more determined to press ahead.

In March 1952, for instance, Guatemala offered United Fruit the labor contract it had long sought. While company officials saw that as a major triumph, Bernays insisted it was a "tactical retreat" by the Communists and "does not mean in any sense that their power has been eliminated." The appropriate response, he added in a letter to company president Kenneth H. Redmond, would be "to carry forward the strong aggressive tactics of the United Fruit Company in pointing the finger at Communism in Guatemala. . . . One other element it seems to me is important, too—that is, that the people of the United States be not permitted to get the impression that all the hue and cry about Guatemala was raised in terms of self-interest. It becomes necessary, therefore, to continue to make visible to the American people what the Communist penetration of Guatemala really is."[33]

In letters to Whitman over the next two years he spelled out the "aggressive tactics" he had in mind. In retrospect, it's clear that those tactics constituted a major escalation in the war of words between the Guatemalan regime and the evolving alliance of the fruit company, key U.S. officials, and other critics of the government in Guatemala.

One way to strike out at the regime would be to issue the "first book on Communist propaganda," Bernays wrote to Whitman. The manual, he explained, would give fruit company executives "the intricate picture of Communist philosophy and propaganda that they are dealing with" and outline the "scientific method of approach" needed to fight back.[34]

The next month he proposed hiring Leigh White, "an outstanding investigating expert" working in Egypt, to undertake a "private intelligence survey" of the "political and ideological situation" in Guatemala.[35] That was the first in a series of references by Bernays to a network of intelligence agents, spies of sorts, that he helped to set up in the Tropics to be coordinated by "the company's 'state department.'" While it's unclear whether White joined up, Bernays's memos to Whitman and to newspaper executives suggest the network did supply valuable information. In a March 1954 letter to *New York Times* foreign editor Emanuel Freedman, Bernays said an "authoritative source" had warned him that the Guatemalan government was preparing to stage a phony plot to justify a crackdown on critics.[36] And in a May letter to David Sentner of the International News Service he said weapons were being funneled from the Moscow embassy in Mexico City to "Guatemalan reds," adding that the information is "not for attribution" and that some of it came from "a very responsible correspondent of ours in Guatemala City" while the rest was from "an equally responsible gentleman in Honduras."[37]

Only select journalists—those on what Bernays called his "confidential list of approximately one hundred special writers interested in Latin America"—received such sensitive information. In an April 1954 letter to Bernays, Whitman said he had learned from a United Fruit vice president, Almyr Bump, about another writer, Paul Jenkins, and "if his writings bear out Bump's belief that he is a 'sound citizen' and if we find him to be a champion of the private enterprise system and anti-communism in Guatemala, etc., then we might want to ask him whether he would care to receive our confidential material."[38]

In June 1952 Bernays broached the topic of psychological warfare, something he'd been pushing since World War I. He presented to United Fruit boss Samuel Zemurray his plan for "psychological activities aimed at developing a better climate of public opinions." Zemurray, Bernays wrote, "recognized that it could not prevent certain situations from arising, but certainly that it should be carried on as a possible insurance against them arising, or as possibly modifying their negative impact on the company." History suggested how valuable such information could be, Bernays argued, writing that "studies of the Nazi criminals by psychologists, the studies psychiatrists make of court cases after the criminal has been sentenced, would indicate that had previous knowledge been had of the situation, one might have coped much more effectively." What kind of information did he have in mind? He spelled that out, too, writing that he wanted "information about the cultural background of the individual, his family background, his early upbringing, his education, development of career and a look at the various incidents and activities in his life that might shed light on his personality."[39]

He also wanted to reestablish the Middle America Information Bureau and to hire Nicholas DeWitt, a scholar from Harvard's Russian Research Center, to do an analysis that would "enable us, if possible, to show the parallelism in the thinking of Guatemalan Communist leaders and the thinking of Marxist or Soviet leaders." DeWitt responded by letter, saying, "It seems to me that this entire subject is a very sensitive one. In view of this, I would like to know at the outset for which purposes and in what form you are planning to use my findings." Bernays wrote back that "if you do not care to have your name associated with this study, we shall, of course, be delighted to keep it confidential." DeWitt is dead, and Harvard colleagues say they aren't sure whether he performed the requested study, but Bernays's files make clear that someone did. A twenty-five-page "content analysis" reviewed nearly 17,000 words spoken by Guatemala's leaders and compared them to statements of Soviet leaders, concluding that there was substantial overlap on matters like how the United States was perceived. In the Guatemalan speeches, the report said, "every item mentioned in almost verbatim form is frequently found in Soviet propaganda messages."[40]

Even as he pushed ahead on other fronts, Bernays always kept a close eye on his press and other propaganda contacts, which he and United Fruit saw as his most effective weapons. In April 1954 he wrote to the *Saturday Evening Post* complimenting it on an article about communism in Latin America and offering to provide—"at no expense, of course"—lists of those who might want reprints, including members of the House and Senate Foreign Relations Committees, the "one hundred special writers," and key officials at the Central Intelligence Agency, the State Department, and the Defense Department. "We also believe," Bernays wrote, "we can be helpful in possibly arranging for some member of Congress to reprint the article, in whole or in part, in the *Congressional Record,* with a possibility of mailings from the *Congressional Record* to a larger list of opinion molders and group leaders."[41] At the same time, plans were under way to mail to American Legion posts and auxiliaries 300,000 copies of a brochure entitled "Communism in Guatemala—22 Facts."

Bernays's schedule for May 1954 reflects the frenetic pace of his activities concerning Guatemala and of the close ties he'd forged with the *New York Times.* On May 1 he talked to Freedman, the *Times* foreign editor. Two days later he spoke to Yarmon, on the *Times* foreign desk, and two days after that he talked again with Freedman. On May 6 he called Freedman and "supplied him with additional information" and spoke with Lissner. The next day he spoke with Lissner twice "regarding Honduras. Passed information on to Mr. Whitman." Bernays was in contact with the *Times* at least once a day nearly every day, also finding time to talk to journalists at the Associated Press, *Meet the Press,* the *New York Herald Tribune,* and other influential media outlets.

Events in Guatemala, meanwhile, were firing up. The Eisenhower administration, which assumed office in 1953, stepped up the pressure on Arbenz. The Guatemalan president responded by hardening his stance, and month by month the situation edged toward confrontation. The final showdown began on June 18, 1954, when Carlos Castillo Armas, an army officer living in exile, crossed the border from Honduras with two hundred men recruited and trained by the CIA— a band Bernays referred to as an "army of liberation." This "invasion," supported by a CIA air attack, quickly achieved its goal, and on June 27 a military junta took control of Guatemala. Armas was named president a week later.

How much of a role did Bernays play in undermining the Arbenz government and in the final assault?

His Library of Congress files show he remained a key source of information for the press, especially the liberal press, right through the takeover. In fact, as the invasion was commencing on June 18, his papers indicate he was giving the "first news anyone received on the situation" to the Associated Press, United Press, the International News Service, and the *New York Times*, with contacts intensifying over the next several days.

Bernays wasn't the only one pressing United's case, of course. The fruit company had powerful friends in the Eisenhower administration, including Secretary of State John Foster Dulles, whose law firm had represented United Fruit in negotiations with Guatemala's former strongman and had served as counsel for the company's railroad subsidiary in Guatemala. Assistant Secretary of State for Latin American Affairs John M. Cabot, whose brother Tom briefly was United's president, was another friend. United Fruit also had influential allies in Congress, including Representative John McCormack, who later became Speaker, and Senator Henry Cabot Lodge, whom Eisenhower named ambassador to the United Nations. Just to be sure, the company hired Washington lobbyist Thomas G. "Tommy the Cork" Corcoran, one of President Franklin Roosevelt's brain trusters, and two other public relations experts—John Clements, a powerful conservative, and Spruille Braden, Truman's assistant secretary of state for Latin America.

And United wasn't the only one pressing for intervention. Senator

Joseph R. McCarthy had launched his search for subversives, the cold war was heating up, and conservatives in Congress and the Eisenhower administration were anxious to take on an apparent Red push in their own hemisphere. Many liberals, afraid of being labeled appeasers, remained silent or joined in sounding the alarm. One writer concluded that "cold war paranoia and sheer ignorance were more powerful than all the manipulations of Edward Bernays and other skillful minions in the pay of United Fruit."[42]

Some of Bernays's lower-level colleagues at the fruit company, meanwhile, resented his lack of hands-on work and wondered how much he accomplished from his perch in faraway Manhattan. "He was what you might call a philosophical adviser during the Guatemalan revolution," says Gale Wallace, who back then was doing PR work for United Fruit based in Latin America. "We didn't think much of his operation; it was long-distance. . . . We were the soldiers, not the people who sat around in the background and dreamed about what to do."[43]

But most analysts agree that United Fruit was the most important force in toppling Arbenz and that Bernays was the fruit company's most effective propagandist. "By early 1954, Bernays's carefully planned campaign had created an atmosphere of deep suspicion and fear in the United States about the nature and intentions of the Guatemalan government," according to the authors of one book about these events. "In the publicity battle between the Fruit Company and the Arbenz government, Bernays outmaneuvered, outplanned and outspent the Guatemalans. He was far ahead of them in technique, experience and political contacts."[44] Herbert Matthews, who'd covered the story for the *New York Times*, agreed that propaganda was the key ingredient in undermining the Guatemalans. "A hostile and ill-informed American press helped to create an emotional public opinion," he wrote. "This, in turn, worked on Congress and, ultimately, on the State Department. Other factors were, of course, at work in Guatemala, but the American attitude would, by itself, have had the effect of strengthening the Guatemalan Reds and making a United States reaction inevitable."[45]

Thomas McCann, the young United Fruit Company PR man, had an even better view of what Bernays was doing and how it influenced events. "My estimate is we were spending in excess of $100,000 a year for Edward L. Bernays, just for his consulting services, which was an enormous amount of money in 1952," McCann recalled. "And everybody in the company hated him, didn't trust him, didn't like his politics, didn't like his fees. . . . The company execs here in Boston and in the Tropics were negative on Bernays because they wanted to do business in the same old way, to foment a revolution and get Arbenz the hell out of there.

"But my sense is we were getting our money's worth, very definitely. I joined the company in '52, just about the time Arbenz made his big move to expropriate our land, and I saw a complete turnaround in the reportage as a result of what Eddie did. . . . There is absolutely no question that Bernays played a significant role in changing public opinion on Guatemala. He did it through manipulation of the press. He was very, very good at that until the day he died."[46]

McCann wasn't the only one who recognized the explosive potential of Bernays's formula: add a wealthy and self-interested private sponsor to sympathetic U.S. operatives, then let a masterful propagandist stir the pot by firing up public opinion, and even toppling foreign governments seemed possible. Or so it seemed to policy makers who would repeat the recipe in Cuba, Nicaragua, and elsewhere across Latin America and around the globe.

. . .

Bernays's war against communism in the Tropics didn't end with the toppling of the Arbenz regime.

Less than two weeks after Armas took over, Bernays wrote to Whitman about ways to build goodwill with the Guatemalan people. He suggested starting a tourist information bureau, sending down a senior medical officer, encouraging U.S. students learning Spanish to write to students in Guatemala, getting the Rockefeller Foundation to fund disease-fighting programs, and sponsoring postgraduate programs for Guatemalan physicians. Those efforts, Bernays explained, would

Eddie, who in the 1930s helped set up the Radio Institute of the Audible Arts to promote his client, Philco, is interviewed at a New York radio station.

Eddie, CBS journalist Walter Cronkite, and Eddie's mother, Anna Freud Bernays, discuss Cronkite's forthcoming broadcast about Mrs. Bernays's brother, Sigmund Freud. She was over ninety at the time.

Eddie had a passion for newspapers that began in the 1950s when he launched the first national survey rating America's 10 best dailies, and continued into his 90s, when he read five papers a day, every day.

In 1924 Eddie launched a national contest in which children were encouraged to carve blocks of soap into everything from animals to characters from Alice in Wonderland. *The soap they used, of course, was Ivory, made by Eddie's client, Procter & Gamble. One youthful participant and his carvings are shown below.*

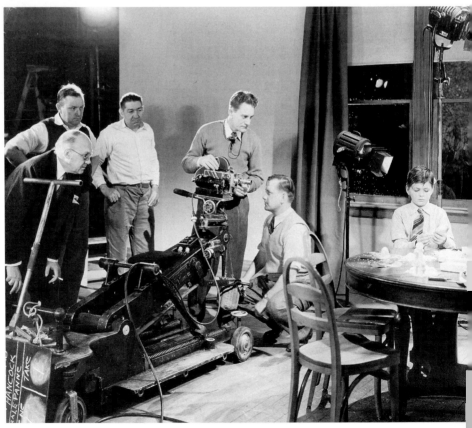

Judges carefully examine soap carvings as part of the contest, which continued for 37 years and used a million cakes of soap a year, inducing untold thousands of contestants between 6 and 86 to spend hour after hour whittling away at the big white Ivory bars.

Newspapers across America ran pictures of Eddie's famous Torches of Freedom parade down Fifth Avenue on Easter Sunday, 1929. Of course none of the stories mentioned that the parade was orchestrated by Eddie on behalf of his client, the American Tobacco Company.

The Green Ball

Uniting Art, Fashion and Beauty

FOR THE BENEFIT OF THE

NEW YORK INFIRMARY

FOR

WOMEN AND CHILDREN

The Waldorf-Astoria

Thursday, October 25th

AT NINE O'CLOCK

Tableaux of Famous Paintings with a Green Motif
Recreated in Living Pictures

and

Fashion Show of Original Models in Green especially
designed by American and French creators and inspired
by Masterpieces of Art

Games—Tableaux and Fashion Show—Supper—Entertainment
Dancing until Three o'Clock

MUSIC by NAT HARRIS and his EMBASSY ORCHESTRA

Reservations and Tickets

THE GREEN BALL COMMITTEE, Room 1525, Chrysler Building

TELEPHONE VANDERBILT 3-9456

American Tobacco was worried that
women might not smoke Lucky Strikes
because the cigarette's green package
would clash with their clothing.
So Eddie set out to change American
women's taste in colors—using events
like the Green Ball to make green the
color of the day.

The Green Ball • THE WALDORF-ASTORIA
OCTOBER 25, 1934

IN AID OF THE NEW YORK INFIRMARY FOR WOMEN AND CHILDREN

OFFICE OF THE COMMITTEE : 405 LEXINGTON AVENUE : NEW YORK : VANDERBILT 3-9451

-2-

And from presidents of two important out of-town department stores come the following comments:

"We believe that such a function will lend distinction to the promotion of fashion and we shall be
very much interested in your plans."

- - - - -

"The writer has attended the Bal de l'Opera a number
of times the last twenty years, and thinks that the
event will help fashion the clothes industry, and
would be a step in the right direction."

while offers of cooperation from designers, manufacturers, etc., have poured in for the Fashion Show, as well
as from editorial sources such as important newspapers,
radio stations, etc.

NOTES FROM PARIS

From Paris we get the following news items on the
"fashionability" of green:

Formal Clothes Register at Paris Night Races

The night racing at Longchamps during the Grande
Semaine brought out the most diverse and formal clothes
seen during the Paris season. The Begum Aga Khan was
stunningly gowned in a full-length dark green velvet coat
with one button at the waist. It had long, tight sleeves
and a looped jabot collar of the same velvet. A tiny
green velvet toque accompanied this coat, which was worn
over a white evening dress and with white gloves and
green slippers.

The Begum, by the way, seems partial to green. From
a leading hat importer we learn that in Patou's collection
one of his most important hats was designed in what they
call "Vert Begum Aga Khan", which is a deep emerald green.

Green Important in Evening Color Scheme

Madame Lucien Robert wore a Lelong green and gold
brocade evening gown with capelet and a little cap turban
trimmed with cross. Many large hats were worn with
short-sleeved evening dresses. Another interesting
costume noted was Augustabernard's famous shirred green
chiffon evening gown with elbow sleeves and train, and a
plain large mousquetaire-type hat.

At Lady Deterding's private gala at the Crillon, a particularly
smart woman wore a fitted coat of stiff black satin lined with bright
green satin, worn over a green net evening dress.

Emeralds Set Off Green Gowns

Mrs. Reginald Fellowes wears two emerald bracelets, one on each
wrist, with a Nile green satin evening gown, and gives herself a very
faun-like appearance with Mercury wing earrings worn on the tops of
her ears instead of in the lobes. Madame Jean Dupuy, the former
Dorothy Spreckels, sets off her pale green satin evening gown with a
beautiful necklace of large pear-shaped emeralds and diamonds with
two strands in the front and one in the back.

Sincerely yours,

THE COMMITTEE

Eddie with Eleanor Roosevelt at a reception in Washington upon publication in McCall's *of the first installment of her memoirs* This I Remember. *Eddie handled publicity for the book, which came out in 1950, including this event at the Carlton Hotel. It drew hundreds of members of Congress, top military brass, and newspaper correspondents.*

OPPOSITE: *Eddie with actress Grace Kelly, NBC-TV chief Robert Sarnoff, and others.*

The National Committee for an Adequate U.S. Overseas Information Program meets with President Eisenhower at the White House in 1956. Eddie is standing to the President's left, and to Eddie's left is famed newsman Elmer Davis. Eddie organized the committee to boost congressional and public support for the U.S. Information Agency.

Eddie and Doris host a birthday party at their Cambridge home with, from left, grandchildren Andrew, Julie, Hester, Polly, Susanna, and Lucas.

help generate "goodwill with the people of Guatemala at this time with due reference to the United Fruit Company getting a share of the credit."[47]

In 1955 he renewed his efforts to get the *New York Times* to write about the region, "exploring further the Communist and other plots against Central American governments, with a view of exposing them to public view in the *Times* and thus focusing national and international attention upon these plots which would help, we believe, to nip them in the bud." And he arranged a two-week trip to Guatemala for Emanuel Freedman, the foreign editor.[48]

Bernays also did all he could to ensure the success of the Armas regime, suggesting that the new president hold a press conference in early 1955, during which, "backed up with facts and figures, he indicates that the economic plight of his country is due to the fact that the previous regime filched *x*-millions from the treasury which would have been used for such-and-such purposes." The same themes reemerged later that year, when Armas visited the United States in a bid to reverse the growing perception of him as repressive and possibly corrupt. "The United Fruit Company man in Guatemala tipped us off as to the questions [Armas] wanted asked at press conferences," Bernays recounted in his memoirs. "He wanted to blame the economic plight of Guatemala on the Communists and to suggest that an economic expert from the United States go to Guatemala and make an independent investigation which would show [that] the devil was Communism."[49]

And in 1956 Bernays came up with the idea of widely disseminating a comparison of the teachings of the Communists with those of the church. "Hate is the driving force of communism," the report concluded, whereas "charity is the impelling motive of Christianity." And under communism "there is no moral law" and "no personal liberty," whereas in Christianity "the moral law is the way which man is created to follow" and "free will means liberty is possible, the liberty of the sons of God to do the right."[50]

Bernays served United Fruit on other fronts as well, such as when the Justice Department filed a civil antitrust suit accusing the company of trying to control banana supplies and prices in the United States and the Tropics. Company officials felt the suit was a bid by the Eisenhower administration to appease critics of the Arbenz overthrow and show that the administration wasn't a puppet of the fruit company. Bernays responded with an inspired campaign. According to McCann, "A series of 'strange coincidence' editorials began to appear in newspapers throughout the country, all questioning why the same government that had received so much help in fighting the 'Red Menace' in Guatemala would suddenly act against its patriotic friend, United Fruit. The year 1954 was near the peak of the McCarthy era, and it was easy to sell the nation the idea that communist infiltration in Washington was so widespread, particularly in the Department of Justice, that the antitrust suit was a way for the Kremlin to strike back."[51]

Bernays's passion for United Fruit subsided only when the company told him, apparently early in 1959, that his services were no longer needed. The new president of the company, he wrote later, "had issued an across-the-board order declaring that all advisers of the company were to go. Castro's expropriation of the company acreage and a resulting decline in profits and dividends were presumably the reasons for this drastic pulling in."[52]

Historians still debate whether or not Bernays and his allies were right in perceiving a Communist threat in Guatemala serious enough to justify U.S.-supported intervention. Some point to CIA documents as confirming the Communists' tightening grip on the country, and insist that without intervention Guatemala would have "gone Red," as did Cuba and, much later, Nicaragua. More agree with Herbert Matthews, who concluded that Arbenz and his followers "were liberal, radical, nationalistic but not, in those early stages, pro-Communist. They were simply tolerant of the Reds. The Communists worked cleverly; the Americans stupidly. We put ourselves in the position of opposing social reforms, leaving the field to the Reds."[53] As for Cuba, McCann wrote, the atmosphere of self-doubt created in the United States by our actions in Guatemala meant that "when a real Communist threat actually did appear three or four years later in

Cuba, the American public and some members of the press were unwilling to believe the truth."[54]

To Bernays, the threat was as real in Guatemala as in Cuba. "Nor have I doubts," he wrote a decade later, "that the Communists wanted to take over Guatemala as a beachhead on this continent." He was less sure, however, about his claims that the regime he helped depose was a puppet of Moscow. "It is difficult to know—and even the experts disagree—whether these trends and events were directed by Russian Communists or whether they took advantage and accelerated what would have taken place anyway," he wrote in his memoirs. "I thought then such events were Communist-furthered, but whether or not they were, they had a deep, upsetting effect and posed a threat."[55]

Most Americans involved in the Guatemala episode, on both sides, managed to put it behind them, but Bernays never could. Each time a book came out questioning his role, he had to answer back, reopening old debates and old wounds—just as he had done with the debates over the post–World War I peace talks and his roles with American Tobacco and Light's Golden Jubilee.

That was especially apparent when Thomas McCann's book, *An American Company*, was published in 1976. It accused Bernays of orchestrating the anti-America demonstration that took place during Arthur Hays Sulzberger's visit to Guatemala in 1949, and which helped convince the *New York Times* publisher that his paper should explore the troubles there. McCann also charged that Bernays had manipulated other publishers and editors he took to the region.

Bernays, who was eighty-four at the time, was furious. He wrote to Crown, McCann's publisher, warning that "in the interests of accuracy and truth and fair play and in your own interests as a publisher, I must point out certain statements in the book which are neither objective or factual, and which may well create embarrassment for you as a publisher. . . . The Communist menace [*sic*] in Guatemala was real and not concocted. Historians and competent and respected eyewitnesses of the situation will attest to that."[56]

His outrage was partly personal. Bernays felt he had helped McCann get his start and treated him like a son. The young PR man's criticism represented the ultimate betrayal. McCann was equally angry and hurt as he sought to understand Bernays's reaction. "I think he was unhappy because I didn't say to him, 'I have a contract to write a book on the United Fruit Company.' He got blindsided on this," McCann explained a year after Bernays died. "As soon as he saw the book was going forward and Crown was printing a substantial number of copies and putting a substantial advertising and promotion budget behind it, he started a letter-writing campaign to all the book reviewers in the country. He said [my book] was full of lies and that his lawyers were looking at this, that for [the reviewers] to report on any of the things I'd said about him [might] constitute a libel action against the reviewer, the paper; he was going to sue everybody. . . . I wrote a letter to Eddie and said, 'I've seen your letter. It has got to stop, and if it doesn't, I'll refer it to my attorney.'

"That ultimately shut him up. . . . But every time my name was mentioned around Bernays he'd just go into orbit. He'd say I'm the worst character—immoral, inaccurate, stupid."[57]

Bernays's venom rose out of more than just wounded pride. He cared deeply about his legacy as a liberal who was anti-Communist but not paranoid like the McCarthyites. The McCann book, to him, represented the unfair rethinking of communism that was then under way in America, applying contemporary values to a very different setting to conclude we'd overestimated the threat and gone further than necessary in places like Guatemala. Worst of all for Bernays, McCann was suggesting that the PR man, rather than having been in control, had been a patsy for the United Fruit Company and for anti-Communists in the U.S. government.

Feeling wronged, Bernays reacted as he always did, by striking out, using his contacts in the press and publishing worlds to hit back as hard as he could.

· · ·

It's not often that figures who play a part in history get a chance to revisit controversies that have plagued them the way Guatemala did

Bernays. But he did, in 1961. The setting this time was South Vietnam, and at first, his history seemed to be repeating itself.

He was advising a New York advertising agency that was working for the government of South Vietnam just as America was ratcheting up its involvement there. And his advice included precisely the sort of propaganda he'd engineered on behalf of Guatemala and, before that, India, complete with a South Vietnam Information Center, endless fact sheets to "give the readers a picture of the country—geographic, economic, educational, ideological," and symbol-laden phrases to "identify the country in the minds of the listener or reader. Here are some possible suggestions that might serve as a basis for further exploration and discussion: 'the bulwark against Communism in Southeast Asia,' 'the little republic in Southeast Asia standing up against Chinese Communistic infiltration,' 'the hard core of resistance against Communism in Southeast Asia.' "[58]

Bernays's special expertise here, as in all his foreign assignments, was handling the press. He had plans for extracting favorable coverage from the *Saturday Evening Post, Foreign Affairs*, the *Atlantic Monthly,* and *Life.* He also knew what to do with TV. On July 19, 1961, he wrote David Brinkley, then with NBC, saying, "The thought has occurred to us that in connection with your forthcoming program you might care to visit South Vietnam, the Republic in Southeast Asia now fighting back Communist infiltration. If you are interested I feel sure the government of South Vietnam would open its facilities and do everything it could to expedite your visit. As you know, South Vietnam is very much in the news today and is regarded as the pivotal state of the free world in that part of the hemisphere."[59]

It's unclear just how long he continued providing such advice, but it wasn't long, and by 1970—at the height of the antiwar movement— he had switched sides, actually proposing to write a paperback book "aimed at men and women interested in having a manual on the how-to of organizing public support for political action at every level to stop the war in Indochina."

Why the switch? Public opinion in the United States was turning around on Vietnam, and Bernays, a master at reading public attitudes, appreciated sooner than most establishment figures how deep-seated the antiwar sentiment was. And this time he'd resolved not to be caught on the unpopular side of history.

So, even as he continued to defend what he'd done in Guatemala, he was offering to put all his insider's know-how to work to stop this latest crusade against communism. "Today, unfortunately, many groups and individuals have had little or no experience with what we call the engineering of consent in a democracy," he wrote in his book proposal. "Many proceed as if no one had even plotted or platted the field before. They act more as if they were carrying out a catharsis and carrying out an effort to identify themselves with this activity, than to use sound proven procedures of communication, public education and public persuasion. . . . The book will attempt to bridge the present gap and to harness enthusiasm, dedication and time to sound methodology."

No matter that he was seventy-eight years old or that few in the antiwar movement knew or cared about all he'd seen, done, and learned in Guatemala. What he was offering them, he told publishers (who never took him up on his offer), was a "practical guide to political and public action by a man who for half a century has practiced in this area of public opinion and public relations."[60]

Uncle SIGI

9

ANYONE WHO KNEW EDDIE BERNAYS KNEW HOW MUCH HE TOOK from his illustrious uncle, Sigmund Freud. But few knew how much he gave back.

Evidence of that give-and-take is sprinkled throughout the scores of letters Eddie and Freud exchanged from 1919 to 1933. The correspondence was at times intimate and at times cold. It reflected Eddie's adulation of the esteemed analyst and Freud's consternation—and fascination—with his consummately American nephew and the novel profession he'd chosen. It also showed seldom seen sides of both uncle and nephew, revealing Freud to be as preoccupied with worldly matters as he was baffled by them, and Eddie to be unrecognizably patient and self-deprecating.

Many of the letters focus on Eddie's role in overseeing the translation into English of Freud's *Introductory Lectures on Psychoanalysis,* a compilation of the famous talks he'd delivered in Vienna between 1915 and 1917. For Eddie, this project, like so many things in his career, began serendipitously. He was in Paris for the post–World War I peace conference. When a colleague said he'd be visiting Vienna, Eddie had him take Freud a box of the Havana cigars he loved but couldn't get during the war. Freud sent back a copy of the lectures, in German, with the inscription "In grateful acknowledgment of a nephew's thought of his uncle."

Eddie recognized the value of the papers, monetarily and histori-cally, to his uncle and to himself. So several months later he showed them to his client Horace Liveright, of Boni and Liveright publishers. "I thought several purposes could be met by publication of the book in English," he wrote forty-six years later. "It would popularize psycho-analysis in America authentically and it would provide stable American dollars for my uncle."[1] The offer of dollars—15 percent of royalties—couldn't have come at a more tempting moment for Freud, who was watching the postwar inflation erode his savings. He autho-rized his nephew to proceed with the translation.

Over the years that followed, Eddie repeatedly claimed credit for bringing Freud to the attention of the American public. While he did play a role, Freud already was known and his fame surely would have spread with or without his nephew. Without Eddie, however, Freud's emotional reactions to the translation might have been lost, reactions he almost certainly would have been more hesitant to share with a nonrelative, but which Eddie saved, and had translated and typed. Those reactions offer almost as much insight into the psychoanalyst's mode of thinking as the lectures themselves.

Consider, for instance, how hard he was to please. Not long after he'd given his okay for Eddie to proceed with the translation from German to English, he sent Eddie's father Ely a terse cable instructing him to "tell Edward stop translation."[2] Eddie responded by cable: "translation finished, introduction written by Stanley Hall also print-ing advertising and publicity contracts all placed, disbursements and obligations to date aggregate three thousands dollars must therefore continue."[3] Freud answered by letter, explaining that he had wanted to back out because he'd heard Eddie was planning to publish the trans-lation in a newspaper, which would be "too American for us over here." There also was the fact that Dr. Ernest Jones, who became Freud's biographer, was about to begin publishing psychoanalytic trea-

Sigi

tises in England and America and wanted the lectures to be among his first publications.[4]

Eddie says that he never had any intention of printing in a newspaper his translation, which was published under the title *A General Introduction to Psychoanalysis*, and that he never owned the publishing rights Jones was worried about. "Rest assured," he wrote his uncle in December 1919, "that I deeply regret that your first authorization should have brought my work and obligations to a point where I could not withdraw. I trust that the book and translation will bring you added fame and glory and also a substantial recompense." To show his good faith, Eddie added, he'd spent $1,000 of his own money on the translation, while Liveright was giving Freud $100 before the book even went on sale and offered him another $10,000 to deliver a series of lectures in America.[5]

Freud turned down the lecture offer, saying "my health and my powers are not up to the point, I would lose very much by the preparations necessary here, and the enormous costs of travelling and of life in America would greatly diminish the sum guaranteed by the firm." But he made clear he appreciated Eddie's efforts, saying, "I am very proud of earning money by the work of my nephew," and he suggested Eddie consider working with the psychoanalytic publishing company Jones was helping set up.[6]

Those and other letters reflect Freud's short temper and constantly shifting moods, one day chastising his nephew and the next pouring on praise. That was partly a result of the stress he was under. Given the way he's venerated today it's easy to assume Freud was an éminence grise during his days in Austria, able to bask in his fame and devote himself to his patients and students. In fact, his country was just coming out of one war and was about to enter another, his revolutionary ideas were coming under attack, his finances were approaching ruination, and his protégés, including Jones, were competing for his attention and support. His New World nephew must often have seemed like yet another source of distress, as well as the most convenient target against whom to vent his frustrations.

Eddie's response to Freud's mercurial states of mind was to remain unperturbed. There was no sign of the temper he'd unleashed on others, family as well as colleagues, who questioned his motives or tactics. He seemed pleased to serve his famous uncle and willing to absorb his outbursts. He relished the notion of acting as a middleman between Freud and important Americans, as he offered to do in a February 1920 letter. The $100 he'd sent from Liveright would be the first of many payments that "will be substantial and continuous over a long period of time," Eddie wrote. Then he told Herr Doktor about a conversation he'd had with "the most important literary agent in America," who "practically begged me to secure for him some publication from you which he might place in one of the very high class American monthly literary scientific publications. Needless to say, such an article would be highly lucrative from your standpoint."[7]

In June Freud wrote again, annoyed that he hadn't received a copy of the newly released translation and hadn't heard from Eddie "for a long time." Eddie calmly explained, as he might to a child, that he'd mailed copies as soon as he received them, that he was passing along a $275 advance on royalties, and that "we have naturally, for your information, made no money on this entire transaction, doing our part as matter of disinterested spirit."[8]

It's easy to see what Freud was getting out of this correspondence: advice about publishing his work, referrals and offers of fees for future writings, and a willing, able, and free financial adviser. His nephew cheerfully attended to the worldly matters that the psychoanalyst knew little about and that he considered unseemly, even though they were essential to his survival and that of his family. Eddie's reward was less tangible. Clearly he basked in his uncle's reflected glory and loved being able to boast later that the interchange which began with a box of cigars "was helpful in introducing psychoanalysis in the United States." But he also relished offering his uncle bits of advice that he would never be able to claim credit for, and he cherished the fact that Freud took him seriously, listened to his advice, and on rare occasions even expressed his appreciation.

Watching Eddie drop his uncle's name over the years, to the point where *Variety* dubbed him a "professional nephew," it's easy to assume he was exploiting the relationship. But their correspondence suggests that if there was exploitation, it went both ways. And it makes clear that the Bernays-Freud relationship was more complex and mutually enriching than was apparent to outsiders.

There were tensions. The translation, for instance, kept resurfacing as an irritant, especially after Freud had a chance to review it and discovered "a number of misprints and misunderstandings." Eddie had hired a Columbia University researcher with a doctorate in psychology to translate the lectures, arranged with another scholar who'd studied with Freud to revise it, and "a large amount of money was spent further in reading, rereading and generally going over the translation." But he'd also been in a hurry, which, Freud said, led to words like *"Verdrengung"* being translated as "suppression" rather than the more accurate "repression."[9]

Freud's anger seemed to subside as positive reviews poured in from newspapers and cash poured in from Liveright. "I had expected it would mean a piece of good business to you," Freud wrote in October 1920, "but I realize from your letters and Felix's account that it all goes to my profit, and I thank you heartily for this demonstration of kindness and helpfulness." He suggested further collaborations with Eddie, including a book to be called *Scraps of Popular Psychoanalysis,* which would have been the ideal merger of Viennese thought and American love of self-improvement.[10]

Eddie, as always, picked up on that encouragement and pursued a series of possible deals for Freud—from a six-month lecture tour of America that would assure him $5,000 and probably net "several times" that, to an offer of $1,000 per article for a series of 3,000-word stories on topics like "The Wife's Mental Place in the Home" and "What a Child Thinks About." Freud's initial response was a two-word cablegram: "Not Convenient." He explained in a December 1920 letter that "I feel deeply grateful toward you on account of the endeavors you make to assist me financially in these hard times and I see it is not your fault if I must refuse your proposals." He turned down the lecture tour for numerous reasons, he said. His health was "not so robust," the offer was "not a very generous one," he wouldn't feel comfortable speaking in English, and Austrian taxes would eat up his profits. As for the articles, Freud was outraged that the American editors refused to sign a contract before gauging public reaction to his initial efforts. "This absolute submission of your editors to the rotten taste of an uncultivated public is the cause of the low level of American literature and to be sure the anxiousness to make money is at the root of this submission," the analyst wrote, adding that "the subjects brought forward in your letter are so commonplace, so far out of my field that I could not give them my attention and my pen."[11]

Receiving that biting response, Eddie remembered in his memoirs, "was exasperating, and I felt frustrated in my effort to be helpful. It was furthermore quite clear that Freud had no idea how widespread his popular appeal was here; nor did he realize that a scientific body of knowledge could be popularized without diminishing its scientific validity."[12] Jones also was taken aback by Freud's tone, explaining, "I cannot help thinking that some of his indignation emanated from feeling a little ashamed himself at having descended from his usual standards by proposing to earn money through writing popular articles. It was the only time in his life that he contemplated doing such a thing."[13]

That exchange didn't deter Freud from continuing to call on his nephew for aid, however, and Eddie continued to oblige. Early in 1921, Freud asked for help for the son of a friend who wanted to emigrate to America; Eddie obtained the needed affidavit. He also got Freud $1,911.08 in royalties due from Liveright, for which Freud was thankful—and more convinced than ever that America was a "queer country." As he wrote Eddie in April 1921, "You did not seem to be puzzled or irritated at all by the attempt of the publishers to rob us of our royalties. You seem to consider it a common business trick and I am sure you know your people. No doubt you were right in engaging an attorney to get the money out of them."[14]

Eddie frequently wrote letters of introduction for American journalists who were in Vienna and wanted to interview his uncle. Freud wasn't always obliging, confessing in a June 1922 letter that he "was

Sigi

not kind" to a female reporter referred to him by Eddie and "she got nothing out of me."[15] Eddie also referred would-be patients, including a wealthy young colleague who, having gotten no better after visiting New York analysts, wanted to be treated by Freud. Freud agreed, although he added, "I would not take him if he be a homosexual and desired to be changed." Eddie responded, "He assures me he is not a homosexual, and that he is writing you in full detail about his case."[16]

While their correspondence focused almost exclusively on business matters, there were exceptions, as when Freud wrote in the fall of 1922 to congratulate Eddie on his marriage: "I heard from Judith that you have married your friend and helpmate and [I] join in her conviction that marital happiness is assured to you." He signed the letter, "Your old uncle, Sigm." Eddie responded that "Doris is proud to be a new niece of Professor Freud, and while she of course will not bask in reflected glory, it is impossible in America not to do that when one is a niece of Professor Freud." The following year, after meeting Doris in Vienna, Freud wrote Eddie to say he found her "a kind, clever and natural girl."[17]

Eddie fared less well in relations with his uncle's friends. Tensions with Ernest Jones and Dr. Otto Rank doomed his plan to participate in other publishing projects. And despite considerable effort, nothing came of his bid to launch a foundation to promote psychoanalysis in the United States. In July 1929 Eddie approached his uncle with another proposal, this time to publish his autobiography, with the promise of an advance payment of "somewhat over $5000.00." Freud responded that "this proposal is of course an impossible one. An autobiography is justified only on two conditions. In the first place if the person in question has had a share in interesting events, important to all. Secondly, as a psychological study. Outwardly my life has transpired quietly and without content and can be dismissed with a few dates. A psychologically complete and sincere life recital would, however, demand so many indiscreet revelations about family, friends, adversaries (most of them still alive), with me as everyone else, that it is precluded from the very outset."[18]

. . .

Had he written a candid autobiography, one of the things Freud would have talked about was his troubled relationship with Ely Bernays and how those strains made it so improbable—and, presumably, satisfying—that he would form close ties years later with Ely's only son, Eddie.

Freud and Ely had once been friends, but that bond became frayed soon after Freud secretly became engaged to Ely's younger sister, Martha. The reason for the break, said Freud's biographer, was that Freud saw Ely as his "most dangerous rival" for Martha's affection. Things got better when, several months later, Ely became engaged to Freud's younger sister, Anna. As Freud wrote in a letter back then: "We freely confess that we were very unjust to Ely. In all important matters he shows himself to be high-minded and understanding."[19]

Freud changed his mind again a few months later. Ernest Jones knew the reasons for this latest break but, apparently not wanting to offend Eddie and other relatives, wrote that they "cannot be given here."[20] Elisabeth Young-Bruehl, in her biography of Freud's daughter, Anna, filled in the gap, relying in part on a letter Jones wrote to Anna. Freud was upset, Young-Bruehl wrote, "when Ely, who had been entrusted with part of Martha's small dowry from an aunt, would not return the money and thus held up Freud's hopes for bringing his long engagement finally to an end." The money was soon returned, however, and it became clear that the funds "had not been embezzled, as Freud thought." Another matter that troubled Freud and his fiancée couldn't be resolved so easily, as Young-Bruehl explained: "Ely's financial troubles were compounded by his infidelity to Freud's sister and [by] a number of illegitimate children to whom he gave money."[21]

Those frictions kept Freud and Ely from communicating for two years and were partly responsible for Freud staying away from Ely's wedding in 1883. A year and a half later, Jones wrote, Freud "was just leaving home when Ely entered to pay a visit; they bowed to each other without a word. Then Freud, taking advantage of Ely's absence, went to call on his sister to congratulate her on the birth of her first child. He made it clear to her, however, that she was not to regard this gesture as indicating any reconciliation with her husband."[22]

The on-again, off-again friendship had warmed again by the time Ely emigrated to America in 1892, and Freud had lent Ely money. Still, bitter feelings persisted, as Freud made clear in a March 1900 letter to his friend Wilhelm Fleiss: "My elder sister Anna and her four children have just arrived there [Berlin] from New York. I do not know what this means and suspect nothing good. I have never had any special relationship with her, as I had, for instance, with Rosa, and her marriage to Ely B. has not exactly improved it."[23]

Ely either was unaware of those resentments or rose above them, repaying Freud's financial generosity tenfold during the war, when the Freuds were desperate for cash. He later donated tens of thousands of dollars to an orphans' fund Freud was helping to oversee, and after Ely's death his widow regularly mailed money to the Freuds. The old enmities seemed to ease with Freud, too, but there are hints in his letters to Eddie that he hadn't entirely forgotten or forgiven. In October 1923, not long after Ely's death, the psychiatrist expressed his regrets, adding, "You know it is hard on me to write more on this subject. Constellations of many years cannot be changed by chance or sudden events." And in a letter two months later he referred to "debts your father left here when he went off to America and never paid in spite of frequent demands, as formed part of his system of cruelty."[24]

The tensions that plagued his father's relations with Freud seemed to have no effect on Eddie, who had his own troubles getting along with Ely. Over the years Eddie made it his mission to collect materials on his uncle and defend him against his many critics. He clipped anything written by or about Freud, saved the dozens of letters from his uncle, and told and retold stories from his youth and afterward about the great psychoanalyst.

Some tales were handed down by Eddie's mother, like the one about Freud as an intense fourteen-year-old. "He sat in the large family drawing room, before maps," Eddie told an interviewer in 1976. "The Franco-Prussian War was on at that time, and he moved the battle lines as indicated in the morning newspaper with little flags that he stuck into the line as it changed from day to day." There also was the story of Freud as slayer of myths: "There had been in 1881 a horrible fire at the Burgtheater. . . . Large numbers of people had died in the holocaust. The Emperor Francis Joseph had built apartment houses on the site of the theater. Nobody was eager to move into them because they thought that the place was fraught with misfortune because of the fire. Sigmund Freud and his newlywed wife moved into this apartment. He was the first to move in, defying all kinds of superstition."[25]

Other tales came from Freud's wife, Martha, and their daughter, Anna, who told them to Eddie and Doris during a visit in 1949, ten years after Freud died. Doris took detailed notes on the encounter, writing about how Anna "sometimes flirts with E [Eddie] like a little girl—moment later a tired old woman. Terribly pleased to see E, who patted her hand, kissed her and treated her like child—no one has ever done that to her before I suppose, and she melted and expanded. . . . 'I never flirt,' she said when I asked. But she does flirt with E. They decided their affection was incestuous—double cousins. E said, 'Its interesting to experiment in this phase of genetics.' A [Anna] said 'Academically or practically?' "

Anna also talked about the family's last months in Vienna, when Nazi storm troopers (the S.A.) and Hitler's elite guard (the S.S.) repeatedly tormented them. "Freud had never shown fear throughout," Doris wrote in her notes. "S.A. invaded their home on Bergasse, 2 to search for money and treasures, 2 with rifles on guard at door. Martha made them sit down, to their embarrassment. Took everything—all money. S.S. came to appraise possessions. In charge was an Austrian Nazi who felt great responsibility to Freud—worried he might be hurt in some way. Posterity would never forgive him. Examined F furniture, silver and valuable antique curios. If value had been 30 thous. kroner they would have been taken over. So this Freud guardian appraised them at 29 thous. Under his personal supervision everything—even kitchen pots, packed by art experts and sent to London." Later, after months of waiting, Anna "finally got passport, took it to F. S.S. asked him to sign paper swearing they hadn't harmed him. F said 'Shall I also write recommendation of S.S.?' Also had to swear he'd never return."[26]

Eddie had his own stories about his uncle, whom he first mentioned on the first page of his autobiography and quoted or otherwise referred to on forty-four other pages—slightly more often than he mentioned his mother or father, and considerably more often than he spoke of his daughters. Also, all of the references to Freud are glowing ones as compared to his constant criticism of Ely. But his memories of Freud weren't as rich as he'd have liked. As a child, he saw the analyst in Austria and "if I had had foresight, my uncle's visit to our farm home on the scenic inland lake in the Austrian Tyrol would have been a memorable occasion and I would today be able to recount everything he said and did. I can truthfully say only that I remember a warm, friendly man, with a beard, who was happy to see his sister, his nieces and his nephew. By one of those memory quirks my recollection instead is of a pair of lederhosen put on in honor of his coming. They were of soft green leather. . . . Instead of being inspired by my uncle's conversation, I was more appropriately inspired by my leather pants."[27] At Cornell, meanwhile, Eddie says he "had social contact with only two professors in my three-and-one-half years." One taught horticulture and wanted to talk about his writings in that field, and the other, "Professor Edward Titchener, the psychologist, learned I was a nephew of Freud and wanted a photograph of my uncle."[28]

Eddie's favorite story grew out of Doris's visit with Freud in Vienna in 1923. "He said to her at that time, 'Edward is one of my sons,'" Eddie wrote in an article thirty-one years later, adding that "this pleased me greatly."[29]

In 1931, when Freud turned seventy-five, Eddie hosted a birthday party at the Ritz-Carlton Hotel that attracted Freud protégé Dr. A. A. Brill, novelist Theodore Dreiser, and attorney Clarence Darrow. Freud couldn't attend, but the group sent him a cable noting that "men and women recruited from the ranks of psychoanalysis, medicine, and sociology are assembling in New York to honor themselves by honoring, on his seventy-fifth birthday, the intrepid explorer who discovered the submerged continents of the ego and gave a new orientation to science and life."[30] Eddie organized a similar celebration, at New York's Harmonie Club, on Freud's eightieth birthday.

His nephew's devotion lasted long after Freud died, as Eddie assumed the role of guardian of his legacy. In a 1952 letter to Princeton history professor Eric Goldman, he took exception to Goldman's calling Freud short and brisk. "Dr. Freud was never brisk," his nephew said. "I would say that if you were looking for the adjective that would least describe him, this is it. A much better adjective might be serious or deliberate." And "he was not little. I would say that he might well have been about 5'8" or 5'9"."[31] In 1971 an interviewer at Columbia University asked about Freud's relationship with his sister-in-law, Minna. "Now, there have been all kinds of direct and indirect implications of immorality in Freud's conduct with his sister-in-law," Eddie said. "There was one by a divinity school teacher at Andover, that Freud had relations with his sister-in-law. Well, that's completely cockeyed—first, based on the character and background of Minna; second, the character and background of Martha; and third, the character and background of Sigmund Freud."[32]

In a 1980 journal article, Eddie wrote that "Freud often has been a victim of distortion by biographers." His relations with his uncle painted a decidedly more upbeat picture, Eddie added. "[H]e had warmth, friendliness, modesty. . . . I learned that he demonstrated compassion early in life. Mother told us that Sigmund, at the age of four, soiled a chair with his dirty hands. He said to his mother, 'Don't worry. When I grow up I'll buy you another chair.'" And when Eddie recounted in the article his long correspondence with Freud, it wasn't the moody or bitter uncle he remembered but the one who "revealed all those basic characteristics I have noted, modesty, warmth, and affection."[33]

Eddie cemented his relationship as adviser and friend to Freud's daughter, Anna, when he visited her in the summer of 1949 and again eight months later when she paid her first visit to America. She wrote Eddie on the eve of that trip, saying, "I look forward to meeting you and Doris again in April, and I hope that we can then repeat the inti-

Sigi

mate and peaceful hours which we had here with you. . . . I cannot tell you how grateful I would be for your help and advice with regard to the American press."[34]

While he seemed consumed by Freud, Eddie was hesitant to discuss how his uncle had influenced him. "The conscious, the unconscious and the subconscious, and the superego were friends at home; just as I suppose a stockbroker discussed market prices of American Radiator and U.S. Steel," he told an interviewer in 1971, recounting how he and his parents often talked about psychology at the dinner table. "And I ascribe whatever I learned about Freud more to absorption than to studiousness in reading of Freud." The interviewer persisted, asking, "Do you think that in your work in projecting the character of corporations and other entities onto public minds, that you were influenced by Freud?"

"Well, I'm glad you raised the question in the words that you did," Eddie said, "because it indicates the misinterpretation that still prevails about public relations. I was seldom interested primarily in projecting characters onto the public. I was much more interested in influencing action and letting the action project itself to the public."[35]

Whether he acknowledged it or not, Eddie was one of Freud's most faithful students and most frequent imitators. He shared Freud's disdain for religion in general and for the Judaism of their forefathers, which both saw as superstitious. He rebelled, as did Freud, against the superego, feeling it stood in the way of his becoming the self-made man he was determined to be. He followed Freud's lead by writing books that laid a framework for his profession. Most of all, Eddie borrowed his uncle's insights into symbols and other forces that motivate people, using them as building blocks for the art and science of public relations.

In the end, however, Eddie was preoccupied with the public arena while Freud was captivated by matters private and inward-looking. Eddie was, in essence, a sociologist while Freud remained a committed psychologist. And while Freud sought to liberate people from their subconscious drives and desires, Eddie sought to exploit those passions.

The Cambridge YEARS

10

LEAVING NEW YORK WASN'T EASY AFTER NEARLY SEVENTY YEARS. But Eddie wanted to finish his memoirs and decided he couldn't do it in the city, with the distractions of work and a bulging social calendar. Once he'd opted to leave, the question of where he and Doris would spend their golden years was merely a matter of applying the same research and reasoning he'd been using with clients for forty-five years.

Their new home had to be in a cultural center, so that they would be stimulated and entertained, and it had to be physically attractive, because they liked to surround themselves with beauty. It had to be a nexus of business and finance, too, because he hoped to keep active professionally. It couldn't be too suburban, because neither of them drove a car. And it had to have good doctors, since he was about to celebrate his seventieth birthday and Doris was sixty-nine.

"Above all," he said later, "I wanted a community in which writing a book was an accustomed action, where people would leave me alone if I told them I was at work."

"I crossed most of the cities off the list immediately," he recounted. "Washington is worse than New York; Providence is provincial. I've spent too much time in Detroit to want to go there; Chicago is hopeless. I wanted a city with a sense of nearness to Europe, so the South and West were out, although the climate at Berkeley is better. Some small cities like Portland, Maine, had attractions, but they lacked the real city flavor."

In the end there was Boston—"really the only city that combined cultural and educational possibilities with a tradition, society, intellectual stimulation, and a feeling for Europe." He refined the search even further by zeroing in on the Harvard Square neighborhood of Cambridge, which "has a mystique all its own. Going to Sage's to shop is the moral equivalent of a good cocktail party."[1]

Actually, Cambridge was the only choice from the start, for two simple reasons: Eddie and Doris's two children lived there, along with their six grandchildren; and Cambridge was just a quick train ride from New York. But simplicity wasn't Eddie's style. Why describe the move as a mundane matter of staying close to family when his own decision-making could be cast as a compelling example of how a methodical approach will produce the right professional and personal choices?

The fact that Cambridge met all his criteria *and* happened to be where his family lived was, as he characterized it in the memoirs he moved there to write, "a rare fulfillment."

. . .

Life in Cambridge was supposed to be serene. Not retirement exactly—Eddie could never conceive of that—but contemplative. The kind of contemplation that seemed to be a matter of course in the ivy-covered community along the Charles River, home to Harvard and MIT, to elegant old thoroughfares like Brattle Street, and to bustling boulevards like Massachusetts Avenue.

Finishing his memoirs didn't take long. He'd started them a decade before leaving New York, with help from young researchers, and he'd been sketching them in his mind for forty years. But he proceeded to take on so many new projects that he told friends he had enough to fill a second volume, which he planned to call *The First Hundred Years*, or maybe *My Second Hundred Years.* In the process he left an indelible handprint on the city that became his final home.

Saving the sycamores along Memorial Drive was one of his earliest passions. The Massachusetts Legislature had proposed building $6 million worth of underpasses so traffic would no longer be slowed at three busy intersections along Memorial, a tree-lined highway on the Cambridge side of the Charles. The problem was that Cambridge residents didn't want the extra traffic that would be drawn to the faster-moving parkway. And they didn't want to lose fifteen to twenty sycamore trees that would have been chopped down so the road could be widened enough to handle the extra traffic.

Eddie went to work. He helped organize the Emergency Committee for the Preservation of Memorial Drive, which made pitches to every interest group Eddie could think of—to mothers who were angry about losing their children's riverfront playgrounds, to real estate executives who worried about devaluing the high-rent apartments along the Charles, to historians who were eager to preserve the historic riverfront, to tax-conscious citizens who were reluctant to underwrite a $6 million road project, and to Harvard University, which wanted to keep its backyard pristine. He even organized the kind of public spectacle he rightly predicted would seduce the media. "This week, in the predawn hours, a patrol of twentieth-century minutemen has been on duty protecting a stand of sycamore trees on Memorial Drive from possible destruction by crews of lumberjacks from the Metropolitan District Commission," the *New York Times* reported on November 15, 1964. "The patrol has instructions to blow a whistle beneath the window of a Harvard housemaster, whose wife has agreed to sound the alarm by telephone. Pickets thus summoned are to assemble at the scene and to place themselves in the path of commission trucks."[2]

The trucks never came, of course, the underpasses never went up, and the sycamores still stand. "To this day, when I drive on Memorial Drive, I often think of Eddie and say, 'Thank God he did something about this, or the trees would be gone,'" reminisced Otto Lerbinger, professor of public relations at Boston University.[3]

Eddie was back at it a few years later, helping to organize the Emergency Committee to Save Homes for Family Life in Cambridge. The committee's name was more of a mouthful this time, and its cause more parochial: blocking the Episcopal Theological School from building a complex of dormitories that the neighbors, including Eddie and Doris, felt would create unwanted congestion. The result, however, was the same: an architect's rendering was all anyone ever saw of the dormitories.

National causes were fair game, too, causes that most despaired of advancing, like improving America's schools. Applying techniques that had worked so well selling bacon, beer, and books, Eddie went to work in the mid-1970s on behalf of the National School Public Relations Association. He gave the group money for a PR library, spoke at its meetings, reviewed manuscripts, wrote introductions to books, and persuaded education agencies from Alaska to Georgia to design and display what he called Flags of Liberty and Learning. At the same time, he was doing all he could for those who were way beyond school age. He worked against age discrimination in Massachusetts and told a congressional committee that mandatory retirement laws constituted "cruel and unusual punishment to those over sixty-five."

Eddie also helped collect money for Armenian earthquake victims and raised the profile of the Massachusetts Society for the Prevention of Cruelty to Animals, Peace Network 2000, Women in Communications, and other nonprofit groups. And his Edward L. Bernays Foundation gave thousands of dollars to causes ranging from race relations to civil liberties, from the Home for Aged and Infirm Hebrews to the League of Women Voters.

There were occasional paying clients as well. The Brotherhood of Railroad Trainmen, for example, hired him to help defeat legislation that would have made them submit to compulsory arbitration in labor disputes. Pat Jackson, who writes a PR newsletter and runs a respected agency in New Hampshire, remembers working with Eddie on that campaign and watching him use his time-tested technique of applying sociology and psychology. Eddie got railroad workers to write people listed in *Who's Who* asking if they thought the legislation was fair, then urged the VIPs to write to Washington and the media. Jackson also remembers that, even though Eddie was only in his early seventies at that time, he "sat at home in Cambridge and would call us all over. . . . He'd just sit there presiding. And all the money was sent to Eddie; he parceled it out. About a year later I was summarily dismissed from all this because I'd asked Eddie, 'Is that the only option? How about this?' Of course you just didn't do that with Ed."[4]

Eddie had vowed to leave his New York lifestyle behind him. Yet his Cambridge world was quickly becoming almost as frenetic, in part because he simply didn't know how to slow down. Like many people who define themselves by their work, he kept working as long and as hard as he could—far longer than most.

But there was something else that spurred him on. In New York, he'd begun to sense that he was becoming passé professionally. Procter and Gamble had left him, along with other longtime clients like United Fruit and the tobacco companies. He was a solo operator in an era when big-name companies preferred big-name PR firms, an aging warrior too seldom summoned to battle. And his techniques often seemed outmoded, if not stale, as when he mobilized scores of "opinion leaders" to endorse whatever his client was selling, failing to see that the public no longer cared what so-called authority figures thought.

If there'd been no professional reason to stay in Manhattan, there also was no personal one. He didn't have many intimate friends, then or ever. He didn't play golf or cards or any of the other things men of his era did to bond, and his short fuse and high expectations made it tough for him to keep friends. He had hundreds of acquaintances, people he could invite to parties, but he had no friends he could confide in or who would confide in him. He couldn't admit any of this to his family, of course, or to himself. So he made his departure from New York seem like an escape from a life that was too busy rather than from one that was suddenly too quiet.

Coming to Cambridge was, in that sense, fighting to hang on. That's why he was so determined to fashion a full life, to let people know he still mattered. And that's why he told interviewers he still had lots of clients willing to fork over $1,000 an hour for his sage advice. Some of those clients recall working with him but only in an informal way and never for $1,000 an hour. The only one who remembered huge payments was Howard Chase, the retired director of public relations at General Mills who was former assistant secretary of commerce and a vaunted PR guru. "I brought Eddie in to a man several years ago who was interested in granting funds to a kind of One World foundation," Chase said in 1995. "Eddie arranged a little lunch of eight people at a club he belonged to, it lasted about one and a half hours. I had neglected to find out in advance what his fee would be, and he came in for $5,000. My wealthy friend was annoyed at me, as he should have been, and I was very much annoyed at Eddie. But of course my friend paid it."[5]

Chub Peabody was more than annoyed, he was screaming mad. He ran for governor not long after Eddie arrived in Cambridge, and he would set aside an hour every day at a downtown hotel to personally solicit funds from large donors. Eddie was invited in, and the two spent about forty-five minutes chatting before Peabody, who went on to win a two-year term, got around to asking for a contribution. Eddie, believing the advice he'd just dispensed was worth more than any cash he could offer, said, "You've just received it."

. . .

Finding the right home was as essential in Cambridge as it had been in Manhattan. For anyone else, it would have been a straightforward matter of consulting agents and perusing ads. But for Eddie it was a delicious challenge, a lot like locating the right city.

He and Doris began by renting on Berkeley Street. All the while Eddie was hiring taxi drivers to show him around Cambridge, cruising neighborhoods at five miles an hour, jumping out each time he saw a home he liked. The process was so frustrating that his regular cabdriver finally ordered him out. Eddie got the message and persuaded the driver to take him to a car dealer, where he bought a light blue Cadillac; he later hired a chauffeur. The taxi rides already had served their purpose, however, yielding a list of streets he liked, and a friend

Cambridge Years

followed up with letters to seven hundred homeowners, asking if they'd sell. Seventy replied but, as Eddie told a reporter afterward, none agreed to part with their dwelling.

"One of the letters, however, offered 'condolences' on my search," he recounted, "and pointed out that the only way houses came on the market in Cambridge was when the owner died. So I changed my method, and began going to as many cocktail and dinner parties in the Harvard Square area as I could. At the third dinner party, my hostess mentioned that a woman she knew had just died, and that she had owned a lovely house on Lowell Street. We're living in it now."[6]

The century-old white Victorian was an unlikely choice. It had ceilings that somehow seemed too high, too few bedrooms for a house that size, and dimensions so awkward that it was difficult to decide how to use the space. More important, Eddie and Doris simply didn't belong in a place that big. Doris adored the backyard, which she called her Central Park, but she needed a motorized chair to negotiate the long stairway. And neither she nor Eddie was prepared to care for such a rambling and rickety home. They'd seen something cozier not far away that Doris loved, but Eddie insisted on the place at 7 Lowell.

It was partly the setting that sold him. Sandwiched between historic Brattle Street and Mount Auburn Street, tree-lined Lowell offered convenience, quiet, and, best of all, one of the most fashionable addresses in Cambridge. The editor of the *New England Journal of Medicine* lived nearby, along with a famous heart surgeon from the Peter Bent Brigham Hospital and an esteemed psychiatrist. Other neighbors had long-standing connections to Brahmin Boston and haughty Harvard. All of which was just right for Eddie, whose home had always constituted an integral part of his persona.

He knew the house was bigger than he and Doris needed, but having plenty of space was very important to Eddie. He planned to do a lot of entertaining, and whenever he inspected a home he imagined it full of guests. Space also had a metaphorical meaning to Eddie: it gave him a feeling of being free and unfettered. That was why he always bought shoes a bit bigger than he needed and wore the crotch in his pants a bit lower than necessary. And it was why his homes, starting back in Washington Square Park, had been substantially larger than they had to be.

His grandchildren certainly didn't mind. They loved to explore the Lowell Street house, hiding in nooks and crannies and dormers; running around in the yard; and, the memory they cherish most, assembling in the dining room for Sunday brunch. "Here's how the ritual worked," recalls Lucas Held, the older son of daughter Doris. "The two families would come over sometime around noon, and a taxicab would be dispatched to Jack and Marion's deli in Brookline. Soon there would appear on their huge seventeenth-century oak table big platters of corned beef and rye bread, smoked salmon, coleslaw, and of course the mandatory strawberry cheesecake."[7]

After lunch Eddie would settle into his soft chair, with his six grandkids assembled around him, and resurrect the stories of Captain Merriwell for this latest generation. "They were wonderful stories with lots of adventures, like in India with a pith helmet," remembers Hester Kaplan, Anne's middle daughter. "He told us another installment every Sunday. He let us sit on his lap and pull his mustache. He was extremely generous, a storybook grandfather."[8] Sometimes he'd top that with a magic show. "He'd take a paper napkin and crumple it into a tight ball," says Lucas, "and he'd put his hand over his mouth and make a series of horrible grimaces. I remember watching with a sense of fascination and fear as he'd bring his hand to . . . his ear and, with more terrible contortions, pull the napkin out of his ear and display it to the assembled crowd of children."

Julie Held, Lucas's sister, was enchanted by those Sundays at her grandparents' house, remembering how, when she arrived, Eddie would "throw his arms open and give me a big bear hug. He'd say, 'Hello, my little friend.' I'd call my grandparents every day when I was between eight and twelve. He'd answer the phone and I'd say, 'Eddie?' He'd say, 'Yessie.'"[9] She also loved Eddie's cartoons, drawings so skillfully sketched and clever that his daughter Doris, who saved a stack of them, is sure he could have been a professional cartoonist.

There were Friday dinners at Joyce Chen's restaurant or the

Harvard Faculty Club, where Doris would pour a packet of Sanka powder over her vanilla ice cream to temper the sweetness. At home Eddie concocted strange meals for the kids and their friends—Coca-Cola warmed on a stove with raisins and other mysterious ingredients, which Julie dubbed a "hot toddy for underage kids," or a dinner consisting of sizzling steak, frozen vegetables, and a glass or two of Asti Spumante. And when they went to camp he sent care packages of pack after pack of spearmint gum, along with a salami. Or, in Hester's case, "Camembert in tins or macadamia nuts—exotic, fancy, odd things."

Sometimes Eddie's different way of doing things seemed charming, but at other times it was annoying. He couldn't recount an old PR campaign without insisting it was precedent-setting, and he couldn't eat a simple bowl of fish soup without pronouncing it "the best fish soup ever." His family knew that exaggeration was an element of his work that long ago had become an element of his personality. They also knew their grandfather really believed the soup was the best, which made it easier for them to accept his hyperbole.

His letters to the grandchildren left little doubt about the joy they gave him. He wrote to "Little Susanna" in 1961, when she was just three, to say that "Mother Goose will be arriving at Francis Avenue in a few days and will speak to you from your record player. Please let her know how you like her and her friends." And his grandchildren wrote back, with Hester, in an undated letter embellished with drawings of a tree, a dog, a house, and a little girl, telling "gampa and grama" that "we go to town evry day. I miss you very much. My cat is Having babies. I learned to swimg."[10]

The fairy tale began to fade as Eddie's grandchildren grew older, however, just as it had with their mothers. "The same characteristics that had made him so wonderful [when I was] a little kid made him difficult to be around later," says Hester. "The focus always was on him, he gave lots of advice, he'd tell you what to do or what you were doing wrong. There never for me was much sense [that] he knew who I was or was particularly interested. . . . When I was in college and won a writing award, he sent a telegram that said, 'Congratulations for carrying on the Bernays tradition.' I didn't know what that was. The gesture was there, but it wasn't quite person-specific."[11]

The old playfulness increasingly gave way to lectures on career choices, on doing the right research, and on considering all the options. He also added his grandchildren to the long list of those to whom he mailed copies of each article he wrote and every story written about him. That sort of preaching "was like something we had to get through. He had to just do it, and then we could get on to the more real stuff," says Julie.[12] But Susanna Kaplan Donahue, his oldest grandchild, says, "I don't think he was ever physically loving. There were no hugs or anything you read about grandfathers in the books."[13]

Eventually his grandchildren had children of their own. And to Hester's sons, Eddie seemed even more bewitching than he'd been to her. She explains that "he'd say they were very virile, very manly. I have no idea what he meant with a one-year-old. But he got great pleasure out of them, and they thought he was fascinating, the oldest man on the face of the earth, teeny and wrinkled with spots all over him. They wanted to be with him. It was cool for them."[14]

His relations with his daughters never warmed the way he imagined they would when he moved to Cambridge. Being nearby merely meant more opportunity for him to intervene in their lives in ways they resented. Tensions ran highest with Anne, the younger and more rebellious daughter. When she and her husband, Justin Kaplan, took off for Berkeley in the summer of 1961, for instance, Eddie wrote to the publisher of the *San Fernando Sun,* to columnist Herb Caen of the *San Francisco Chronicle,* and to the book editors of the *San Francisco Examiner, San Francisco News-Call Bulletin,* and *Berkeley Daily Gazette.* He just wanted to say they were coming and that Kaplan was writing a biography of Mark Twain while Anne had worked for "the avant-garde magazine *Discovery.*" He also mentioned that Anne was his and Doris's daughter and Sigmund Freud's grandniece. The next year, although Anne had made clear that she didn't want Eddie to promote her first book, *Short Pleasures,* he sent out press releases and dropped a line to Doubleday suggesting a full-fledged promotion campaign.

Anne knew he meant well, but she was tired of his interference and frustrated by how little he understood her world. "*Discovery* had been dead for six or seven years," she recalls, "and his promotions were horrible, just awful."[15] Justin says the letters to California journalists were typical: "When we went to Europe he wrote to a lot of old fart ambassadors we had no interest in seeing under any circumstances. . . . My bigger issue with him was reality versus appearance. He didn't understand what the point was of doing good work if you weren't recognized for it."[16]

Things with daughter Doris were better, but not by much. She liked the idea of having her father and mother nearby and of having her three children really get to know their grandparents. And her parents did stop by regularly to play with the kids, but they never baby-sat, and the children seldom visited them without their parents. That was partly because of the older Doris's back pain, which limited her mobility, and partly because, as young Doris recalls, Eddie "didn't want to be part of my life. He wanted to continue in his direction, and his direction and my direction were very different."[17]

· · ·

Eddie had considerably more time to spend with his wife during the Cambridge years. Doris no longer had a household staff to manage, and they no longer spent long hours at the office. That meant more time to stroll down Brattle Street, holding hands, or to sit and read in the backyard. "They did so well together," says Frank Genovese, who befriended them shortly after their move to Cambridge. "They were both so bright; they had ideas and encouraged each other. It was rather wonderful to watch them interact."[18]

Their partnership seemed most seamless during the garden parties they hosted on the lawn behind the house. The backyard was abuzz with artists exchanging gossip with writers, and politicians trading tales with diplomats from as far off as India. Sometimes there was an orchestra. Doris would take hold of Eddie's arm and expertly navigate him through the crowd, stopping to let him greet a friend or chime in with a story. Eddie needed to surround himself with people to feel alive. He relished those gatherings as he had his soirees decades before in New York. "He wanted to have the feeling of having lived in very deep ways and wanted to enjoy himself," says Camille Roman, a close friend from those years. "One time we were talking about poetry. I was asking him jokingly could he remember any, and Eddie took up the challenge with all he'd memorized from Longfellow and Kipling. Doris was astounded and said, 'I didn't know you knew any of that.' "[19]

Everette Dennis, a journalism educator, recalls getting to know the Bernayses in 1977, when he began a fellowship at Harvard. "I went to his house at eleven A.M., and there was this elfin man who answered the door. In his usual style he offered tea or coffee, then gave me the grand tour. I thought I'd be there an hour. Then Doris came in. She was magnificently attractive, with huge piercing eyes, hair pulled to the back of her head, a great presence, and she said, 'Oh, you're still talking. You should get a bite of lunch.' I wanted to excuse myself, but I did stay for lunch, and I remember them serving these ghastly German wines, and he liked to top it off with slivovitz. Then he said, 'Let's talk a while longer,' and I was there until four in the afternoon. . . . When my wife moved to Boston we had dinner almost weekly for about a year. We always went to their place; only once could we get them out anyplace. He said, 'I hate to do social bookkeeping. Come to our house and you don't need to do a quid pro quo.' "[20]

Tit-for-tat had its place, however, as in 1971, when an obituary of Mrs. Florence Sutro Anspacher mentioned "the Bernays Foundation, of which the late Edward L. Bernays, the public relations consultant, was president." Remembering how Mark Twain had rebutted the "greatly exaggerated" reports of his death, Eddie relished the prospect of calling the newspaper to point out the error. But he didn't want them to simply run a retraction; he'd learned years before that denying a rumor only made people believe it more, and he understood that the newspaper was embarrassed enough to do whatever he asked. So he asked for a story on a lecture series he was sponsoring at Boston University. The lectures weren't nearly significant enough to be reported in the paper under normal circumstances, but they were announced the next day in an article noting that the obituary had "inadvertently stated that Mr. Bernays was deceased."[21]

Three years later he and Doris rebounded again, this time from an armed robbery that would have set back a couple of any age and been disabling to most octogenarians. The burglar crawled in through a window in the pantry and, when Eddie came down to investigate the noise, the intruder confronted him with a gun. "The guy said, 'I'm here to rob you,'" Anne remembers, "and Eddie said, 'You don't need that gun. Just put it down and tell me what you want.' [The burglar] put the gun down and took a mink coat and a typewriter, maybe an electric shaver, but he never got upstairs."[22] Later, when the shock of what had happened sank in, Eddie and Doris temporarily moved to the Ritz-Carlton Hotel in Boston, then to the Copley Plaza, and they considered relocating to an apartment in the more sedate suburbs of Brookline or Newton. They ultimately stayed in Cambridge, but only after installing a fortresslike array of locks and bolts, along with impenetrable window screens, that kept them locked in as efficiently as it kept others out.

Those generally peaceful years together didn't last long enough, however. And like so much else in Eddie's life, things weren't as serene as they seemed. Doris wasn't taking to their new life the way Eddie was. She'd had intimate friends in New York and never got over leaving them behind. While Cambridge club society welcomed her, she found chatting with bright but unfulfilled matrons too boring for words.

Doris also finally had time to reflect on her career and her family, which proved unsettling. She was a talented writer who had always wanted to be a novelist but had failed to complete any of the several novels she began. She also had doubts about having spent so much time and energy on public relations, a field she'd been dragged into by Eddie. And it can't have been easy for her to watch her daughter Anne finish her novels and have them published, or to see Anne show her disdain for public relations by quickly spurning Eddie and Doris's offer to take over their PR business.

Then there was the way Eddie treated her. He'd always had

conflicting expectations—wanting her to be the twenty-four-hour-a-day partner he kept telling interviewers about, but not realizing how much backbreaking work that involved. He'd never been an equal partner at home, and he never was willing to give Doris the credit she deserved for her pioneering work in public relations. He'd never truly consulted her before deciding to move to Cambridge or before any of their many moves in New York. So while she relished spending more time with him in retirement, it was also a strain. She confessed to her son-in-law, Justin Kaplan, that she sometimes felt "like a prisoner. I think she meant imprisoned by Eddie. He wouldn't even let her sit out in the backyard by herself. He kept a short leash on her."[23]

Eddie insisted he was simply protecting her after their robbery and a mugging nearby, but really it had as much to do with his insecurities as wanting to protect her. He cherished her support and friendship, but wanted them all to himself. He was overprotective of her in overt ways but didn't protect her nearly enough from physical and emotional pain.

Her discomfort was apparent to all three of Anne and Justin's children, although they weren't sure where it came from or what it meant. Doris had "a slightly imperious air to her. Very imperious. Pretty cold, I thought," says Hester. "Eddie was the center of attention at that point. Grandmother would be watching, listening, and make a very regal appearance. She'd descend the staircase with a Queen Elizabeth–like pocketbook, triangular and stiff with a short handle."[24] And while Eddie relished the spontaneity of the children, Doris seemed preoccupied with how to put things back in order.

Julie Held has a less grim image of her grandmother, recalling how she "called us kids 'duckie dear'. . . . When *Playgirl* came out, . . . she wanted a copy. One of us got her *Playgirl*—it might have been my aunt and uncle—and she was very disappointed. 'Oh,' she said, 'it doesn't show the pecker.'"[25]

Doris did enjoy writing poetry, especially when Eddie helped get it published. But she sometimes seemed terribly sad, and the more depressed she got, the worse the pain in her back became. Finally, not long after the robbery, her older daughter gave her the name of a psychiatrist. She went and seemed to be improving, but Eddie wasn't happy about his wife needing therapy. First he insisted on attending one of her sessions; then he made her stop. "My father put his foot down and said, 'You can't see this person anymore.' It may be because he was threatened; he probably understood he was an issue," says Anne.[26] Justin recalls meeting Eddie and Doris for lunch in Boston one day when "she had just come back from her shrink. The conversation at the table was extremely unpleasant, with Eddie saying, 'I don't want you to see that person again.' The general argument was that it wasn't doing her any good and that this person was learning things that probably weren't any of her business. It was a very, very powerful confrontation on this issue of her seeing a shrink."[27]

Eddie seemed to have forgotten that he'd spent much of his life touting the merits of psychoanalysis as practiced by his uncle Sigmund. "He was an ambivalent keeper of the flame, to say the least," says his daughter Doris, herself a therapist. "He could see psychoanalytic theory or Freudian theory in its applicability to groups, its sociological applicability, and he was a very quick study in that sense. In a more personal sense, he didn't have a clue what it was all about. He never understood it."[28]

It also was becoming increasingly clear that Doris wasn't well. She'd always had a bad back, caused in part by a tumble she'd taken as a youth and aggravated by arthritis. She had developed cataracts in both eyes, and she used a big tortoiseshell hearing aid. Twenty years earlier cancer had forced her to have a breast removed. In addition, a doctor's report in January 1980 said she had blocked arteries throughout her body and a leaky heart valve. She'd had heart-related chest pains "for at least fifteen years" and, at some point, had suffered a heart attack, all of which likely resulted from her cigarette smoking.[29] Her illness might explain why, as her granddaughter Polly remembers, "she always ate antacids and had crusty stuff around her lips."[30]

Antacids weren't all she was eating. She took Lasix and Aldactone to remove bodily fluids and digoxin to strengthen her heartbeat. There were Darvocet and nitroglycerin pills for pain, Maalox for indigestion, Senokot for constipation, Dalmane to sleep, and Persantine to boost her circulation.[31]

Nothing she was taking helped her get back her appetite, but Eddie knew the trick. When it came to a physiological problem like that, he was at his most charming and creative. He would take breakfast to Doris's bedroom every morning, sometimes including treats like vanilla ice cream with her favorite topping, Sanka. He also served lunch, and when she insisted she wasn't hungry, he would talk about politics or poetry—anything to distract her long enough to take one bite, then another, until she had eaten just enough to sustain her.

She couldn't sustain herself for long, however. Six months after her 1980 medical examination Doris suffered a massive stroke that began as a clot and ultimately caused her brain to hemorrhage. She died ten days later.

. . .

His wife's death was the hardest adjustment Eddie ever had to make. As had happened with so many other things in his life, his reaction was brimming with contradictions.

First he fell into despair. Life seemed pretty pointless when you'd lost your companion of fifty-eight years and your best friend. He'd always been resilient, but Doris had always been around to help him bounce back. "We were at his home when Doris was in a coma. We spent six to eight hours with them," Camille Roman says. "My husband observed how Eddie came unglued when Doris died. He said, 'Eddie had Doris between him and the world. She was his grounding.'"[32]

Then there was denial. Eddie wasn't good at directly confronting any emotional issue, and death was especially tough for him. The same had been true when his mother died. It was why he couldn't talk about his own mortality. And it was especially apparent now. "After my grandmother died," Hester remembers, "he was all business. After reading Kübler-Ross's book [on adjusting to the death of loved ones] he stated he'd passed all of the stages, and this was within two days!"[33]

Finally there was the release that often comes along with denial. Without Doris as his "moral anchor," Eddie at first "acted like someone let out of jail," his daughter Anne says. "He partied, he stayed out till three in the morning, he went out everywhere. Anywhere anyone invited him he went. He started drinking a lot of wine."[34] Anne's husband, Justin, remembers that at first Eddie "appeared to be thoroughly traumatized. He was walking around in a daze for several weeks; he was really stricken. But then some amazing transformation occurred, and he took on another life altogether. He appeared to be younger and act younger. He went to all kinds of weird parties. He went to a gay bar and said, 'A man kissed me.' It was as if ten to fifteen years had dropped off his life suddenly. But he still kept the bedroom exactly the way it had been, including her little four-drawer jewelry case that was open with necklaces dripping out of it."[35]

Eddie's older daughter, Doris, once again saw those seeming contradictions as two sides of the same reaction to the trauma of losing his lifelong partner. He was so devastated, she says, that he described his deceased wife as "a part of himself, like an arm or a leg." But then he brought in "a string of young women to help him get back to life."[36]

Eddie hired the women to keep him company in return for room and board. Most were in their twenties or thirties, and all were bright and attractive. Most kept their regular jobs, spending time with him in the morning and evening, and all were astonished at the active life he maintained as he neared ninety. Up by 5:30 A.M., he'd start the day by reading the *Boston Globe*, the *Boston Herald*, the *New York Times*, the *Wall Street Journal*, and the *Washington Post*. "I'd leave for work about eight, but always spent about fifteen minutes with him in the morning to make arrangements for the day," recalls Cindy Strousse, a public relations woman who was about to turn thirty when she moved in with Eddie a couple years after Doris died.[37] "I'd go into his room, and he'd be sitting there dressed, at a chair and table. He'd tell me all the important things he'd read about."

During the day Eddie would have visitors, of whom some came for advice, others to chat. When new guests came, he often played the "chair game," inviting them to sit on Doris's electric stair climber.

Once they were strapped in, he'd run ahead, beat them to the top, and stand there grinning, eyes sparkling. He regaled his visitors with stories about his Easter Sunday Torches of Freedom parade, Light's Golden Jubilee, or some other classic campaign—stories that he could repeat word for word and that never failed to charm. Once his guests left, he would read his mail, which still came in stacks, pasting the best letters into notebooks, which he added to his Library of Congress collection. Twice a week he walked the ten blocks to Harvard Square to do his banking and other business, never taking out denominations bigger than five dollars.

He was still writing prolifically, mainly letters to the editor, like one in 1975 to *Harvard* magazine bemoaning the "startling omission" of public opinion and communications courses from the curriculum at the John F. Kennedy School of Government. There were book reviews, too, and twenty years of correspondence with people like *Grinnell Herald-Register* publisher Al Pinder in Iowa, whom he'd met by chance in the late sixties. Finally there were his handwritten "for your information and comment" notes to old friends and casual acquaintances, passing along articles of interest, most often about him.

Setting up routines and looking for ways to keep busy are part of the adjustment that all retirees make, and the task is always tougher when they lose a longtime spouse, as Eddie had. But staying in control was more important for him than for most. And being alone was more difficult. He didn't especially like reading books. He didn't like watching television. He'd always thrived on contact with people—talking on the telephone, getting together with friends, and inviting over a houseful of people to fill the empty space whenever he felt lonely.

Life in Cambridge was supposed to put him at the center of a crowd, but it wasn't working out that way. He desperately wanted to be accepted into the Harvard community, to be taken seriously as the author and creative thinker he saw himself as. But Harvard had never acknowledged journalism as a pursuit worthy of its attention, let alone the unsavory craft of public relations. The best Eddie could manage was to forge ties with less lofty schools like Boston University, Northeastern, and Emerson College. They had schools of journalism and courses in public relations, and were grateful for Eddie's expertise and for the largesse of the Bernays Foundation.

Winning acceptance by the wider Cambridge community wasn't much easier. The people of Cambridge weren't sure what to make of Eddie's light blue Cadillac or his heavy-handed tactics. And, like the literati of Harvard, they didn't know, or care to know, much about public relations. Eddie's wife had been adept at assimilating into the local culture and had been welcomed into Cambridge's inner sanctums. But Eddie, who was less intuitive and less flexible, was never really accepted.

Boston Brahmins were also wary of this Jewish PR man, wary enough that while the august Boston Symphony Orchestra gladly accepted his advice, it never invited him to become a board member. Decades earlier, and for similar reasons, Manhattan's Metropolitan Opera had denied him the private box he so desperately wanted. It wasn't that he especially liked opera, but a box at the Metropolitan was as clear a sign as there was of status in 1930s New York.

In his old age Eddie's family was a disappointment, too. His grandchildren were growing up and, with the exception of his grandson Andrew, moving away. It was late to suddenly forge a close relationship with Anne. And while he was in touch every day with his older daughter, Doris, they never really became close—in part, she thinks, because Eddie was afraid of depending too much on anyone.

Still, he had too much energy and was too resourceful to give up. And it wasn't like him to stew about lost opportunities, a trait his daughters think was a key to his longevity. He found the companionship he craved with his new young friends, like Cindy Strousse. By the time she got home in the evening, Eddie would have finished his reading and writing and cooked dinner, "usually chicken that his wife taught him how to cook," Strousse says. "He'd broil it on one side, and it'd always be burnt and dry. He'd throw vodka on it. And there'd be canned peas or canned asparagus. During the day he'd eat candy and stuff—M&M's and anything chocolate. He'd put it in his pocket and munch on it all day. . . . Every night he'd watch Dan Rather, his favorite news. The TV would be on really loud because he couldn't hear. I'd always turn it down a little bit, and he'd turn it up and always say he wasn't hard-of-hearing. Every night Dan Rather would say, 'Good night,' and Eddie would say, 'Good night, Dan.'

"He didn't want somebody like me there to take care of him," Strousse adds. "He just wanted to know that at the end of the day there'd be somebody there to talk to. The relationship he and I had was one where sometimes he was the grandfather and I was the grand-daughter, sometimes I was the mother and he was the son. One time, when he hurt his back, I looked down and he'd forgotten to put his socks on. Sometimes when he was home with me he'd take his den-tures out. Someone would knock on the door, and the dentures would be in his pocket. I'd pat my teeth, and he'd put one hand into his pocket and casually put his teeth in his mouth.

"Sometimes we were like sister and brother. We'd fight about actual things and have to get out a book and prove who was right and who was wrong. We knew each other that well and knew which buttons to press. . . . He was very generous, but he was not generous in terms of money, not at all. He was generous in terms of giving of himself. There were some lines he and I never crossed, and money was absolutely one of them."[38]

Eddie also reached out to several Cambridge neighbors, especially Sherry Houghton. "He was very chivalrous with me. He perceived me as a lady of quality and treated me as such," she recalls. "The name Houghton didn't hurt; my former husband's brother gave Houghton Library to Harvard. A group of us would be sitting around and he'd ask 'Mrs. Houghton' what she would do under the circumstances. It wasn't 'Sherry,' which is what he always would call me. With others around it was 'Mrs. Houghton.' I don't think he had enough important people around him anymore, so he liked making me more important than I was."

Still, Eddie was good enough company that Houghton invited him to her son's graduation from Saint Mark's prep school. "He was pleased to go out and sit at this little boarding school in the terrible heat and be an observer, be a member of the family. If you didn't have any idea who this guy was you'd have said, 'There's somebody's great-great-grandfather who thoughtfully came to his graduation.' Not in the slightest, Eddie could have been taking notes for a book. He was constantly observing, and commented afterward on the trend in subject matter for valedictory speeches and asked, 'Did you notice how informally many parents were dressed?' This inquiring mind is what kept him alive."[39]

Entertaining helped, too, and he maintained his tradition of hosting garden parties and ad hoc dinner gatherings. The former were less elegant than they had once been, with wine now served in paper cups. And the dinners featured what guests called Chicken Bernays, which meant raw in the middle. Sherry and cheese were the standard hors d'oeuvres, while the main meal was accompanied by overcooked vegetables, inexpensive German wine, and, for dessert, ice cream or Oreo cookies.

But just when people thought they knew what to expect, Eddie would surprise them, as he'd always done. "I brought Claude Bertrand, a French press critic and fetishist about food, there once and said, 'You've got to remember this is an old man and you're about to have a terrible meal,'" says Everette Dennis. "We arrived and Eddie was dressed up, for a change; he had on a black suit and looked very nice. He bowed at the door and spoke fluent French. We had a very fine wine before dinner, and when we walked in to the dining room there was an entire big salmon, three to four feet long, poached salmon, with exquisite food. He figured a Frenchman was coming to dinner. He wasn't just dealing with some guy like me from Minnesota. That said a lot about him in many ways, and it was the only edible meal I ever had with him."[40]

After Doris died, his closest friend was Herbert Patchell, a Renaissance man who'd taught at the Cambridge Center for Adult Education and Northeastern and who was perpetually troubled by allergies and migraines. Hired by Eddie to do yard work and other odd jobs, which helped him pay his bills, Patchell always ended up sticking around to eat, talk, and enjoy Eddie's company, much as Eddie did his.

Patchell distinctly remembers about Eddie's special voices, like the one he used with his daughters. "I knew about some strains in the family, and he was genuinely concerned, preoccupied. His voice with them was really a loving voice. I wish my parents had used a voice like that." And there was the "pathetic ninety-eight-year-old voice" Eddie would use when he answered the phone. "If it was a client he'd say, 'Just a minute,' and hold the phone against his body for ten to fifteen seconds, then answer as himself in a deeper voice that was much more vigorous, with all his vim poured into it."

Eddie came alive each year as the New England winter finally faded. "We'd go to Mahoney's Garden Center in Winchester," Patchell says. "I'd get terrible spring fever, and here's this fellow twice my age, and he'd get exactly the same response every year. It reinvigorated him. Coming back from Mahoney's he'd never miss an opportunity to look over a good-looking woman. One day we both commented on a woman with a great figure who turned out to be a guy in drag. He said, 'Imagine, someone at my age making a mistake like that.'"[41]

His age hadn't done anything to lessen his libido, and Doris's death gave it even freer rein. "On one of my visits to his house, I think it was for his ninetieth birthday when there was a big party going on downstairs, I said to him, 'To what do you attribute your longevity?'" recalls Mary Ann Pires, one of many young PR women who tell similar stories. "He stooped toward me, looked me right in the eyes, and said, 'I always kissed the girls on the lips.' There was a sign right over his bed saying, 'Be sure and kiss Eddie good night.'"[42] Sherry Jahoda had a similar experience: "He was always interested in women. As I was walking out of the music room to the porch, he gave me a big kiss on my mouth, which was very unexpected. That was after his one hundredth birthday."[43]

He'd always had a magnetic appeal to girls. "He'd go into any room, and before you knew it all the women were around him, absolutely adoring him," says his son-in-law Justin.[44] The older he got, the more the young girls indulged him by letting him kiss them or hold their hands, sure that this ninety-year-old elflike legend had to be harmless.

· · ·

Something else happened as Eddie got older: people flocked to him, especially people from the PR world who saw him as an icon and mentor.

He'd invite to his home students from Boston University, Emerson College, and other area schools, then dispatch them to the store for cheese, cold cuts, and beer, and let them stay late into the evening as he told story after story. "With the guys he'd sit around drinking and apparently would drink them under the table," remembers Cathryn Kaner, who at the time was getting her master's in public relations at Boston University. "He liked the young women and was very eager to show he was still a vital, sharp, energetic human being."[45] They didn't seem to mind that they'd often have to repeat things, loudly, so he could hear. Or that he'd tell the same story he'd told the last time they were there. After all, he was a legend, the man they'd read about in their textbooks.

When she turned twenty-five, Kaner adds, she invited him to her birthday party "in a cramped, roach-infested apartment in Allston. Not only did he attend (and was one of the last guests to leave), but a few days later I received a letter in the mail from him saying what a good time he had and requesting that I come with nine of my friends to his place for supper so that we could continue the festivities."

It wasn't just students who were captivated. Longtime practitioners stopped in, too, to see this man who'd been there at the beginning. "I went one time to his house in Cambridge in 1990," recalls Joe Trahan, who teaches PR at the University of Tennessee. "He'd just had eye surgery, and the woman taking care of him said, 'He can't see you.' He heard, and he said, 'Tell him to come on up.' He showed me his library and the photos on the wall of people he'd been a counselor for. It was like a who's who in history from the 1900s to today. We spent five hours together walking and talking."[46] Pires was taken on a similar tour, where "Eddie said, 'There I am with Tom.' The Tom turned out to be Edison. And 'Henry and I were together for a meeting,' where the Henry was Ford. The original Ford."

Shelley and Barry Spector took an even longer walk through history, visiting Eddie in Cambridge on twenty different occasions and capturing on videotape eighty hours of conversation that amounts to a greatest-hits record of his long career. "He was my hero, meeting the guy who founded the very industry you're in and seeing him suddenly come to life. He was ninety-three when I met him. To most people that's very old, but he seemed at the time more like seventy-three," says Shelley, who with her husband runs a PR firm with offices in New York and New Jersey. The Spectors were so impressed with Eddie and his stories that they've transformed their New Jersey office into a Bernays museum, complete with his desk, copies of pictures that lined his Cambridge office, and other memorabilia.[47]

The Spectors weren't the only PR people who were interested in what Eddie had to say. He was one of the hottest properties on the national public relations speaking circuit in the 1980s and early 1990s. He had overcome his fear of flying and appeared at conferences and conventions from Boston to Puerto Rico and from Florida to Washington. Peter Hollister served as host when Eddie, who was 100 years old then, appeared before a PR group in Cincinnati. "I think it was the last major trip he made," Hollister said. "His short-term memory was not particularly strong, but his long-term memory was absolutely wonderful. At one point he was talking about his work with President Woodrow Wilson, and he went down the list of his Fourteen Points as if he had designed them the day before."[48]

Hester, his granddaughter, recalls a colleague asking her to arrange a meeting with Eddie: "She went over and saw him and said it was the most important hour she'd ever spent with anybody. . . . That was probably his greatest gift."[49]

Europeans also wanted to hear what this stooped little man with white hair had to say. Eddie toured Barcelona in 1990, meeting the chief of the Catalonian parliament, the mayor of Barcelona, and scores of PR professionals. "All over the city we put banners with his photograph, saying, 'Welcome, Edward.' We made some parties here and in other cities and a gala dinner at the palace," says Elvira Vazquez, the Barcelona businesswoman who arranged the trip.[50]

Not everyone was enamored with Eddie, however. Barbara Hunter, who was president of the Public Relations Society of America in 1984, recalls that she "shared several platforms with him. At that point, he used a lengthy prepared speech (somewhat dog-eared), and delivered it all, whether or not it fitted into the time he was allocated. I remember being left with fifteen minutes to sum up an entire two-day conference because it was virtually impossible to dissuade him from finishing his entire address, which took well over an hour."[51]

And not everyone found his advice prescient. Joseph T. Nolan approached Eddie in 1954, when Nolan was an editor at the *New York Times.* At that time the newspaper unions were threatening to strike, and he was considering quitting the paper for a job in public relations. "'Tell me, young man,'" Nolan remembers Eddie saying, "'how much money would you expect to make in public relations?' At the time, my dad was earning about $25,000 as an Assistant School Superintendent in Connecticut, so I replied: 'I think $25,000 would be a good round number to aim at.' Bernays was aghast. 'Young man,' he said, 'here in New York the garbagemen make more than that. Good day, sir!' Some thirty years later, I reminded him of the incident when we were on the same speaking program at the University of Florida, he representing PR counseling agencies and I corporate public relations (Chase Manhattan and later Monsanto Chemical). He graciously acknowledged he had made a 'mistake or two,' over the years, in picking his associates, and perhaps this was one of them. The concession emboldened me to ask: 'Ed, why do you punish yourself—at your age and with your money and prestige—running all over the country making speeches?'

"Without a moment's hesitation, he replied, 'Sheer ego, my boy, sheer ego!'"[52]

That response was more insightful than normal for Eddie, and more candid. He was used to getting recognition for his achievements and loved it. Over the years he received hundreds of keys to cities and citations, many so obscure they ended up in cardboard boxes in the back of his basement. But he was also awarded France's prestigious Officer of Public Instruction (1926), Denmark's King Christian X Medal

(1946), the Veterans of Foreign Wars' Award of Appreciation (1955), and the City of New York's Bronze Medallion of Honor (1961).

The older he got, the more people felt he was worthy of recognition. After he moved to Cambridge he was honored by Ohio University, Suffolk University, Babson College, the Royal Society of Arts, the Art Institute of Boston, Emerson College, and Boston University. The Public Relations Society of America gave him its 1976 Golden Anvil Award, its highest honor for individuals. Massachusetts governor Edward King presented him with a proclamation in 1982, and in 1991 Boston mayor Raymond Flynn proclaimed an "Edward Bernays Centennial Jubilee Day." In 1984 artist Patricia Marshall Tate completed a portrait of him—in familiar pink shirt, burgundy tie, light blue vest, and darker blue jacket, with a wall of books in the background—commissioned by the National Portrait Gallery. While working with Eddie had been "delightful," Tate wrote a friend, it was "rather like trying to paint a grasshopper—with his dashes to answer the doorbell, the telephone, at a loss for anything else, a dash to the kitchen to bring me a glass of sherry. . . . From the way he flies around all over the country, and all by himself, he scarcely appears frail! A human marvel."[53]

His birthday also became a bigger deal over time, to the point where, when he turned ninety-five, the party was held in the ballroom at the Cambridge Marriott Hotel to accommodate the five hundred celebrants. For each celebration there was a special planning committee, like the Committee of Ninety for his ninetieth birthday, which included U.S. Senator Jacob Javits of New York, Massachusetts governor King, and *Meet the Press* moderator Lawrence E. Spivak. Eddie's one-hundredth-birthday party featured a video called *100 Years in the Life of Edward L. Bernays.*

Sometimes there were several parties for the same birthday, as in 1981 when several hundred turned out in Chicago for his ninetieth as an encore to the Boston bash. "I arranged the ninetieth birthday Public Relations Society of America celebration in Chicago," recalls veteran PR man Frank LeBart, who was also vice chairman of the Boston Committee of Ninety. "That was one of his finest hours, with a couple

Cambridge Years

thousand people in a huge ballroom and representatives of PRSA and other PR associations. Everyone lighted a candle in a semidarkened ballroom. It was a very exciting moment, and he loved that. 'Ego-titillating' is a phrase he always used."[54]

His one hundredth, at the fashionable Charles Hotel in Cambridge, was equally festive, and he had an equally good time. "Somebody decided it was necessary to give one of those stupid silver bowls com-memorating the occasion with his name and the date, so he said some-thing nice," remembers Cathryn Kaner. "As he was leaving the stage he put the bowl on his head. He loved the attention." Joan Schneider, who runs her own PR agency in Boston, chaired the one hundredth party and said she was impressed "when I asked Edward if he wanted to make a speech and he said, 'Of course I'll make a speech. I've been alive one hundred years, and I have a lot to say.' I was so nervous about speaking for two minutes to introduce him, and he got up at age one hundred and spoke for twelve minutes with no notes. It was totally cohesive. . . . He got a standing ovation."[55]

Another common element in the parties was the role Eddie played in planning them. "I was on the Committee of Ninety, supposedly organized by someone else on his ninetieth birthday," recalls Everette Dennis, "but all of us knew we'd been picked by Eddie. He acted sur-prised, 'Oh, me?' when in fact he organized and manipulated every bit of it."[56]

One Last RIDE

11

IT STARTED THAT STEAMY DAY IN JUNE 1988 WHEN JOAN VONDRA swept into Eddie's life. She brought with her not only delicious parties and a final go-around at sex but also an alleged abduction and accusations of elder abuse and thievery. All of which was electrifying for someone with Eddie's sense of adventure—like a last ride on a roller coaster. It also was a bit unnerving for someone ninety-six years old.

Joan, who was half Eddie's age and half a foot taller, was hired to keep him company at dinner and sleep there overnight. But her role kept evolving, from nurse to social secretary, from hostess to friend. In the end—as she told anyone who asked—she was Eddie's lover. Her financial arrangement also evolved, from room, board, and medical expenses, when all she did was spend the night, to that plus a $32,500 salary and money for a car and clothing when she became a full-time employee. "It was difficult to get to know him at the beginning," she recalls, "because he lived such a busy life. . . . He wasn't coming back until I already was in bed."[1]

Before long, however, Eddie and Joan were inseparable. She arranged his garden parties and dinner parties. She helped set up interviews with the British Broadcasting Company, National Public Radio, and an assortment of newspapers. She traveled with Eddie across America and to Spain, and she managed the household staff. She also saw him through a series of health problems. Not long after she moved in, Eddie came down with a severe flu. "It became a crisis," Joan says. "It happened in one weekend, and he went down from 143 to 117 pounds. His daughter Doris and I were taking care of him. I didn't think the doctor held too much hope he'd be alive."

Another time she came home and found that Eddie looked "strange" and couldn't talk. "I immediately called the doctor and said, 'Edward is not talking,'" she remembers. "The doctor said he'd had a minor stroke. I called friends, but by this point Edward had his coat on and was walking down the street, swinging his arms side to side to inflate his lungs and get more oxygen to his brain. He'd already walked halfway to the hospital by the time I got through calling everybody. His speech came back in the emergency room, and he became a little ornery. He didn't want to wait for the doctors and for all the tests to come back. He wanted to go home."[2]

Joan was a strong, sturdy woman, but she says running around after Eddie exhausted her, twice sending her to the hospital. Still, the good times far outnumbered the bad, and even at its worst, life with Eddie seemed preferable to her earlier life. Joan had married at twenty-one, had two sons, and helped put her husband through school before they divorced. She married again and was divorced almost immediately when it became clear it wouldn't work. She changed jobs frequently, starting as a secretary and ending as a buyer for high-tech firms, and she helped care for a handicapped brother. Before moving in with Eddie she had shared a two-bedroom apartment with her brother and mother, who she says rifled through her personal things. "I wasn't really happy to be back living with my mother and brother in Somerville, having been out of the house so many years. My old friend Rosian Zerner knew I was anxious to make a change and told me about this man in Cambridge."[3]

Life with "this man" Eddie opened a whole new world for Joan Vondra. She was wined and dined in Cambridge, Washington, Barcelona, and everywhere else they went together. She met people she'd only seen on television like former *Meet the Press* moderator Lawrence Spivak, ex–network newsman Marvin Kalb, and Librarian of Congress Emeritus Daniel Boorstin. She shared in the spotlight that never seemed to leave Eddie his last years, and she was delighted when he hung a picture of the two of them in his office alongside photographs of him with Henry Ford and Thomas Edison. And she helped host parties the likes of which she'd never even attended. There were bashes each spring around Harvard commencement and parties for her birthday in July. Sometimes a classical pianist lent a quiet touch; other times she and Eddie rolled up the rugs so guests could dance to a seven-piece band. Once they brought in 125 jazz and ragtime musicians to entertain 200 friends. There was a party even when Eddie was deathly ill with what looked like the flu. "Everybody and his uncle came, and he just rallied," Joan says. "We set up a coffee table in the bedroom with sherry. Edward always loved a party."[4]

"There always were those kinds of people coming and going," Joan recalled eight years afterward, her voice lifting as she conjured up old thrills and then softening as she realized they were unlikely to be repeated. "I remember in the early years something social was going on this week and each succeeding week. Edward would love to see to all the details, to stay on top of things. He really taught me how to put those things together, how to have interesting mixtures of people and be very eclectic. After he had schooled me I would carry on on my own."[5]

· · ·

Joan became so comfortable at carrying on that at some point her role began to blur. She began acting more like the mistress of the house than hired help. Her relationship with Eddie befuddled their hosts when they traveled together on Eddie's speaking tours. Was she his secretary or his colleague? His nurse or his girlfriend? Pictures from their trip to Spain show Eddie with wispy white hair and sagging skin standing next to Joan, who, with wavy blond hair, black dress, and fur coat, looked like his daughter. The caption refers to him as "Mr. Bernays" and to her as "his companion." Eddie and Joan understood the consternation they were creating, and they loved it. He'd always enjoyed raising eyebrows. She relished the attention, and the way people suddenly treated her with deference.

The issue of sex was even more confusing. Joan openly discusses their intimacy, saying that when he was in his late nineties they had sex "every day—oh, yeah. Edward was very, very capable, let me tell you, very capable. Edward was not a man very easily sated." Even while he was involved with her, he'd chase friends she'd invited over and young students who came to interview him, kissing and trying to fondle them. "Edward must have been something in his youth, I tell you," Joan says. "I had great difficulty with this in the beginning, great difficulty dealing with it and learning to overlook it."[6]

Their relationship was also ripe with romance, or so she says. Like the time they were in Dearborn, Michigan, for an anniversary of Light's Golden Jubilee, and they stayed in a honeymoon cottage. "He really pretended to be the new husband," she recalls. The last time they were intimate, she adds, was when he was 101. "It wasn't every day. . . . I wasn't living there then. I was visiting him at that point."[7]

Eddie also hinted to friends and relatives that he had a sexual relationship with Joan, and to some he bragged about it. But when questioned during the later legal proceedings, he denied they'd been intimate. Maybe they weren't, or maybe he couldn't remember. More likely, acknowledging having sex with a paid companion would have violated his deep-seated class consciousness. Joan, he insisted, "had her own room and bath" and he never knew her in the "biblical sense."[8]

Many of Eddie's friends thought that Joan was just what he needed to keep tuned in and toned up. Her energy was high and her spirit youthful. She loved his stories and attended to his needs. She was willing to let him remake her the way he'd reshaped so much of his world. "Edward and Joan had a really good thing going. He was happy," says Joan Schneider, a Boston PR executive who chaired Eddie's one-hundredth-birthday bash. "She really loved him, she was really there for him, she took care of him."[9]

But others saw the relationship as increasingly skewed. Joan, after all, was young enough to be Eddie's granddaughter. He was in his late nineties, an age at which a man can easily be taken advantage of. And she'd gradually taken it upon herself to decide when he should be available to family and old friends. That was when they started wondering what was going on.

Herbert Patchell, Eddie's gardener, companion, and close friend, went from a fan to a foe as he saw Joan's influence grow and Eddie's autonomy wane. "I watched her evolve from housekeeper to lady of the house, completely self-anointed," Patchell says. "Edward was playing a game he always played with people, particularly women, and Joan had been thrown into a world she didn't believe existed. I was fully in support of her, 100 percent, the first three years. I knew things were going on, with her seeing other men and abusing the privilege of the house, but she made Edward as happy as any time I knew him. The last three years were the nightmare years."[10]

Eddie's daughter Doris also liked Joan at first and liked the attention she was paying to her father. His daughter Anne found her at least tolerable. By the summer of 1993, however, both were nearly as alarmed as Patchell.

It was their fear of financial finagling that first got Eddie's daughters worried. Anne received a call from a vice president at Sotheby's auction house saying that Joan wanted to sell all of Eddie's artwork, his furniture, and even his house. Doris worried that her father was bouncing checks from the Edward L. Bernays Foundation, and his bank statements were no longer being forwarded to his longtime accountant. Joan, who had tripped on a doormat in his house, was suing him, although she subsequently withdrew the complaint and filed for workers' compensation.[11]

Anne and Doris feared that their father was losing his short-term memory and that Joan was exploiting his vulnerability, so they asked a court to award them control over his finances. The judge was sufficiently confused by the claims and counterclaims that in September 1993 he appointed a lawyer as guardian *ad litem* and asked her to talk to all of the parties and sort out their stories.

· · ·

Events on the ground were outpacing those in the courtroom. The day after the daughters went to court, Joan went to the bank with Eddie and withdrew $27,000. Then the two of them obtained a domestic partnership agreement from the city of Cambridge. Doris testified later that $50,000 of her father's assets was unaccounted for dating back to 1992, and thousands more in Joan's credit charges continued to accumulate through the fall of 1993. The family also couldn't determine what had happened to Eddie's Social Security checks.[12]

Joan said the cash from the bank was used to hire an attorney to allow Eddie to retain control over his finances and that Eddie hid the money as soon as they got home. She denied taking any money, although she acknowledged letting Eddie buy her clothes and gifts. As for her call to Sotheby's, she said Eddie himself called first, having two conversations about auctioning off two paintings and a sculpture. The problem was that there simply wasn't enough money to maintain a house that big, and the parties he loved were expensive. Sometimes, she added, she used her own money to pay for things and was never reimbursed.[13]

To Joan, it was shaping up as a battle between the money-hungry daughters on the one hand and her and Eddie on the other. An experienced street fighter like Joan Vondra wasn't about to roll over and surrender.

The stakes were also rising for Anne and Doris. They were sure Joan was behind Eddie's dismissal of his longtime doctor and lawyer. And they were frightened by other things they'd seen themselves and heard from Patchell and from Kelai Li, a music student who was Eddie's live-in cook and later his caretaker. There were stories of Joan having parties at the Lowell Street house with her friends, of masseurs visiting regularly, of Joan not keeping fresh food in the house, and of her yelling at Eddie when he accidentally set off the house alarm. "Men came to the house, and she had many boyfriends—Peter, Victor, Alex, and Bill," Li told the court-appointed lawyer. "Peter lived with her here in the house and came at night and left in the morning. Joan said, 'Sex with Peter was very good.' Dr. Bernays would not like another person to stay here but Dr. Bernays didn't know."[14]

The daughters finally decided they'd heard enough, and in August 1993 Doris fired Joan. Two days later Joan and Eddie drove off without telling anyone. Doris told the police she was afraid Eddie had been abducted, since Joan had filled two cars with his medications, papers, and "a substantial amount" of his clothing. Then a lawyer friend of Joan's called to say someone would be by to pick up Eddie's passport. The FBI was called in to work with the Cambridge police. A private investigator searched Joan's room and, according to Doris, found "a dildo, marijuana pipe, empty wine bottles, and vague pornography." The room was disturbingly disorganized, she added, "with papers strewn everywhere, clothes not sorted but just stuffed in things, drawers pulled open. There were old wrappers and newspapers. It was really appalling, and in all the closets and under the bed were boxes, many of them unopened, that she got from mail order or television. Dozens and dozens of boxes."[15]

Eddie and Joan were found two days later at a Day's Inn in Woburn, about twenty minutes from Cambridge, where she'd signed in as "Linda Parks." Eddie, Doris reported later, was "alert, lively, unaware of where he was and did not know that he had been gone for more than a night. He was pleased with the attention and had no idea of the passport or boxes of clothing."[16] That same day a judge issued a restraining order preventing Joan from seeing Eddie.

Joan's version of what happened was markedly different. She told the guardian *ad litem* that shortly before the alleged abduction Eddie had an angry exchange with Doris in which he said, "I'm the parent and you're the child. Remember that." Joan also said that going away was Eddie's idea, as was getting his passport. They first headed for Cape Cod, then changed direction and headed north to Maine, making it as far as a hotel in Amesbury, Massachusetts. They spent the next night in Woburn. Joan was trying to say good-bye even as Eddie was insisting she couldn't be forced to go. He also told her he didn't have much longer to live and his children would soon inherit everything. He kept repeating that he "couldn't understand why the children couldn't wait."[17] Looking back years later, Joan, who hopes to write a book about her time with Eddie, called the whole incident a "big fiasco. They [Anne and Doris] saw their chance to get rid of me, and they pounced on it, with help from Kelai and Herbert Patchell. The last chapter hasn't been written on that yet," she added, apparently referring to a defamation lawsuit she filed in 1997 against Patchell and the newspaper that published a column by him accusing her of elder abuse.[18]

She denied abusing Eddie in any way. As for being involved with other men, she acknowledged that she "dated during the relationship, and Ed was initially very jealous, and then Doris spoke to him about my private time being my private time." While she lived with Eddie, she had relationships with two other men, Joan said, but Eddie knew about and approved of both attachments. "Emotionally it was difficult to give my heart to anyone else until it [her romance with Eddie] was really over," she added. "I loved Edward. I also used men in defense because Edward was also physically demonstrative with others. . . . Although at the time he was a man of ninety-seven, he behaved like a sixty-five-year-old and had that kind of mentality and could perform like a younger man daily. He used two muscles—his cerebral and his penile."[19]

Joan saw herself as a victim caught in the cross fire between Eddie and his daughters. "The daughters," she told the court lawyer, "are trying to portray me as a villain." Eddie's relationship with Anne and Doris, Joan added, was "not physically demonstrative. It was more remote. I don't think he was father of the year. His daughters saw him about five times a year. . . . [Eddie] would not openly be affectionate or demonstrative to them. Instead of saying 'Thank you,' Ed would pat Doris' elbow."[20]

That analysis is surprisingly similar to one that Eddie's granddaughter Hester, who was no fan of Joan's, gave the court guardian. "My grandfather's relationship with his daughters was one that was controlling, judgmental, opinionated, and he had a disdain for people who were not as smart as he," Hester said. "He is scary because he is opinionated and forceful, and the daughters were coward [*sic*] by him. They didn't step in until it was late because they knew they couldn't control him."[21]

· · ·

Sifting through all of the conflicting accounts wasn't easy for Linda Kaloustian, the lawyer from Andover, Massachusetts, who served as guardian *ad litem*. She interviewed or received material from three dozen people, including Joan, Doris, and Anne. And she got thirty-five or so letters from people who supported Joan, many of whom wrote in response to a campaign organized by a friend of Joan's.

One of Kaloustian's most valuable sources turned out to be Eddie himself. He was almost 102 and had lost much of his short-term memory, but he still had sufficient sense and savvy to make a compelling case and give a distinct shape to the events swirling around him. As always, he took charge from the start, switching roles at one point to interrogate Kaloustian about her background and the purpose of her work for the court and later quizzing her about her marital status, her husband's occupation, and the backgrounds of her children. "Dr. Bernays informed the GAL [guardian *ad litem*], 'I am 102 years old. Mental and physical capacity has no relation to age,'" Kaloustian wrote. "'As far as my work and mental capacity, it's no different than when I was 57½ years old. Physicians will validate that my mental and physical age is like 59 years old.'"[22]

Eddie proceeded to answer a series of questions aimed at helping Kaloustian decide what to recommend regarding his daughters' bid to take charge of his finances. He said Joan had "worked here for five years, twenty-four hours a day, and was like a member of the family living in the home. . . . I signed a power of attorney to Joan to go shopping to the grocery store, and she used my signature for groceries. That was the only purpose. . . . I trusted Joan. I know her mother, brother, and sister and they are all respected and respectable people."[23]

He also was diplomatic about his daughters, saying, "I have a pleasant relationship and they are mature, but not so young women. If there were difficulties, they would help me. My daughters are highly intelligent." As for their relationship to Joan, Eddie said, "My daughters and Joan saw each other seldom. They have quite a social life and I don't imagine that they were wild about each other. Some relative may feel what right does an outsider have to be so close. I don't know if this applies. Maybe my daughters liked her; maybe they liked her a little."[24]

He was most adamant about the alleged abduction: "You mean the kidnapping? Couldn't do it. Cockeyed idea that I was kidnapped and then it was [made] public by the newspapers. . . . I was never kidnapped. This was an accusation. We just drove around. We often did this. We went to Gloucester, so going off was no great novelty. There is nothing to this story. Why is there such great interest in this? I can't see the drama. The article in the newspaper is a good news story about a fifty-year-old who abducts a one-hundred-year-old."[25]

Although he may have liked Joan, he insisted he never considered marrying her. "She's half my age! Whose idea was this? She was a good worker and ran the house and the employees." He was equally resistant to turning over his finances to his daughters: "Independence is an important aspect of life. I don't want to be in a position where I say, 'Mommy, can I buy an ice cream? I haven't a dime.' People shouldn't confound age with stupidity. I still earned fees until ninety-five."[26]

At the end of his last talk with the court-appointed lawyer Eddie said, "As an attorney, the more you charge, the more you'll be respected." Kaloustian thanked him for the advice.[27]

Kaloustian's 103-page report, dated December 1, 1993, was never made public. She ended it by outlining her version of what happened during the soap opera–like years near the end of Eddie's life. There may have been dependency and manipulation in Eddie and Joan's relationship, she suggested, but it went both ways: "He enjoyed being with articulate and intelligent people, and Joan maintained a speech, interview, and travel schedule while insuring that his health was not jeopardized by this lifestyle. She wanted to preserve the image of the man who made such an important contribution to our society." In return, Joan was "introduced to a highly sophisticated group of people and a lifestyle that she probably never would have encountered were it not for Ed Bernays. He was her teacher, and she learned quickly. . . . Joan Vondra also positioned herself for a future in the public relations field."[28]

Despite Eddie's denial, Kaloustian concluded that "an intimate relationship developed." Yet she goes on to say that "Joan Vondra thought she was more like a wife, and Ed Bernays thought of her as a very important member of the household, like a family member, but still an employee."[29]

On other crucial issues the guardian *ad litem* sided with Eddie's daughters. She said that Joan "made statements to Ed Bernays and others in an attempt to create a mistrust of his daughters and cause a divided front of 'us against them.'. . . There is no 'Daddy Dearest' book to the best of the GAL's knowledge." And she recommended that Joan be made to "provide a complete accounting of expenditures and reasons therefore in order to address the issue of whether financial impropriety or exploitation did or did not exist." When Eddie's memory troubles are factored in, Kaloustian concluded, "Dr. Bernays does not have the present ability to care for his property. . . . Dr. Bernays does not have the present insight to understand the legal proceedings, and his ability to engage counsel is questionable because he does not remember doing so." Kaloustian said Eddie's daughters were the "appropriate" people to manage his money, a choice that was later affirmed by the judge.[30]

· · ·

By the time that decision was made, however, Eddie had already spent most of his money.

As far back as 1931 he had been netting more than $60,000 a year, which would be more than $700,000 in current terms. But while he was earning a fortune, he was also spending a fortune—renting a full floor of the Sherry Netherland Hotel for his family, for example, and before that the Washington Square house and all the summer homes and expensive furnishings, not to mention the limousines, chauffeurs, and servants. And he gave away a lot through his foundation, which still has more than $450,000 in assets. If he'd bought rather than rented in those early years he might have cashed in on the soaring values of Manhattan real estate, and if he'd taken more investment cues from his robber baron clients he might have gotten richer without having had to work so hard.

He did sometimes show flashes of financial brilliance, as when he unloaded much of his stock just before the recession of the late 1970s. "That was just before the crash and he came out with a nice profit," recalls Charles Seidenberg, Eddie's accountant during his three and a half decades in Cambridge. "After that he pretty much stuck with government issues, Treasury bonds. Those produced a pretty good income even then. . . . He got a little fidgety about going back into the stock market."[31]

Eddie and Doris came to Cambridge with enough money to buy the Lowell Street home and have about half a million dollars left to invest, Seidenberg estimates. That wasn't much, considering all they'd made over the years. But it was enough to earn $25,000 to $30,000 a year in interest, which was sufficient to live very comfortably in the 1960s, especially since they owned their home outright. And Eddie supplemented that with an occasional fee from a paying client.

The problem was that Eddie lived about twenty years longer than the average retiree, which meant that he had to get by mainly on interest income for more than thirty years—and he spent money faster than most people on fixed incomes. "He lived the good life and spent and eventually had to dig into principal to come up with cash," says Seidenberg. "He needed to carry on his household. He wanted to stay there, and his house was very big on upkeep." Things were bad before Vondra moved in, and afterward expenses mounted even faster. "He liked to give parties and entertain people, and he had to get cash somewhere," his accountant remembers. "The only way to do it was to cash in some of his securities."[32]

By the time his children took over, there was hardly any money to manage, and they had to take out a reverse mortgage on the Lowell Street house just to pay his bills. Eddie hated having anybody know about his finances, even his children. He also hated mortgages. He hated owing money to a bank or anyone, but heat alone came to nearly $1,000 a month in the winter, when his age and thin blood required keeping the house at 80 degrees. Then there were insurance premiums for everything that could be insured—an obsession with Eddie. And paying for the housekeeper, taxes, food, bottled water, cable TV, three newspapers a day, medical bills and medicines, and maintenance on a very old home.

The result was that after he died in 1995, after the house was sold for $1.1 million, and after taxes, lawyers, and other debts were paid, there was about $600,000 to divide between Anne and Doris—far from the fortune the public and most of his friends assumed he'd left.

His children remain mystified as to how Eddie managed to die with so few assets. "Money was very much a verboten topic" in the Bernays household, Doris recalls. "But sometime in later life Eddie told me he hadn't spent his money wisely. It's the only time he ever told me he regretted anything."[33]

· · ·

By the time his daughters took over his finances, Eddie's senile dementia had progressed so far that he probably didn't realize how bad things were. And the whole struggle pitting Joan against Anne and Doris seemed to have sapped his strength.

Or maybe he was finally yielding, despite his determination not to, to the fact that he was past one hundred. Even then, according to his physician of twenty-five years, Dr. Victor Gurewich, he remained in remarkable shape. He'd been on medication to control blood clotting for decades—"probably longer than any patient in history," Gurewich says, since he was one of the earliest patients of the doctor who pioneered use of those drugs—and "all his cerebral problems were transient; there never was any permanent deficit." As for his state of mind, the doctor adds, "I never saw him depressed, up to the very end. He was constantly in good spirits. I also never heard him complain. He never had a single complaint in his whole life with me, and as his physician I found that quite remarkable."[34]

Still, those who knew him best saw a change for the worse from 1993 on. Herbert Patchell recalls a visit with him that year. A couple of friends were sitting around the kitchen table when one asked Eddie what his average day was like. "He described a typical day of ten years ago, with phone calls, reading the *Times*, doing this and that. In fact he had slept the entire day. It was just before Christmas, and he had cancer of the bladder. . . . It was a detailed reconstruction of something that hadn't gone on for a decade."[35]

Eddie also for the first time had to write out speeches so he wouldn't repeat himself. He would forget names, which he'd never done before, as well as birthdays and words. And in his interview with the guardian *ad litem* he said at one point that Joan had worked for him for twenty years rather than five, he didn't remember discharging his doctor, he wasn't sure what it meant to sign up as Vondra's domestic partner, he couldn't recall what year it was or how old he was, and he didn't know how many grandchildren he had or what their names were. "Anne Kaplan has children too," he told Kaloustian, "but I forget what they do. They are all very busy."[36]

Doris recalls stopping by Lowell Street near the end of her father's life: "He'd be sitting there reading a newspaper upside down. That was poignant, but it also was very brave; he just wouldn't let go. There was a bulldog quality to his mind. I could see him literally stretching his capacities."

While he had bladder cancer and clotting troubles, he ultimately succumbed to what Gurewich called old age, or "the cells just giving up." Doris says it was more like "starving himself to death, which is not uncommon. . . . We fed him by mouth, fed him medication under the tongue with a dropper. . . . He just gradually faded away. He withdrew more and more and eventually went into a coma and died. The fading [continued for] weeks and weeks. He was in the coma only for a day."[37]

Patchell was there by Eddie's side at the end, early in 1995. "He was very alert when he died," his friend remembers. "Kelai and I were with him the entire week, right around the clock. . . . He had alert moments; sometimes we had half-hour discussions."[38]

Joan came by, too. "He didn't want me to leave," she recalls. "He had tears in his eyes. I would talk to him. I said, 'Edward, remember those years in New York when you walked everywhere? You'd leave the limousine with your wife and kids.' I said, 'All that walking served you well. You're still as sturdy as ever.' "[39]

There was no funeral service or funeral. Eddie didn't believe in

Last Ride

either, although he probably would have liked the memorial service his daughters held at the Harvard Faculty Club, with tributes from Anne, Doris, and grandson Lucas, along with Patchell and other friends. He'd left no instructions as to what to do with his body. That was unusual for a man who planned everything, but it was consistent with his overwhelming fear of death. His children decided to have him cremated, as he had done for his father seventy-two years before.

Today his daughter Doris has Eddie's ashes, along with those of his parents, Ely and Anna Bernays. She's considering sprinkling them somewhere in New York, near one of the places he lived or worked, but she knows just what Eddie would have said about such a sentimental scheme: "Don't be silly. That's a lot of mumbo jumbo."[40]

A Question of PATERNITY

12

IT WAS JUST THE SORT OF OBITUARY EDDIE MIGHT HAVE CRAFTED for himself. The first paragraph proclaimed him "an early leader in the public relations field who devised or developed many techniques for influencing public opinion." The second credited him with enlarging the "narrow concept of press agentry" into a bold bid to "influence and change public opinion and behavior." The article called his campaign on behalf of Lucky Strike green "a brilliant success" and his soap sculpture contests "legendary." It said his "niche in cultural history seemed assured," it credited him with turning against smoking in his later years, and, of course, it noted that he was Sigmund Freud's nephew. His death was announced on page one and his obituary spanned four columns inside, a true sign of significance in the *New York Times*, a paper his own surveys had cited as America's finest. And, best of all, the headline called him the Father of Public Relations, although it set the title in quotation marks, implying that the editors weren't entirely sure.[1]

The *Times* wasn't alone in lionizing Eddie Bernays. Headlines in the *Boston Globe*, *USA Today*, the *Financial Times*, the New York *Daily News*, the *Providence Journal-Bulletin*, and scores of other papers also referred to him as the Father of Public Relations. The *Washington Post* didn't raise the issue of the profession's paternity in its headline, but the second paragraph of its obit reported that "Mr. Bernays . . . often was called 'the father of public relations.'"

Regal titles were nothing new for Eddie. As far back as the 1930s reporters had devised catchy monikers for this PR pioneer: the Baron of Ballyhoo, Sire of the Big Sell, Master of Mass Psychology, High Priest of Press Agents, Pontiff of Publicity, Pope of Propaganda, Prince of Propaganda, and Prince of Puff. In 1935 *Time* declared him "No. 1 U.S. Publicist," a phrase that was regularly repeated by other publications. In recent years, profilers from the *Washington Post*, the *San Diego Union*, and the *Boston Globe* settled on the less poetic but more historically significant appellation "Father of Public Relations," a phrase used so often that it almost became an extension of his name.

But was he the legitimate father?

Or was he merely so good at his chosen profession that he managed to invent his own epithet, and a disputed one at that?

Those questions might not mean much if they weren't so central to the way the world has defined Eddie's legacy, and the way he defined it. And if the public relations profession weren't so central to American society today. And if the mere mention of him as that profession's "father" didn't continue to fuel such passionate debate among PR professionals. Denny and Glenn Griswold, pioneers in writing about public relations and longtime colleagues of Eddie's, began chronicling that controversy as long ago as 1948, and it has heated up since then. "The position of Edward L. Bernays in the history of public relations," the Griswolds wrote, "is more debatable and more often debated than that of any other man."[2]

. . .

If "father" is taken literally as founder, or first, the verdict on Eddie is easy: he wasn't it.

The true father probably was Aaron. Back in biblical days God anointed him spokesman for his brother Moses, charged with explaining to the Hebrews why it was time to pack their bags and head across the desert. It also could have been Julius Caesar, who wrote commentaries on his campaigns in Gaul to promote his fortunes in Rome. Or maybe it was the ministers of propaganda for the Catholic church, named to fend off attacks from Martin Luther and his followers. In America, the first PR men were Samuel Adams, Thomas Paine, and the other patriots who, Eddie wrote, "used oratory, newspaper exposure, meetings, or correspondence to rally public opinion to their cause, and as a matter of fact, historical research indicates that Thomas Jefferson wrote the Declaration of Independence as a public relations pronouncement."[3]

The modern era of public relations dates back to the early 1900s, when America's business leaders realized that persuasion rather than coercion was the best method of getting their way with the public and with the government. That meant letting people know how business operated, tempering business excesses to conform to public mores, and hiring specialists to interpret business to the people and vice versa.

Scott M. Cutlip, America's premier PR historian, has analyzed those early beginnings and concluded that recognition of publicity as a legitimate corporate function began in 1888, when Mutual Life Insurance Company set up a "literary bureau" to put out the word on its products. A year later George Westinghouse hired a newspaperman from Pittsburgh to help him do battle with Thomas A. Edison. The first real PR agency, Cutlip says, was the Publicity Bureau, set up in 1900 in Boston by George V. S. Michaelis, Herbert Small, and Thomas O. Marvin. Its clients included Harvard University, the Massachusetts Institute of Technology, and the American Telephone and Telegraph Company.[4]

But while few in or out of the profession today remember Michaelis and his partners, Ivy Ledbetter Lee still stands out among the early pioneers, and to many he's the legitimate claimant to the title of father.

Ivy Lee started out as a reporter for the *New York Journal*, the *New York Times*, and the *New York World*, but he quickly realized that reporting wouldn't earn him the status and money he wanted. In 1903 he began doing publicity work for political candidates. About a year later he opened an agency, Parker and Lee—the third of the modern era. While he represented some of America's biggest corporations, from the Pennsylvania Railroad to Bethlehem Steel, he's best known for helping transform the public personae of America's best-known entrepreneurs, John D. Rockefeller Sr. and his son, John D. Jr. The Rockefellers were used to being called robber barons and heartless industrialists, but they couldn't ignore the vilification that followed the Ludlow Massacre of April 20, 1914, when operators of a Rockefeller coal mine in Colorado dispatched private guards and militia against striking miners, burning "to a crisp" two mothers and eleven children. In the first of a series of successful efforts to muffle the impact of the massacre and rehabilitate the Rockefellers, Lee struck back with press notices that cast the strikebreaking as a blow for "industrial freedom."

While many of his efforts on behalf of the Rockefellers remain controversial, Lee managed, with them and other clients, to set a standard for his profession that elevated it from the hucksterism and press agentry of an earlier era. He insisted that actions by a company speak louder than words. He made openness and accuracy the watchwords for PR counselors and made informing the public, rather than ignoring or fooling it, the mission. And he preached that the greatest service a PR man could perform for business would be to publicize its policies in "the language of the man who rides in the trolley car and goes to ball games, who chews gum and spits tobacco juice." Lee was so convincing that corporate titans started hiring him and his colleagues, often at high salaries and in high-level posts, to the point where the *New York Herald Tribune* referred to him as "A Physician to Corporate Bodies." Lee liked the title so much he reprinted the story as a pamphlet.

There were other labels, however, that he neither liked nor repeated: "Little Brother of the Rich," "Minnesinger to Millionaires," "paid liar," and "Poison Ivy." He also was charged with misleading the press and spreading mine owners' lies after the Ludlow Massacre. Worst of all were accusations that in the mid-1930s he had counseled German industrial giant I. G. Farben on how to battle the bad press that the new Nazi regime was getting. Lee's defenders insist he was working with Farben to get Hitler to reform.

Despite the controversy, many chroniclers of his era and ours regard Lee as the closest thing public relations has to a patriarch. *Time* magazine in 1939 proclaimed him the "first great exponent" of public relations, referring to Eddie as one of Lee's "younger rivals."[5] Veteran PR man John W. Hill agreed, calling Lee "unquestionably the father of the modern practice of public relations counseling." Eddie, Hill noted, was "another pioneer" who "by his writings and speeches, has done much to call attention to public relations."[6] And *Literary Digest* in its 1934 obituary called Lee "number 1 publicity man for big business," adding that Eddie was a "runner-up to Lee in the art of selling industry to the people."[7]

Where Eddie fits into the chronology of the early pioneers depends in part on where one puts the starting point. It could be as late as 1919, when he opened his first office, or as early as 1912, when he first hooked up with his former classmate Fred Robinson and started working at the *Medical Review of Reviews*. In either case, he's more than a decade behind Michaelis and nearly as far in back of Lee. He also was preempted by newspaperman William Wolff Smith, who opened a "publicity business" in Washington in 1902, Hamilton Mercer Wright, who in 1905 became the first to undertake publicity for a foreign country, and Pendleton Dudley, who opened his firm in 1909 and stayed active until his death at age ninety in 1966.

Cutlip, in a 1991 letter to the *New York Times*, said his research had turned up even more pioneers and convinced him that "when Edward L. Bernays opened his publicity office in a remodeled house at 19 East Forty-eighth Street in New York City in the summer of 1919, his was the eighth such agency, not the first."[8]

· · ·

Chronology isn't the only basis for determining paternity, however, especially when one considers fatherhood in the broader context of establishing theoretical, practical, and ethical guideposts for later generations. In this sense, Eddie has a compelling claim to the title.

In 1923 he became the first to teach a university course specifically entitled public relations, at New York University, although in 1920 the University of Illinois had offered a less ambitious course on publicity techniques.

Also in 1923 he became the first to publish a book outlining the theory and practice of public relations, *Crystallizing Public Opinion*, although two other publicity men had published a less ambitious guide a month or so before. *Crystallizing* "stood alone among works dealing specifically with public relations in having exerted any influence outside the narrow public relations world or much influence within it," social historian J. A. R. Pimlott wrote in 1951.[9]

Through fourteen other books and scores of articles, Eddie established himself as public relation's most prolific—and articulate—philosopher and spokesman. He built on the abstract offerings of Gustave Le Bon and Walter Lippmann, showing how public relations men were just the ones to tame and mold the mass mind and make sense of a world where technology seemed out of control and the old order seemed to be crumbling. He showed how his uncle Sigmund Freud's insights into what drives individuals also explained how to move groups. And he admonished his colleagues to see that the real tools of their trade were the laws of social science, of research and opinion-molding, just as their real ethical test was whether they could advance the public good along with their clients' private interests.

Not only were Eddie's theories on his profession the first to be promulgated, but they've also lasted longer than anyone else's. His writings still are cited in public relations courses across America, and of all the early pioneers his is the name today's PR students are most likely to recognize.

But whether or not they've read his writings, contemporary PR scholars and practitioners are sure to have heard how he put those ideas to work in the real world. Light's Golden Jubilee remains a classic example of how to transform an anniversary into an international sensation. His work in Guatemala is a model for American corporations on how to flex their economic and diplomatic muscles. And his

Torches of Freedom crusade has instructed a whole new generation of tobacco PR men on how to use symbols—and secrecy—to win over a whole new generation of smokers. More generally, Bernays's Big Think continues to be the mind-set that separates the most creative and successful PR professionals from the rest of their overpopulated field, much as it distinguished Bernays from his less bold and creative contemporaries.

"It has been the custom to hold up Ivy Lee as the greatest example of what a newspaperman may do when he enters upon publicity work," Stanley Walker wrote in 1934. "But it is probable that Bernays is the more important as an American phenomenon. He is more of a psychologist, or psychoanalyst, than Lee. . . . Bernays has taken the sideshow barker and given him a philosophy and a new and awesome language."[10]

Richard Tedlow of the Harvard Business School, writing forty-five years later, agreed that Bernays was at least Lee's equal. Lee, he said, "should be viewed as the representative public relations man of the Progressive era, but that position was occupied by Edward L. Bernays in the postwar period. . . . Lee was tongue-tied when asked to explain his job, but Bernays sallied forth in books, articles, and speeches not only to define public relations counseling (a term he coined in 1920) but to outline its methodology and suggest a code of ethics. While Lee thought of his trade as an art which would not outlive his career, Bernays conceived of public relations as the ongoing science of the 'group mind' and 'herd reaction.'"[11]

The popular press also typically sided with Eddie. He "was conditioning the Mass Mind for Richard Bennett long before Ivy Lee took over the job of merchandising John D. Rockefeller," John T. Flynn wrote in *The Atlantic Monthly* in 1932.[12] "Edward L. Bernays," columnist Sid Bernstein wrote in *Advertising Age* in 1975, "probably has more right than anyone to be called the father of modern public relations."[13] Perhaps the best sign of Eddie's relative impact was the fact that he was the only PR man included in *Life* magazine's 1990 listing of the 100 most important Americans of the twentieth century. "It was he and future wife Doris E. Fleischman," *Life* wrote, "who coined the phrase 'counsel on public relations' for the business they opened in 1919, the prototype for the 2,000 or so PR firms today."[14]

. . .

Eddie Bernays may have been a prototype for the profession, or even its progenitor, but over the years many PR professionals have been slow to acknowledge his pioneer status. And some are mortified at the notion that what America's 125,000 public relations people do today has anything in common with what he was doing half a century ago.

That's partly a natural reaction to the disdain he showed them. Eddie did write more books, articles, and speeches defining and promoting public relations than anyone then or since, but for most of his life he refused to join the Public Relations Society of America or any other PR group. And PR people generally didn't make it onto the guest lists for his legendary salons and soirees.

Asked about his hesitancy to hook up with organizations like PRSA, Eddie, as always, had a well-rehearsed and high-minded response: "I have never attended a meeting of this group. In fact I was a member of the organization only for one year, as a gesture of good will to a good friend. And in that period of time my only connection was to pay a year's dues. I firmly believe and still do that the organization should from its start have required the highest standards of character and professionalism of its prospective members. But that was not in the cards because the organization depended upon numbers for its sustenance."[15]

That's only part of the story, however. Eddie was indeed a loner, someone who staked out new territory and relished the notion that he was so far ahead of his times that his colleagues couldn't understand or appreciate him. And he did preach a standard of ethics that was tough for any group or individual to meet. But he hadn't always been eager to go it alone, and his later determination to do so wasn't always a matter of choice.

As early as 1927 he chaired a committee of fourteen leading PR men who, using the American Medical Association and American Bar Association as models, hoped to create an organization to "clean up the evil practices in publicity." The group, realizing the sensitivity of its mission, resolved to push ahead quietly, but that resolve was shattered by a long article in *Editor and Publisher* on the industry, its troubles, and the move to clean it up. While most committee members declined to talk to the magazine, Eddie released a statement that took up a full column, a move that, as he later acknowledged, offended his fellow committee members and doomed the organizing effort.[16]

Eddie tried again in 1938, inviting to his home twenty or so leading PR men, but again the bid was killed by premature publicity that he apparently initiated. "This unpublicized, high-powered group calls itself the Council on Public Opinion," *Time* reported. "Chairman is the nation's No. 1 publicist, dark, Machiavellian Edward L. Bernays."[17] The 1938 meeting did have two effects: it inspired John W. Hill, founder of the huge Hill and Knowlton public relations firm, to form an elite association of PR professionals called the Wisemen, and it ensured that Eddie, who'd offended Hill and others through stunts like the self-aggrandizing article in *Time*, wouldn't be invited to join the new group.

He'd also been excluded two years earlier when the National Association of Accredited Publicity Directors was formed. In fact, as Cutlip reports, the association "had a rule that when a member mentioned Bernays, he had to drop a quarter in a pot. The money was used to buy drinks at the end of the year."[18]

Eddie became such a pariah partly as a result of envy. He was making more money than most of his contemporaries. He had more high-profile clients, threw more high-flying parties, and got more highly favorable press.

Anti-Semitism also probably played a role. Eddie didn't practice his religion and at times was actively antagonistic to it. Still, nearly everyone knew he was Jewish, if only because he perpetually advertised his relationship to Freud, who everyone knew was Jewish. And it wasn't always easy being a Jew in a business world dominated by white Anglo-Saxon Protestants at a time when Jew-baiting was widespread. "He talked to me openly about things he had to work out because he was Jewish, social exclusions, trying to work with the WASP political establishment," recalls Camille Roman, a close friend from the Cambridge years.[19]

Bernays also had a knack for saying and doing things that made colleagues cringe. Like staging old-style stunts such as the Torches of Freedom parade and writing books like *Propaganda* and *Engineering Public Consent*, whose very titles drew the ire of the press and raised the eyebrows of a public already wary of the hidden hands of PR men. Worst of all, he relentlessly advocated government regulation of the profession, to the dismay of his colleagues. "The licensing drive was extremely controversial for a lot of reasons," explains Frank LeBart, a former top PR man at Exxon and John Hancock Insurance who was Eddie's close friend. "A lot of the more senior practitioners were very uncomfortable about requirements for accreditation, and many refused to take an exam. There also was a group who felt strongly that government has no role in public relations. It's a profession that functions under the First Amendment, and any hint of government regulation or control is highly undesirable. . . . Eddie's motives were good with this, but he overdid it. He never gave a speech where he didn't include it."[20]

His liberalism on issues ranging from labor unions to race relations was one more reason many in the craft despised him. Eddie "never shared their devotion to big business or their conservative politics," writes Tedlow, the Harvard Business School professor. "Symbolic of his ideological distance was a remark he made at a convention in 1945. The customary words of criticism had been directed at unions when Bernays asserted that the record would not be clear 'if we don't say a few words about the strategy of the revolutionary employer. I think we all know men who are revolutionary in their attitudes and actions to kill off the labor unions.' 'Oh, no, no, no, no!' moaned George Kelley of Pullman in reply. 'Don't speak that way of them.'"[21]

If the substance of his message was difficult for colleagues to digest, his arrogance in delivering it really made them choke. LeBart recalls one such instance where Eddie "was having what in effect was a debate over licensing with Phil Leslie, and while Leslie was speaking against it Eddie was sitting in the front row reading the *New York Times.* Some of those things did not endear him to people."[22]

But what most angered his colleagues, even those who rank him as a premier pioneer, was his perpetual self-promotion and the way he actively lobbied for fatherhood status. That's why Hill kept him out of the Wisemen in 1938, and Hill grew even angrier over the years as Eddie began to claim credit for bringing him into public relations. "It was a total legend that Bernays helped bring Hill into the business," says Loet Velmans, former chairman of Hill and Knowlton. "Hill had very little respect for Bernays."[23]

Howard Chase, who ran the PR departments at General Mills and General Foods, admired Eddie as "a very, very complicated man of diverse talents." But he also saw him "as a man of fantastic arrogance and egocentricity. The word 'chutzpah' applied to him as much as anybody I know. He alienated almost everybody else in the field. . . . He was never quite accepted by people he regarded as his peers because of his self-promotion, his very bland assumption that the field really didn't exist before Bernays."[24]

William H. Baldwin, a venerated figure in the early days of public relations, also was torn. On the one hand, in a letter Eddie quoted in his memoirs, Baldwin said, "Bernays had more to do with developing acceptance for PR and public relations counsel than any half dozen other persons." But in the same letter he made clear that "I date the emergence of public relations from the work that Ivy Lee did for John D. Rockefeller Sr. in the Colorado strike." And in a later missive Baldwin clarifies his earlier reference to Eddie, writing, "I have always felt that Bernays did make the first major breakthrough in getting public awareness of public relations, but that this was but a by-product of self-publicizing."[25]

Bill Ruder, a longtime PR consultant in New York, puts it more simply: "My overall impression of Bernays is that he only had one client, and that was Edward L. Bernays."[26] But Sidney Blumenthal says that was natural given the profession he'd chosen. To accuse Eddie of self-promotion, Blumenthal wrote, "is like accusing a fish of swimming."[27]

Eddie probably wouldn't have minded being accused of touting his own accomplishments, since he believed they were substantial and felt he was the only one able to present them accurately. When it came to shaping his legacy, Eddie unabashedly drew on every PR strategy and tactic he'd tested over a lifetime.

First he crafted a compelling historical argument about the five stages of PR history in America—one that set him apart as the originator of the fifth and decisive stage. Parts one through three run from colonial days through Cornelius Vanderbilt's "Public be Damned" era of the late 1800s. Stage four, according to Eddie's manifesto, was the "Public be Informed" period, where Ivy Lee helped businesses see how vital it was to give people truthful information. "But as I look back on the time," Eddie wrote, "the emphasis was on words and not on changed action to conform to public demand and public desire."

Enter stage five: "Period of Mutual Understanding," a time when public relations came to mean "not a one-way street for giving information to the public for our clients but rather one of interpreting the public to the client as a basis for their action and, after the action had been carried out, interpreting the client to the public."[28] It also happened to be a time when Eddie was getting back from Paris, opening his PR office, and setting a model for the new two-way network.

Coming from Eddie, such a take on history seemed a bit self-serving, no matter how accurate it was. But it assumed an aura of respectability when it was endorsed in 1948 by Eric F. Goldman, an esteemed historian at Princeton University and former editor of *Public Opinion Quarterly*. "Bernays moved along with the most advanced trends in the public relations field, thinking with, around, and ahead of them," Goldman wrote in *Two Way Street*, his treatise on the history of public relations in America. In Goldman's view there were three, not five, crucial stages in that history, with Lee originating the second and Eddie standing as father of the third and most critical stage. The kind of PR Eddie sketched out in his pioneering book *Crystallizing Public Opinion*, Goldman wrote, "marks the third stage in the evolution of public relations thought in the United States. The public was not to be fooled, in the immemorial manner of the press agent. It was not merely to be informed, according to the formula of Ivy Lee's 1906 'Declaration.' The public was to be understood—understood as an intricate system of group relationships and by an expert with the technical equipment, the ethics, and the social view associated with the lawyer, doctor, or teacher. Public relations was to be a two-way street—and a street in a good neighborhood."[29]

But there were several things Goldman didn't tell his readers: Eddie had come up with the idea for *Two Way Street*, and the idea of Goldman as its author. He'd helped Goldman find a publisher, and he was deeply involved in the editing and packaging. And Eddie purchased from Goldman, for $900, "all rights, title, and interest" in the book.[30]

Eddie had learned with clients like American Tobacco and Mack Truck just how much more compelling an argument was when it came from a respected, seemingly disinterested expert. And Goldman, who went on to become a top aide to President Lyndon Johnson and later a Johnson biographer, was just the expert Eddie was looking for. Judging from extensive correspondence between them contained in Eddie's and Goldman's files at the Library of Congress, it appears that Goldman wrote the book on his own, although Eddie made lots of editing suggestions, both technical and substantive, many of which Goldman took. Goldman did acknowledge in the book's foreword the "cooperation" of seven PR pioneers, including Eddie, and he said all the information he'd gathered was "used solely as my historical sense dictated"—precisely the wording Eddie had proposed in a letter to Goldman dated October 15, 1947, except that Eddie had proposed "dictates" instead of "dictated."[31]

Historians were just one of several influential audiences Eddie courted to make his case for paternity. He also sweet-talked the press from the very start, with impressive results. The *American Mercury* in 1930 ran an eight-page profile arguing that Eddie's "rank as public relations counsel is at least the equal of Ivy Ledbetter Lee's" and saying "Eddie can foretell the future."[32] Two years later the *Atlantic Monthly* published a ten-page story that gushed, "Bernays himself is quite the newest type of public relations specialist, so intelligent and so free from the conventional inhibitions that he assumes almost the character of a phenomenon."[33] Around the same time the *Jewish Tribune* complimented him on "the high standard of ethics which he has always maintained and upon which he insists," the *New York World-Telegram* called him "a prophet to the people for the profit of his clients," the *Literary Digest* wrote that he "helped make press-agentry a 'science,'" and *The New Yorker* said he "is an idealist of the most profound order."[34] The compliments continued to flow into the 1950s, '60s, '70s, '80s, and '90s, with *Printer's Ink* writing in 1959 that Eddie had "written more and spoken more than anyone else to raise the status of public relations," and the *Washington Post* in 1984 calling him "the Father of Us All."[35]

Not all of his coverage was favorable, of course. The trade press in particular went after him, believing that PR men were costing them advertising revenues by getting free publicity for clients. *Editor and Publisher* in 1928 called Eddie "Machiavelli at his best, or Bismarck at his worst," and in 1929 it said he was "the most modern, smoothest, highest paid and most effective of all the expert tribe of propagandists and space grabbers."[36] The *Guild Reporter*, meanwhile, said he had "turned the space-grabbing racket into a science."[37] But Eddie knew the media well enough to realize that even negative stories "made me known to the journalistic field."[38]

There were lots of other ways to get out his version of his history, all of which he tapped. He expounded his role in public relations in each university course he taught, and he used his nonprofit foundation to sponsor contests that bore his name and promulgated his definition of PR. He ran ads in magazines and newspapers that trumpeted his books, his devotion to all-American values like democracy, and his client services, although he later told an interviewer that "we never went out after clients."[39] And, recognizing the importance of encyclopedias in defining a profession and its pioneers, he got H. L. Mencken to use his definition of the profession—and his contention that he'd coined the phrase "public relations counsel"—in his 1945 version of

The American Language. Eddie's office, meanwhile, put out a bio that called him "a notable, unique example of how a profession grew up with a man," and in retirement he used his birthday parties to generate news coverage of himself, nearly all of which matter-of-factly referred to him as the Father of Public Relations.

That was more than he'd ever done for any client, but it wasn't enough.

There still was the question of how a future biographer—and he was sure there would be one—would interpret what he'd done. To be really certain, he quietly tried to recruit someone he felt was up to the job. "He and I had a lengthy correspondence the last third of his life, and I think he thought I'd write his biography. Everything he ever did he sent me a copy of, and it always had a handwritten note on it," recalls Ray Eldon Hiebert, Ivy Lee's biographer and a journalism professor at the University of Maryland. "I just didn't want to do another public relations person."[40] Similar notes went to other esteemed authors, from Eric Goldman to Daniel J. Boorstin, the former Librarian of Congress. But his most promising candidate was PR historian Scott Cutlip, with whom he engaged in a decade of letter-writing.

Cutlip, who was teaching at the University of Wisconsin, desperately wanted Eddie to donate his personal papers to Wisconsin's State Historical Society. The society was trying to build its PR collection, Cutlip was trying to advance his academic career, and Eddie had what everyone acknowledged was the best collection of historic material on the profession. Decades later Cutlip disparaged Eddie's "indefatigable zeal in promoting himself as the father of public relations and in using excessive hyperbole in the retelling of his public relations endeavors."[41] But in 1955 he had offered only kind words, writing to Eddie with the promise that "if we were to be favored as the depository for your papers I would undertake, promptly, the task of organizing and indexing the papers and then preparation of a book manuscript on your pioneering work in this field. . . . I think much of the story of public relations' evolution can be told in terms of your career."[42] Eddie loved the idea of Cutlip as his biographer, but he realized his papers would be more widely read—and available to more potential biographers—if he left them to the world's biggest, most prestigious depository, the Library of Congress.

The more than eight hundred boxes of documents he left to the library appear to be an unabridged version of his professional life, one that includes material he knew would be unflattering to him and his clients. His willingness to tell all sets him apart from most fellow practitioners and suggests that, despite his resolve to forge a favorable legacy, he was confident that history would judge him kindly from an honest reading of the record. Yet the fact that he saved nearly everything he ever wrote or received also sets him apart, making clear that he believed he was an epic figure who would remain interesting to future generations. And as he sketched out how he would hand over his papers he couldn't resist using them to tout himself. John McDonough, a Library of Congress historian, wrote after meeting with Eddie in the fall of 1965, "As one of the country's leading public relations men, Mr. Bernays is not unmindful of the benefits of promoting himself. He therefore proposed the following: When the legal tangle involving the gift is worked out, LC should make arrangements for a formal, symbolic presentation of the gift. . . . If LC would supply a photographer, Mr. Bernays would see to it that his guests would number some of the following: Vice President Humphrey, Senator Paul Douglas, Senator Saltonstall, Senator Fulbright, and from the Supreme Court—Abe Fortas and William O. Douglas."[43]

The papers would tell part of his story, Eddie believed, but he would tell the rest in his 849-page autobiography, immodestly titled, *Biography of an Idea: Memoirs of Public Relations Counsel Edward L. Bernays*, his 478-page oral history at Columbia University, and his dizzying collection of books, articles, and speeches, all of which set a decidedly upbeat, self-important framework for his life story that he hoped would guide anyone writing about him afterward. "I am not unmindful of the fact that most people who are interested in setting up any image about themselves for posterity had better play a part in doing it themselves," Eddie confessed to Boorstin in 1959. "Those who write about other human beings are given to so much ego-projection, so much bias and distortion, that even in one's lifetime the truth suffers."[44]

Still, he wasn't content. Posterity would have all his papers and his personal perspective on his life story. But he felt it was important that biographers and historians also have a road map to everything he'd written and everything that had been written about him over his long career, one that included capsule versions of the writings, since he'd learned long before that busy authors had limited attention spans. So, in a truly unusual move, he hired a doctoral student to compile a 774-page annotated bibliography on him and his wife Doris. This work—*Public Relations, the Edward L. Bernayses and the American Scene: A Bibliography*—included 24 pages and 185 entries just on things the *New York Times* had said about him. There were hundreds of pages more of long excerpts from each book, periodical, and film that mentioned him, or that he contributed to. And there were references to nearly every speech he delivered and letter to the editor he wrote. Borrowing techniques he'd used in promoting the published works of clients, he sought and received endorsements of the bibliography from sixty people. *New York Times* reporter Will Lissner said he found the summaries "very informative and useful," and Stanley Marcus of Nieman-Marcus said he was delighted to have it for his library.

Roscoe Ellard, a Columbia Journalism School professor who reviewed an earlier, ninety-two-page version of the bibliography for *Editor and Publisher,* said it usefully sketched the history of PR in America. Still, he couldn't help observing how odd it was for such a work to be commissioned, noting wryly that it had happened only twice before that he knew of—with Napoleon and Abraham Lincoln.[45] PR veteran Bill Riis also thought it odd, although not for Eddie, as he wrote, "No one but Bernays would think of selling his own personal clipping book. The trick is, it won't sell."[46] Riss was right: Eddie was stuck with twenty-five cases of copies, which he kept in his basement. But the bibliography found its way to scores of libraries and other research centers and is available to anyone interested in reading or writing about him.

Eddie knew friends and colleagues thought he was a self-promoter. He pleaded guilty, but insisted it wasn't a crime. "I myself have always thought that I was modest personally," he told an interviewer in 1971, "but I haven't refrained from occasionally being what might be considered immodest professionally, because unless you present the facts, those who may not be in sympathy with you may distort them."[47]

. . .

Making the case for his position as father of the profession got easier as he grew older. Fewer and fewer other old-timers were around to contend for the title, and critics squirmed at taking on someone as old as Eddie. Also, as he got grayer and more stooped, and neared the magical age of one hundred, he increasingly looked like a father figure—or a grandfather figure. And the press, ever seduced by a facile moniker like "Father of Public Relations," found it ever easier to repeat without feeling any obligation to explain.

As Eddie aged, his claims got bolder and tougher to substantiate. This may have happened because his memory was fading or, more likely, because with each repetition the tales grew a bit grander, to the point where even he wasn't sure what was strictly factual and what was embellished.

This pattern was particularly apparent when it came to Ivy Lee, his button-down archrival for the title of father. Sometimes Eddie's assertions were simply wrong, as when he said his in-house PR newsletter, *Contact*, was a "new" idea, even though he must have known that Lee had been publishing a similar bulletin for at least two years. Other times there were shadings of gray, as when Eddie insisted he'd coined the term "counsel on public relations" even though he'd acknowledged in 1949 that Lee sometimes "called himself a councillor in (or on) public relations." And every chance he got, Eddie praised Lee—but cast his accomplishments in a way that made clear their limits. "He [Lee] made an impact certainly in high business quarters, because his clients were the establishment," Eddie told a Columbia University interviewer in 1971. "From the standpoint of professionalizing or rationalizing the field as a) a field of study, b) a profession, c) a field of growing public importance, his influence in my time was not very great. . . . Lee's impact remained within his circle, rather than with the broader public."[48]

Eddie's memoirs also drew charges of self-aggrandizement. "Some have said that there are gross inaccuracies that cannot be attributed to a normal distortion of memory," said a review in the winter 1966 edition of *Public Relations Quarterly,* although it didn't identify the "some" and only vaguely alluded to the alleged distortions. T. J. "Tommy" Ross, who was Ivy Lee's partner, wrote that "I got it [Eddie's autobiography] yesterday and so far have read only the chapter on George Washington Hill. It is outrageous—as well as inaccurate. Even the address of the company is incorrect."[49] William H. Baldwin, the PR pioneer, said the book's "title was conceived in sin and the text whelped in iniquity," while Cutlip wrote that it contained "errors and exaggerations."[50] And a review in the November 20, 1965, *Editor and Publisher* said that Simon & Schuster, Eddie's publisher, had been "bombarded" with "letters saying that Mr. Bernays is 'not the founder of public relations, nor coiner of the phrase.'" Simon and Schuster officials say that, more than thirty years later, they can't locate those letters, and presume they were discarded years ago.

The autobiography also drew its share of praise, however. The *New York Times* wrote that "the reader will be swept along by the richness of Mr. Bernays's material," and the *Columbia Journalism Review* said it was "a much better book than students of his ponderous theoretical works had reason to expect." Even *Editor and Publisher* conceded that it was "only heavy to hold, but is light as gossamer in spirit."[51]

Eddie used the praise to help promote the book, and, as always, he took on his critics. When Cutlip suggested the 849-page autobiography was "a bit long and crowded with detail," Eddie wrote back saying that "a number of the reviews from competent critics stated that the book wasn't long enough and didn't go into detail enough." And to the suggestion of errors and embellishments, Eddie responded, "I welcome your word about errors and exaggerations too, for a second edition of the book is coming out soon. Naturally, in a 320,000 word book, errors are bound to creep in. And we have caught some typos and others. I'd be delighted if you were willing to pass them on, so that I can examine them for possible use. As to exaggerations, I would be glad to have them too, although you may be referring to value judgements, which obviously would differ with the person making the judgement ."[52]

In his later years, when he was out of the limelight of New York and writing less, Eddie made the case for himself as a PR pioneer in a quieter way, person by person. He welcomed historians, public relations luminaries, and others to his home, giving each a special tour of the "ego shelf" in his den, a floor-to-ceiling collection of volumes by or about him. Then he led them upstairs to his study, where the walls were lined with photos of him with President Eisenhower, Thomas Edison, and other figures from history. Special guests might be invited to dip into his stacks of scrapbooks on the Green campaign, or Light's Golden Jubilee, and for critics he would peruse his files, pulling out just the right letter or memo to prove his point.

He also hit the speaking circuit more often than ever, pressing his interpretation of the history of the profession and his role as pioneer. Sue Bohle, who runs a PR firm in Los Angeles, remembers one speech he gave at age ninety-nine where all he had for notes were "little torn sheets of paper. When he got done he got a standing ovation. People put their hands beside their faces and said, 'I don't know if he really was the first, but who cares.'"[53]

He even put aside past prejudices and, in old age, joined a few public relations groups. He linked up with his fellow practitioners partly because his disdain, and theirs, had tempered over time. An equally important reason was that younger practitioners were eager to meet and lionize their last living legend, and he wasn't about to resist. And when he joined, he did so with that special Bernays flair. "I was president of the International Public Relations Association of which Ed was one of our very distinguished members," says William J. Corbett. "I recall his writing us a letter asking if we have any kind of program to abate the dues for people over 90, and then he wrote again asking if we could reduce the dues for anyone over 100. I thought that was quite humorous."[54]

To his grandchildren, all the tours, speeches, and other promotions sometimes seemed a bit much, especially when they'd watch him buy a book and immediately turn to the index to see if he was mentioned. But they tried to keep their sense of humor about it all, and so did Eddie. Hester remembers that "Polly once extracted the fortune from a cookie and wrote on the back of it, 'You will be the Father of Public Relations.' Eddie loved it."[55]

· · ·

Eddie also would have loved the debate that continues to swirl over whether he really was the father of his profession. He would relish the fact that he still inspires such loyalty from his defenders and such venom from his detractors.

University of Michigan historian David Lewis tried to sort out the conflicting evidence in 1970, when he asked PR practitioners nation-wide to rank the "most outstanding" people in their profession. Ivy Lee got the most first-place votes (22), followed by John W. Hill, Pendleton Dudley, Carl Byoir, and, in fifth place with sixteen votes, Eddie. Lewis wrote that Lee "is generally regarded as the first public relations practitioner in the present sense of the term," while his respondents said that Eddie "gave profession its theoretical underpin-nings. . . . First to emphasize social role of public relations. . . . Made field respectable; elevated it to profession."[56]

The survey, Lewis explained years later, reinforced his belief that Eddie "would not have had to exaggerate at all to be one of the great figures in public relations."[57]

Samplings like Lewis's, however, are just a snapshot of how PR practitioners at a given moment in history feel about their forebears, and given how much longer Eddie lived than his rivals and how inten-sively he promoted himself, it's almost certain he would have scored higher if Lewis had repeated his survey twenty years later. Even more significant is what individual PR people think about Eddie today.

"I think Bernays's greatest achievement was living so long," John Reed, a respected PR man in Washington, says when asked to assign

Eddie a place in PR history. Bill Ehling, who founded the PR department at Syracuse University, takes a similarly dim view: "If we are going to have someone who we can look back to as making an impact on the field I'd like to think it would be someone who did something more than getting women to smoke cigarettes and running people down to help Coolidge get reelected."

But Shelley Spector, who runs a public relations agency in the New York City area, insists that Eddie "had as much impact on twentieth-century society as his uncle Sigmund Freud had on his field of psychology." Ray Gaulke, chief operating officer of the Public Relations Society of America, says, "No one this century had as much impact on public opinion as Edward Bernays." And Harold Burson, founder of the world's largest PR firm, Burson-Marsteller, says that while Lee clearly came first and was a superior tactician, "from a theoretical standpoint on an organized basis I'd probably have to say he [Eddie] was the father. . . . To my knowledge no one has come up with anything better. We're still singing off the hymn book that he gave us."

Both sides are right, in part. Bernays clearly wasn't the first modern PR practitioner. Ivy Lee deserves that title, or maybe George Michaelis. But Bernays was the profession's first philosopher and intellectual. He saw the big picture when few others did, and he was the first to appreciate the nexus between theory and practice or, as he would have said, between the art of PR and the science. And in doing so he was the first to demonstrate for future generations of PR people how powerful their profession could be in shaping America's economic, political, and cultural life.

Yet Edward L. Bernays's most compelling claim to the title of Father of Public Relations goes beyond that art and science. It was his life itself. At work he thought bigger and bolder than anyone had before, to the point of getting women to fall in love with the color green. He brought the same preoccupations home, setting the tone with his wedding-day publicity stunt and feeling more comfortable offering his daughters PR advice than listening to their growing pains. Most of all, in his relentless bid to shape his own legacy, he offered a perfect portrayal of the full array of PR tactics and strategies, of

Father of

manipulations and embellishments, and how they could be used to redefine reality.

Bernays embodied the profession of public relations the same way that fellow *Life* magazine honorees Martin Luther King Jr. and Henry Ford were the fathers, respectively, of civil rights and the automobile, even though they, like Eddie, weren't really the first.

If he can claim credit as PR's progenitor, however, Eddie Bernays must also accept at least some responsibility for what his progeny have done. For he remains, in the end, a role model for propagandists who take us to war as well as those who work for peace. He inspires corporate strategists who peddle deadly tobacco products as well as those who are convinced that doing good is good for their business. And he is the father of the spinmeisters who manipulate our perceptions of politicians as well as those who inspire officeholders to serve the public that elected them.

Notes

CHAPTER 1: *Starting with* **SYMBOLS**

1. Doris Fleischman, "Notes of a Retiring Feminist," *American Mercury*, February 1949.
2. Edward L. Bernays, notes for his memoirs, Bernays Papers, Library of Congress.
3. Bernays, *Biography of an Idea: Memoirs of Public Relations Counsel Edward L. Bernays* (New York: Simon & Schuster, 1965), 38.
4. Ibid., 54.
5. Ibid., 61.
6. Letters from Elizabeth Hazelton Haight to Bernays, December 1, 1914, and to Mary Vida Clark, November 20, 1914. Bernays Papers, Library of Congress.
7. Bernays, *Biography*, 81.
8. Metropolitan Musical Bureau, undated press packet for Ballet Russe tour, Bernays Papers, Library of Congress.
9. Bernays, *Biography*, 112.
10. Adella Hughes, *Music Is My Life* (Cleveland: Cleveland World Publishing, 1947), 203.
11. *New York Dramatic Mirror*, December 4, 1915.
12. Bernays, *Biography*, 102.
13. Ibid., 132.
14. Bernays, Samuel Hoffenstein, Walter J. Kingsley, and Murdock Pemberton, *The Broadway Anthology* (New York: Duffield, 1917), 6–7.
15. *Musical America*, May 26, 1917.

16. Letter from R. H. Van Deman, chief of Military Intelligence Branch, U.S. War Department, April 22, 1918, Library of Congress.

17. Ernest Poole, *The Bridge: My Own Story* (New York: Macmillan, 1940), 422.

18. Letter from George Creel to Ernest Poole, June 7, 1918, Library of Congress.

19. *New York World*, November 21, 1918.

20. George Creel, *How We Advertised America* (New York: Harper, 1920), 409.

21. James R. Mock and Cedric Larson, *Words That Won the War* (Princeton, N.J.: Princeton University Press, 1939), 322.

22. Bernays, *Biography*, 167.

CHAPTER 2: *Lighting Up* **AMERICA**

1. Edward L. Bernays, *Biography*, 383.

2. Letter from Nickolas Muray, November 1928, Bernays Papers, Library of Congress.

3. Letter from Dr. George F. Buchan, Box 85, Library of Congress.

4. Letter from Arthur Murray, June 30, 1930, Library of Congress.

5. Memo from Bernays to American Tobacco, April 19, 1929, Library of Congress.

6. Memo from Bernays, "Candy Advertisement of the Future," Box 86, Library of Congress.

7. Correspondence between Bernays and American Tobacco, Box 85, Library of Congress.

8. Letter from George W. Hill to Bernays, November 17, 1928, Library of Congress.

9. Memo from Bernays to Hill, November 18, 1929, Library of Congress.

10. Bernays, *Biography*, 386.

11. Letter from Hill to Bernays, December 11, 1928, Library of Congress.

12. *Saint Petersburg Times*, February 2, 1984.

13. Quoted in Bernays, *Biography*, 386.

14. Ibid., 386.

15. Ibid., 387.

16. Memo, "System Outline for Easter Smokers," Library of Congress.

17. *New Mexico State Tribune*, dispatch from United Press, April 1, 1929.
18. Bernays, *Biography*, 387.
19. Memo from Bernays to Hill, May 27, 1929, Library of Congress.
20. Letter from Bernays to O. V. Richards, February 14, 1930, Library of Congress.
21. Bernays, notes for his memoirs, Library of Congress.
22. Letter from Bernays to Miss Blackmar, May 13, 1931, Library of Congress.
23. Letter from James E. Clark to Bernays, February 5, 1929, Library of Congress.
24. *New York Evening World*, April 1, 1929.
25. *Shreveport Times*, March 31, 1929.
26. *New Mexico State Tribune*, April 1, 1929.
27. Reminiscences of Edward L. Bernays, 1971, Columbia University Oral History Research Office, 473.
28. Jane Webb Smith, *Smoke Signals: Cigarette Advertising and the American Way of Life* (Chapel Hill: University of North Carolina Press, 1990), 23.
29. Michael Schudson, *Advertising: The Uneasy Persuasion* (New York: Basic Books, 1984), 186–87; and interview with Schudson, 1996.
30. Allan M. Brandt, "Recruiting Women Smokers: The Engineering of Consent," *Journal of the American Medical Women's Association*, January–April 1996.
31. Bernays, *Biography*, 374.
32. Ibid., 375.
33. Ibid., 375–76.
34. Ibid., 378.
35. Bernays Reminiscences, 477.
36. Bernays, *Biography*, 400.
37. Ibid., 389.
38. Ibid., 391.
39. Bernays office advisory on Green Ball, Library of Congress.
40. Bernays, *Biography*, 394.
41. Ibid., 393.
42. Ibid., 392.
43. *Vogue*, November 1, 1934.
44. Bernays, *Biography*, 394.

45. Edwin P. Hoyt, *The Supersalesmen* (New York: World Publishing, 1962), 73.
46. Robert Sobel, *They Satisfy: The Cigarette in American Life* (Garden City, N.Y.: Anchor Books, 1978), 96.
47. Bernays, *Biography*, 395.
48. Memo from Bernays to R. W. Richards, January 21, 1931, Library of Congress.
49. Memo from Bernays to American Tobacco, December 23, 1930, Library of Congress.
50. Bernays, *Biography*, 396.
51. Letter from Bernays to the editor of the *Boston Globe*, September 15, 1972.
52. Letter from Bernays to Paul M. Hahn, May 22, 1933, Library of Congress.
53. Letter from Bernays to Hahn, May 23, 1933, with attached reports from German medical magazines, Library of Congress.
54. Letter from Bernays to Hahn, December 10, 1932, Library of Congress.
55. Campaign outline by Dr. Clarence W. Lieb, Box 86, Library of Congress.
56. Interviews with Anne Bernays and Doris Held, 1996.
57. Notes for speech by Edward L. Bernays to Massachusetts Thoracic Society, March 28, 1964, Library of Congress.

CHAPTER 3: *The Big* THINK

1. *The Nation*, February 16, 1927.
2. Brochure from National Small Sculpture Committee, Box 323, Edward L. Bernays Papers, Library of Congress.
3. Interview with Oliver Gale, 1996.
4. Report by Henry Bern to Procter and Gamble Public Relations Department, April 30, 1959.
5. Bernays, *Biography*, 680–81.
6. Copy of Dixie Cup ad, Box 200, Library of Congress.
7. Undated pamphlet on Texas beer ordinance, Library of Congress.
8. *Forbes*, September 23, 1985.
9. Bernays, *Biography*, 333.

10. Memo from Bernays to Serge Obolensky, October 19, 1949, Library of Congress.

11. Letter from Justice Felix Frankfurter to President Franklin D. Roosevelt, May 7, 1934.

12. Bernays, *Biography*, 445.

13. Ibid., 455.

14. Geoffrey C. Upward, *A Home for Our Heritage: The Building and Growth of Greenfield Village and the Henry Ford Museum, 1929–1979* (Dearborn, Mich.: Henry Ford Museum Press, 1980), 60.

15. *The Nation*, August 14, 1929.

16. *The New Yorker*, November 9, 1929.

17. *Atlantic Monthly*, May 1932.

18. Leonard W. Doob, *Propaganda* (New York: Henry Holt, 1935), 195.

19. Letter from Thomas A. Edison to Bernays, October 22, 1929, Library of Congress.

20. Mary Barr Mavity, *The Modern Newspaper* (New York: Henry Holt, 1930), 87.

21. David L. Lewis, *The Public Image of Henry Ford* (Detroit: Wayne State University Press, 1976), 224–25.

22. Interview with David L. Lewis, 1996.

23. *Editor & Publisher*, October 12, 1929.

24. Lewis, *Public Image*, 225.

25. Interview with Scott M. Cutlip, 1996.

26. *Editor & Publisher*, October 12, 1929.

27. Ibid., October 26, 1929.

28. Letter from Bernays to N. H. Boynton, March 23, 1929, Library of Congress.

29. Interviews with Oliver Gale and Robert G. Eagen, 1996.

30. Bernays, *Biography*, 364.

31. Correspondence between Bernays and Henry Luce, April 1923, Library of Congress.

32. Letter from Paul Garrett to T. Stacy Capers, December 24, 1963, State Historical Society of Wisconsin.

33. Gale interview.

34. Bernays, *Biography*, 541–42, 556.

35. Ibid., 354.

36. Bernays, notes for his memoirs, Library of Congress.
37. Interview with Sylvia Lawry, 1996.
38. Sally Bedell Smith, *In All His Glory* (New York: Simon & Schuster, 1990), 70–71, 132–35.
39. Interview with Hester Kaplan, 1996.
40. Interview with Doris Held, 1996.
41. Letter from David L. Lewis to the author, June 19, 1996.

CHAPTER 4: *Setting the* SPIN

1. *New York Times*, October 18, 1924.
2. *New York Review*, October 18, 1924.
3. *New York World*, October 18, 1924.
4. Edward L. Bernays, *Biography*, 341.
5. Strategy of the Campaign, undated memo on Hoover reelection bid, Bernays Papers, Library of Congress.
6. Bernays, *Biography*, 650.
7. Recommendations to the O'Dwyer Campaign Committee, undated, Library of Congress.
8. Recommendations to Poletti Campaign, undated, Library of Congress.
9. Reminiscences of Charles Poletti, 1978, Columbia University Oral History Research Office, 610–11.
10. Bernays, *Biography*, 653.
11. Reminiscences of Edward L. Bernays, 1971, Columbia University Oral History Research Office, 243.
12. Bernays, notes for his memoirs, Library of Congress.
13. Bernays Reminiscences, Columbia University, 233.
14. Unpublished Bernays interview with Henry Morgenthau III, 1978.
15. Bernays Reminiscences, Columbia University, 400, 405.
16. Bernays, *Biography*, 699.
17. Correspondence between Bernays and Clare Boothe Luce, 1946, Library of Congress.
18. Reminiscences of Robert H. Jackson, Columbia University Oral History Research Office, 618.
19. Bernays, notes for his memoirs, Library of Congress.
20. Interview with George Kovtun, 1996, and letter from Kovtun to author, July 16, 1996.

21. Bernays Reminiscences, 1971, Columbia University, 23.

22. Bernays Reminiscences, 24.

23. Interview with Camille Roman, 1996.

24. Bernays Reminiscences, 197.

25. *PR Quarterly*, spring 1988.

26. Bernays Reminiscences, 199–200.

CHAPTER 5: *Rationale for a* **PROFESSION**

1. Edward L. Bernays, *Propaganda* (New York: Horace Liveright, 1928), 9–10.

2. Ibid., 10, 159.

3. Edward L. Bernays, *Biography*, 291.

4. Bernays, *Crystallizing Public Opinion* (New York: Boni & Liveright, 1923), 56.

5. Ibid., 122, 173.

6. Ibid., 64.

7. Ibid., 212.

8. Interview with Stuart Ewen, 1996.

9. Stuart Ewen, *PR! A Social History of Spin* (New York: Basic Books, 1996), 163.

10. Scott M. Cutlip, *The Unseen Power: Public Relations. A History* (Hillsdale, N.J.: Lawrence Erlbaum, 1994), 177.

11. Marvin N. Olasky, *Corporate Public Relations: A New Historical Perspective* (Hillsdale, N.J.: Lawrence Erlbaum, 1987), 80–81, 83.

12. Mencken, Henry Louis, *The American Language* (New York: Alfred A. Knopf, 1936), 288.

13. Ernest Gruening, "The Higher Hokum," *The Nation*, April 16, 1924.

14. Bernays, *Propaganda*, 45, 69.

15. Cutlip, *Unseen Power*, 182, 186.

16. *Journalism Quarterly*, Winter 1956.

17. Bernays, *Public Relations* (Norman: University of Oklahoma Press, 1952), 345.

18. Reminiscences of Edward L. Bernays, 1971, Columbia University Oral History Research Office, 3.

19. Bernays, "Attitude Polls—Servants or Masters?" *Public Opinion Quarterly*, fall 1945.

20. Suzanne A. Poliquin, "My Learning Experience with 'the Father of Public Relations,'" October 1983, provided to author.
21. Letter from Melvin N. Poretz to author, 1996.
22. *Public Relations Journal*, March 1970.
23. Bernays Reminiscences, Columbia University, 78–79.
24. Bernays, *Take Your Place at the Peace Table* (New York: International Press, 1945), 1.
25. *American Political Science Review*, August 1945.
26. Olasky, *Corporate*, 94–95, and interview with Olasky, 1996.
27. Henry F. Pringle, "The Mass Psychologist," *American Mercury*, February 1930.
28. John T. Flynn, "The Science of Ballyhoo," *Atlantic Monthly*, May 1932.
29. Bernays, *Propaganda*, 46.
30. Bernays, *Biography*, 757.
31. Ibid., 411.
32. Letter from Joseph Freeman to Floyd, April 17, 1952, Joseph Freeman Collection, Hoover Institution Archives, Stanford University.
33. Letter from Freeman to Floyd, June 5, 1952, Stanford University.
34. Bernays article, *Communication World*, International Association of Business Communicators, November 1986.
35. Bernays, *Biography*, 652.

CHAPTER 6: *Getting* **PERSONAL**

1. Interview with Doris Held, 1996.
2. Anne Bernays, "You Give Me the Answer, I'll Tell You the Question," *Mosaic*, fall 1966.
3. Interview with Anne Bernays, 1996.
4. Letter from Ernest Jones to Anna Freud, November 10, 1952.
5. Edward L. Bernays, *Biography*, 6–7.
6. Doris Fleischman Bernays, *A Wife Is Many Women* (New York: Crown, 1955), 71.
7. Letter from Ely Bernays to Edward L. Bernays, July 12, 1905, Bernays Papers, Library of Congress.
8. Edward L. Bernays, *Biography*, 20–21.

9. Ibid., 30–31.

10. Letter from Ely Bernays to Edward L. Bernays, October 1, 1909, Library of Congress.

11. Letter from Edward L. Bernays to Ely Bernays, January 30, 1912, Library of Congress.

12. Edward L. Bernays, *Biography*, 51.

13. Ibid., 84–85.

14. Ibid., 222.

15. Doris Fleischman Bernays, *Wife*, 62.

16. Edward L. Bernays, *Biography*, 219.

17. Doris Fleischman Bernays, *Wife*, 190.

18. Edward L. Bernays, *Biography*, 216.

19. Ibid., 221.

20. Ibid., 217.

21. Doris E. Fleischman (Bernays), "Notes of a Retiring Feminist," *American Mercury*, February 1949.

22. Doris Fleischman Bernays, *Wife*, 1.

23. Interview with Pat Jackson, 1996.

24. Interview with Camille Roman, 1996.

25. Edward L. Bernays, *Biography*, 221.

26. Doris Fleischman Bernays, *Wife*, 171.

27. Susan Henry, "In Her Own Name? Public Relations Pioneer Doris Fleischman Bernays," Presentation to Association for Education in Journalism and Mass Communications at California State University, July 1988.

28. Anne Bernays interview.

29. Held interview.

30. Doris Fleischman Bernays, *Wife*, 59.

31. Ibid., 206.

32. Edward L. Bernays, *Biography*, 233.

33. Insurance report from Continental Appraisal Company, January 19, 1937.

34. Edward L. Bernays, *Biography*, 805.

35. Ibid., 234.

36. Anne Bernays interview.

37. Held interview.

38. Unpublished Edward L. Bernays interview with Henry Morgenthau III, 1978.
39. Edward L. Bernays, "Applying Mass Psychology to Eliminate Race Prejudice," *American Hebrew*, December 9, 1932.
40. Held interview.
41. Susan Henry, "In Her Own Name?"
42. Anne Bernays interview.
43. Doris Fleischman Bernays, *Wife*, 167.
44. Doris E. Fleischman (Bernays), "Notes of a Retiring Feminist."
45. Anne Bernay interview.
46. Held interview.
47. Roman interview.
48. Interview with Mary Ann Pires, 1996.
49. "Valentine's Day Love Stories," *Christian Science Monitor*, February 14, 1980.
50. Edward L. Bernays, draft article for *Women's Handbook*, Library of Congress.
51. Letter from Edward L. Bernays to Judith Bernays Heller, July 28, 1948, Library of Congress.
52. Edward L. Bernays, *Biography*, 810.
53. Held interview.
54. Doris Fleischman Bernays, *Wife*, 28–29, 33.
55. Anne Bernays interview.
56. Ibid.
57. Ibid.
58. Held interview.
59. Edward L. Bernays letter to Swarthmore College, Library of Congress.
60. Edward L. Bernays letter to Doris Held, October 29, 1952, Library of Congress.
61. Held interview.
62. Anne Bernays interview.

CHAPTER 7: *At the* **OFFICE**

1. Interview with James Parton, 1996.
2. Interview with Anne Bernays, 1996.

3. Interview with Walter Wiener, 1996.

4. Interview with Luther Conant, 1996.

5. Interview with Stanley Silverman, 1996.

6. Interview with Robert Hutchings and letter from Hutchings to author, 1996.

7. Parton interview.

8. Conant interview.

9. Interview with Tom McCann, 1996.

10. Anne Bernays interview.

11. Interview with Ralph Bugli, 1996.

12. Interview with Molly Schuchat, 1996.

13. Interview with Elizabeth di Sant'Agnese, 1996.

14. Hutchings interview.

15. Interview with Peter Straus, 1996.

16. Interview with Cynthia Donnelly, 1996.

17. Conant interview.

18. Bugli interview.

19. Henry F. Pringle, "The Mass Psychologist," *American Mercury*, February 1930.

20. "PR's Edward L. Bernays: Creating Acts That Make News That Raises Sales," *Printer's Ink*, December 4, 1959.

21. Wiener interview.

22. Letter from Joseph Freeman to Floyd, November 21, 1951, Joseph Freeman Collection, Hoover Institution Archives, Stanford University.

23. Ibid., April 17, 1952.

24. Ibid., May 25, 1952.

25. Ibid.

26. Ibid., June 5, 1952.

27. Edward L. Bernays, *Biography*, 612, 622.

28. Ibid., 561–66.

CHAPTER 8: *Going to* WAR

1. Letter from Edward L. Bernays to Edmund Whitman, April 21, 1952, Bernays Papers, Library of Congress.

2. Bernays, Reminiscences, 1971, Columbia University Oral History Research Office, 52.

3. Edward L. Bernays, *Biography*, 189.

4. Ibid., 227.

5. Ibid., 702–4.

6. Ibid., 727.

7. Letter from Bernays to Rayan Sen, May 26, 1952, Library of Congress.

8. Letter from Sen to Bernays, June 2, 1952, Library of Congress.

9. Memo from Bernays to United Fruit, May 8, 1942, Library of Congress.

10. Charles Morrow Wilson, "Middle America and U.S.," Middle America Information Bureau, Library of Congress.

11. Memo from Bernays, "Instructions and Suggestions for Writers and Researchers Preparing Material for Use by the Middle America Information Bureau," Library of Congress.

12. Interview with Samuel Rovner, 1996.

13. Memo from Bernays to United Fruit, September 11, 1947, Library of Congress.

14. Bernays, *Biography*, 755.

15. Ibid., 750.

16. Diane K. Stanley, *For the Record: United Fruit Company's Sixty-Six Years in Guatemala* (Guatemala City: Centro Impresor Piedra Santa, 1994), 113.

17. Memo from Bernays to Whitman, March 21, 1951, Library of Congress.

18. Memo from Bernays to Whitman, November 14, 1950, Library of Congress.

19. Memo from Bernays to Whitman, July 23, 1951, Library of Congress.

20. Letter from Bernays to Arthur Hays Sulzberger, August 30, 1951, Library of Congress.

21. Letter from Bernays to Whitman, June 28, 1951, Library of Congress.

22. Letter from Will Lissner to Bernays, July 25, 1951, Library of Congress.

23. Letter from Bernays to Whitman, March 12, 1952, Library of Congress.

24. Bernays cable to Winchell, March 6, 1954, Library of Congress.

25. Whitman letter to Bernays, March 15, 1954, Library of Congress.

26. Bernays, *Biography*, 761.

27. Thomas McCann, *On the Inside: A Story of Intrigue and Adventure, on Wall Street, in Washington, and in the Jungles of Central America* (Boston: Quinlan Press, 1987), 45–46.

28. Bernays, *Biography*, 761.

29. Interview with Morton Yarmon, 1996.

30. Interview with Lissner, 1996.

31. Interview with Sidney Gruson, 1996.

32. Letter from Herbert Matthews to Bernays, November 17, 1966, Bernays family album.

33. Letters from Bernays to Whitman, March 12, 1952, and to Kenneth H. Redmond, March 13, 1952, Library of Congress.

34. Letter from Bernays to Whitman, April 21, 1952, Library of Congress.

35. Letter from Bernays to Whitman, May 12, 1952, Library of Congress.

36. Letter from Bernays to Emanuel Freedman, March 26, 1954, Library of Congress.

37. Letter from Bernays to David Sentner, May 10, 1954, Library of Congress.

38. Letter from Whitman to Bernays, April 9, 1954, Library of Congress.

39. Letters from Bernays to Whitman, June 6, 1952, and May 21, 1953, Library of Congress.

40. Letters from Bernays to Nicholas DeWitt, April 2 and April 22, 1954, and from DeWitt to Bernays, April 20, along with undated "Content Analysis of Pronouncements of Guatemala's Political Leaders," Library of Congress.

41. Letter from Bernays to Caskie Stinnett, April 8, 1954, Library of Congress.

42. Piero Gleijeses, *Shattered Hope: The Guatemalan Revolution and the United States, 1944–1954* (Princeton: Princeton University Press, 1991), 131.

43. Interview with Gale Wallace, 1996.

44. Stephen Schlesinger and Stephen Kinzer, *Bitter Fruit: The Untold Story of the American Coup in Guatemala* (Garden City, N.Y.: Doubleday, 1982), 90.

45. Matthews, *The Cuban Story* (New York: George Braziller, 1961), 124.

46. Interview with McCann, 1996.

47. Letter from Bernays to Whitman, July 13, 1954, Library of Congress.

48. Letter from Bernays to Whitman, January 6, 1955, Library of Congress.

49. Letter from Bernays to Whitman, January 24, 1955, Library of Congress, and *Biography*, 772.

50. "Comparison of the Teachings of Communists and the Church," reprinted from the *Texas Catholic*, July 3, 1954, Library of Congress.

51. McCann, *On the Inside*, 59–60.

52. Bernays, *Biography*, 775.

53. Matthews, *Cuban Story*, 123–24.

54. McCann, *On the Inside*, 55–56.

55. Bernays, *Biography*, 757, 768.

56. Letter from Bernays to Nat Wartels, July 6, 1976, Library of Congress.

57. McCann interview.

58. Letter from Bernays to Willoughby Chesley, June 14, 1961, Library of Congress.

59. Letter from Bernays to David Brinkley, July 19, 1961, Library of Congress.

60. Bernays, book proposal, May 25, 1970, Library of Congress.

CHAPTER 9: *Uncle* SIGI

1. Edward L. Bernays, *Biography*, 253.

2. Sigmund Freud cable to Ely Bernays, September 24, 1919, described in *Biography*, 254.

3. Bernays cable to Freud, October 9, 1919, Bernays Papers, Library of Congress.

4. Letter from Freud to Bernays, September 27, 1919, *Biography*, 254–55.

5. Letter from Bernays to Freud, December 18, 1919, Library of Congress.

6. Letter from Freud to Bernays, January 4, 1920, Library of Congress.

7. Letter from Bernays to Freud, February 5, 1920, Library of Congress.

8. Letters from Freud to Bernays, June 17, 1920, and from Bernays to Freud, June 30, July 12, and August 2, 1920, Library of Congress.

9. Letter from Freud to Bernays, July 20, 1920; *Biography*, 259; Letter from Bernays to Freud, August 8, 1920, Library of Congress.

10. Letter from Freud to Bernays, October 2, 1920, Library of Congress.

11. Letters from Bernays to Freud, November 19 and November 27, 1920. Cable from Freud to Bernays December 1, 1920, and letter from Freud, December 19, 1920. Library of Congress.

12. Bernays, *Biography*, 264.

13. Ernest Jones, *The Life and Work of Sigmund Freud: The Last Phase, 1919–1930* (New York, Basic Books, 1957), 29.

14. Letter from Bernays to Freud, March 19, 1921, and letter from Freud to Bernays, April 24, 1921, Library of Congress.

15. Letter from Freud to Bernays, June 28, 1921, cited in *Biography*, 266.

16. Letters from Freud to Bernays, June 19, 1921, and from Bernays to Freud, July 5, 1921, Library of Congress.

17. Letters from Freud to Bernays, October 2, 1922, and September 14, 1923, and from Bernays to Freud, October 16, 1922, Library of Congress.

18. Letter from Bernays to Freud, July 24, 1929, cited in *Biography*, 275. Letter from Freud to Bernays, August 10, 1929, Library of Congress.

19. Jones, *Sigmund Freud: Life and Work, The Young Freud, 1856–1900* (London: Hogarth Press, 1953), 129–30.

20. Jones, *Young Freud*, 131.

21. Elisabeth Young-Bruehl, *Anna Freud: A Biography* (New York: Summit Books, 1988), 31.

22. Jones, *Young Freud*, 131–32.

23. Jeffrey Moussaieff Masson, *The Complete Letters of Sigmund Freud to Wilhelm Fliess, 1887–1904* (Cambridge, Mass.: Harvard University Press, 1985), 406.

24. Letters from Freud to Bernays, October 20 and December 8, 1923, Library of Congress.

25. Reminiscences of Edward L. Bernays, 1971, Columbia University Oral History Research Office, 300–1.

26. Doris Fleischman Bernays, August 19, 1949, notes from visit to Freuds, Library of Congress.

27. Bernays, *Biography*, 17.

28. Ibid., 34.

29. Bernays, "My Uncle Sigmund Freud," *New Leader*, November 15, 1954.

30. Bernays, *Biography*, 276.

31. Letter from Bernays to Eric F. Goldman, June 19, 1952, Library of Congress.

32. Bernays Reminiscences, Columbia University, 310.

33. Bernays, "Uncle Sigi," *Journal of the History of Medicine and Allied Sciences*, April 1980.

34. Letter from Anna Freud to Bernays, December 15, 1949.

35. Bernays Reminiscences, Columbia University, 339–40.

CHAPTER 10: *The Cambridge* YEARS

1. *Boston Magazine*, "The Engineer of Consent," March 1964.

2. *New York Times*, November 15, 1964.

3. Interview with Otto Lerbinger, 1996.

4. Interview with Pat Jackson, 1996.

5. Interview with Howard Chase, 1995.

6. *Boston Magazine*, March 1964.

7. Interview with Lucas Held, 1996.

8. Interview with Hester Kaplan, 1996.

9. Interview with Julie Held, 1996.

10. Letter from Edward L. Bernays to Susanna Kaplan, January 26, 1961, and undated letter from Hester Kaplan to Bernays, Bernays Papers, Library of Congress.

11. Hester Kaplan interview.

12. Julie Held interview.

13. Interview with Susanna Kaplan Donahue, 1996.

14. Hester Kaplan interview.

15. Interview with Anne Bernays, 1996.

16. Interview with Justin Kaplan, 1996.

17. Interview with Doris Held, 1996.

18. Interview with Frank Genovese, 1996.

19. Interview with Camille Roman, 1996.

20. Interview with Everette Dennis, 1996.

21. *New York Times*, July 22 and July 23, 1971.

22. Anne Bernays interview.

23. Justin Kaplan interview.

24. Hester Kaplan interview.

25. Julie Held interview.

26. Anne Bernays interview.

27. Justin Kaplan interview.
28. Doris Held interview.
29. Letter from Dr. Victor Gurewich to Dr. B. Thomas Hutchinson, January 18, 1980, Bernays papers, Library of Congress.
30. Interview with Polly Kaplan, 1996.
31. Gurewich letter.
32. Roman interview.
33. Hester Kaplan interview.
34. Anne Bernays interview.
35. Justin Kaplan interview.
36. Doris Held interview.
37. Interview with Cindy Strousse, 1996.
38. Ibid.
39. Interview with Sherry Houghton, 1996.
40. Dennis interview.
41. Interview with Herbert Patchell, 1996.
42. Interview with Mary Ann Pires, 1996.
43. Interview with Sherry Jahoda, 1996.
44. Justin Kaplan interview.
45. Interview with Cathryn Kaner, 1996.
46. Interview with Joe Trahan, 1996.
47. Interviews with Shelley and Barry Spector, 1996.
48. Interview with Peter Hollister, 1996.
49. Hester Kaplan interview.
50. Interview with Elvira Vazquez, 1996.
51. Letter from Barbara Hunter to author, May 7, 1996.
52. Letter from Joseph T. Nolan to author, May 2, 1996.
53. Letter from Patricia Tate to Mr. Stewart, July 17, 1985, Susanne A. Roschwalb Papers, American University, Washington, D.C.
54. Interview with Frank LeBart, 1996.
55. Interview with Joan Schneider, 1996.
56. Dennis interview.

CHAPTER 11: *One Last* RIDE

1. Interview with Joan Vondra, 1996.
2. Ibid.

3. Vondra interview and Report of Guardian *ad Litem*, "In Re: The Matter of Edward L. Bernays," Probate and Family Court, Commonwealth of Massachusetts, December 1, 1993.

4. Vondra interview.

5. Ibid.

6. Ibid.

7. Ibid.

8. Guardian report, 6.

9. Interview with Joan Schneider, 1996.

10. Interview with Herbert Patchell, 1996.

11. Guardian report, 16, 19, 27–28.

12. Ibid., 20–22, 31.

13. Ibid., 59–62.

14. Ibid., 17–18, 39.

15. Guardian report, 23, and interview with Doris Held, 1996.

16. Guardian report, 26, 66.

17. Ibid., 62–66.

18. Vondra interview.

19. Guardian report, 56, 67.

20. Ibid., 54–55.

21. Ibid., 36–37.

22. Ibid., 2.

23. Ibid., 2.

24. Ibid., 3–4, 7.

25. Ibid., 4–5.

26. Ibid., 9.

27. Ibid., 14.

28. Ibid., 98–99.

29. Ibid., 98, 101.

30. Ibid., 100–3.

31. Interview with Charles Seidenberg, 1996.

32. Ibid.

33. Held interview.

34. Interview with Dr. Victor Gurewich, 1996.

35. Patchell interview.

36. Guardian report, 4–13.

37. Held interview.

38. Patchell interview.

39. Vondra interview.

40. Held interview.

CHAPTER 12: *A Question of* **PATERNITY**

1. *New York Times,* March 10, 1995.

2. Glenn and Denny Griswold, *Your Public Relations: The Standard Public Relations Handbook* (New York: Funk & Wagnalls, 1948), 634.

3. Edward L. Bernays, "Public Relations: Yesterday, Today and Tomorrow," address to Publicity Club of Chicago, May 15, 1981.

4. Scott M. Cutlip, *The Unseen Power: Public Relations. A History* (Hillsdale, N.J.: Lawrence Erlbaum Associates, 1994), 2, 10.

5. *Time,* April 3, 1939.

6. John W. Hill, *The Making of a Public Relations Man* (New York: David McKay, 1963), 16.

7. *Literary Digest,* November 17, 1934.

8. *New York Times,* January 18, 1991.

9. John Alfred Ralph Pimlott, *Public Relations and American Democracy* (Princeton: Princeton University Press, 1951), 11.

10. Stanley Walker, *City Editor* (New York: Frederick A. Stokes, 1934), 143–44.

11. Richard S. Tedlow, *Keeping the Corporate Image: Public Relations and Business: 1900–1950* (Greenwich, Conn.: Jai Press, 1979), 39–40.

12. John T. Flynn, "The Science of Ballyhoo," *Atlantic Monthly,* May 1932.

13. Sid Bernstein, "We Can Use a Bit of Flag Waving," *Advertising Age,* August 11, 1975.

14. *Life,* fall 1990.

15. Letter from Bernays to Cutlip, November 29, 1975, Bernays Papers, Library of Congress.

16. *Editor & Publisher,* April 2, 1927.

17. *Time,* January 24, 1938.

18. Cutlip, *Unseen Power,* 216.

19. Interview with Camille Roman, 1996.

20. Interview with Frank LeBart, 1996.

21. Tedlow, 158.

22. LeBart interview.

23. Interview with Loet Velmans, 1996.

24. Interview with Howard Chase, 1995.

25. Letters from William H. Baldwin to Eric F. Goldman, January 22, 1948, and to Harry A. Bruno, October 16, 1965, Baldwin Papers, State Historical Society of Wisconsin.

26. Interview with Bill Ruder, 1996.

27. Sidney Blumenthal, *The Permanent Campaign* (Boston: Beacon Press, 1980), 29.

28. Bernays address to Publicity Club of Chicago.

29. Eric F. Goldman, *Two-Way Street: The Emergence of the Public Relations Counsel* (Boston: Bellman, 1948), 16, 19.

30. Memo to Bernays from Goldman, March 10, 1948, Library of Congress.

31. Goldman, *Two-Way Street*, and letter from Bernays to Goldman, October 15, 1947, Library of Congress.

32. *American Mercury*, February 1930.

33. *Atlantic Monthly*, May 1932.

34. *Jewish Tribune*, Dec. 7, 1928; *New York World-Telegram*, April 9, 1935; *Literary Digest*, June 2, 1934; *New Yorker*, Aug. 28, 1926.

35. *Printer's Ink*, Dec. 4, 1959, and *Washington Post*, May 23, 1984.

36. *Editor & Publisher*, Feb. 25, 1928, and October 26, 1929.

37. *Guild Reporter*, March 21, 1938.

38. Edward L. Bernays, *Biography*, 780.

39. Reminiscences of Edward L. Bernays, 1971, Columbia University Oral History Research Office, 98.

40. Interview with Ray Eldon Hiebert, 1996.

41. Cutlip, *Unseen Power*, 160.

42. Letter from Cutlip to Bernays, April 6, 1955, State Historical Society of Wisconsin.

43. Memo to his Library of Congress file from John McDonough, October 18, 1965, Library of Congress.

44. Letter from Bernays to Daniel J. Boorstin, February 13, 1959, Library of Congress.

45. *Editor & Publisher*, June 9, 1951.

46. Memo from Bill Riis, undated, State Historical Society of Wisconsin.

47. Bernays Reminiscences, 271.

48. Bernays Reminiscences, 104–5; Bernays notes for New York University journalism course, February 17, 1949, Library of Congress.

49. Letter from T. J. Ross to Harry Bruno, October 20, 1965, State Historical Society of Wisconsin.

50. Letter from Baldwin to Bruno, October 16, 1965, State Historical Society of Wisconsin; letter from Cutlip to Bernays, January 6, 1966, Library of Congress.

51. *New York Times*, November 29, 1965; *Columbia Journalism Review*, Winter 1966; *Editor & Publisher*, November 20, 1965.

52. Letter from Bernays to Cutlip, January 8, 1966, Library of Congress.

53. Interview with Sue Bohle, 1996.

54. Letter from William J. Corbett to author, May 4, 1996.

55. Interview with Hester Kaplan, 1996.

56. David L. Lewis, "The Outstanding PR Professionals," *Public Relations Journal*, October 1970.

57. Interview with Lewis, 1996.

Bibliography

Adams, Frederick Upham. *Conquest of the Tropics: The Story of the Creative Enterprises Conducted by the United Fruit Company.* New York: Arno Press, 1976.

Albig, William. *Modern Public Opinion.* New York: McGraw-Hill, 1956.

Allen, Frederick Lewis. *Only Yesterday.* New York: Harper, 1931.

———. *Since Yesterday.* New York: Harper, 1940.

Baldwin, Hanson Weightman, Collection at Yale University Library.

Beechnut Packing Company—Bartlett Arkell Collection, Canajoharie, New York, Library and Art Gallery.

Bent, Silas. *Ballyhoo: The Voice of the Press.* New York: Boni & Liveright, 1927.

Bernays, Anne. *Growing Up Rich.* Boston: Little, Brown, 1975.

Bernays, Doris Fleischman. *A Wife Is Many Women.* New York: Crown, 1955.

Bernays, Edward L. Bernays Papers, Library of Congress.

———. Cornell University files.

———. *Crystallizing Public Opinion.* New York: Boni & Liveright, 1923.

———. *Democratic Leadership in Total War.* Cleveland: Western Reserve University, 1943.

———. *The Later Years: Public Relations Insights, 1956–1986.* Rhinebeck, N.Y.: H&M, 1986.

———. *An Outline of Careers.* New York: Doubleday, Doran, 1935.

———. *Private Interest and Public Responsibility.* New York: Cooper Union, 1939.

———. *Propaganda.* New York: Horace Liveright, 1928.

————. *A Psychological Blueprint for the Peace—Canada, U.S.A.* Toronto: Southam Press, 1944.

————. *Public Relations.* Norman: University of Oklahoma Press, 1952.

————. *Speak Up For Democracy.* New York: Viking Press, 1940.

————. *Take Your Place at the Peace Table.* New York: Gerent Press, 1945.

————. Bernays, Robert H. Jackson, and Charles Poletti, *Reminiscences,* Columbia University Oral History Research Office.

————, Samuel Hoffenstein, Walter J. Kingsley, and Murdock Pemberton. *The Broadway Anthology.* New York: Duffield, 1917.

Bernstein, Irving. *The Lean Years: A History of the American Worker.* Boston: Houghton Mifflin, 1983.

Biography of an Idea: Memoirs of Public Relations Counsel Edward L. Bernays. New York: Simon & Schuster, 1965.

Black, Sam. *Practical Public Relations.* London: Pitman, 1976.

Blumenthal, Sidney. *The Permanent Campaign.* Boston: Beacon Press, 1980.

Boorstin, Daniel J. *The Image: A Guide to Pseudo-Events in America.* New York: Vintage Books, 1961.

Borkenau, Franz. *World Communism: A History of the Communist International.* Ann Arbor: University of Michigan Press, 1962.

Burton, Paul. *Corporate Public Relations.* New York: Reinhold, 1966.

Childs, Harwood Lawrence. *An Introduction to Public Opinion.* New York: Wiley, 1940.

————. *Public Opinion: Nature, Formation, and Role.* Princeton, N.J.: D. Van Nostrand, 1965.

Collier, John. Collection at Yale University Library.

Cook, Blanche Wiesen. *The Declassified Eisenhower: A Divided Legacy of Peace and Political Warfare.* New York: Doubleday, 1981.

Cox, Reavis. *Competition in the American Tobacco Industry.* New York: Columbia University Press, 1933.

Crawford, Kenneth Gale. *The Pressure Boys: The Inside Story of Lobbying in America.* New York: Julian Messner, 1939.

Creel, George. *How We Advertised America.* New York: Harper, 1920.

Cutlip, Scott M. *A Public Relations Bibliography.* Madison: University of Wisconsin Press, 1965.

————. *Public Relations History: From the 17th to the 20th Century.* Hillsdale, N.J.: Lawrence Erlbaum, 1995.

————. *The Unseen Power: Public Relations. A History.* Hillsdale, N.J.: Lawrence Erlbaum, 1994.

————, Allen H. Center, and Glen M. Broom. *Effective Public Relations.* Englewood Cliffs, N.J.: Prentice-Hall, 1985.

Dixon, Marlene, and Susanne Jonas, eds. *Revolution and Intervention in Central America.* San Francisco: Synthesis, 1983.

Dobbyns, Fletcher. *The Amazing Story of Repeal: An Exposé of the Power of Propaganda.* New York: Willett, Clark, 1940.

Doob, Leonard W. *Propaganda: Its Psychology and Technique.* New York: Henry Holt, 1935.

Douglas, Ann. *Terrible Honesty: A Mongrel Manhattan in the 1920s.* London: Picador, 1995.

Eastman, Max. *Great Companions: Critical Memoirs of Some Famous Friends.* New York: Farrar, Straus & Cudahy, 1959.

Ewen, Stuart. *PR! A Social History of Spin.* New York: Basic Books, 1996.

Flannagan, Roy Catesby. *The Story of Lucky Strike.* New York: Steidinger Press, 1938.

Fox, Richard Wightman, and T. J. Jackson Lears, eds. *The Culture of Consumption: Critical Essays in American History.* New York: Pantheon, 1983.

Freud, Sigmund. *Group Psychology and the Analysis of the Ego.* Vienna: International Psychoanalytical Press, 1922.

Fried, Jonathan, ed. *Guatemala in Rebellion: Unfinished History.* New York: Grove Press, 1983.

Fuhrman, Candice Jacobson. *Publicity Stunt.* San Francisco: Chronicle Books, 1989.

Gauvreau, Emile Henry. *Hot News.* New York: Macaulay, 1931.

————. *My Last Million Readers.* New York: Dutton, 1941.

Gleijeses, Piero. *Shattered Hope: The Guatemalan Revolution and the United States, 1944–1954.* Princeton, N.J.: Princeton University Press, 1991.

Goldman, Eric F. *Two-Way Street: The Emergence of the Public Relations Counsel.* Boston: Bellman, 1948.

Griswold, Glenn and Denny. *Your Public Relations: The Standard Public Relations Handbook.* New York: Funk & Wagnalls, 1948.

Guhin, Michael A. *John Foster Dulles: A Statesman and His Times.* New York: Columbia University Press, 1972.

Harral, Stewart. *Public Relations for Higher Education*. Norman: University of Oklahoma Press, 1942.

Hiebert, Ray Eldon. *Courtier to the Crowd: The Story of Ivy Lee and the Development of Public Relations*. Ames: Iowa State University Press, 1966.

Hill, John W. *The Making of a Public Relations Man*. New York: David McKay, 1963.

Hoyt, Edwin P. *The Supersalesmen*. New York: World Publishing, 1962.

Immerman, Richard H. *The CIA in Guatemala: The Foreign Policy of Intervention*. Austin: University of Texas Press, 1982.

Inman, Samuel Guy. *A New Day in Guatemala: A Study of the Present Social Revolution*. Wilton, Conn.: Worldover Press, 1951.

Irwin, Will. *Propaganda and the News: Or, What Makes You Think So?* New York: McGraw-Hill, 1970.

James, Daniel. *Red Design for the Americas: Guatemalan Prelude*. New York: Day, 1954.

Jonas, Susanne. *The Battle for Guatemala: Rebels, Death Squads, and U.S. Power*. Boulder, Colo.: Westview Press, 1991.

Jones, Ernest. *The Life and Work of Sigmund Freud: The Last Phase, 1919–1930*. New York, Basic Books, 1957.

——. *Sigmund Freud: Life and Work, The Young Freud, 1856–1900*. London: Hogarth Press, 1953.

Josephson, Matthew. *Edison: A Biography*. New York: McGraw-Hill, 1959.

Kaplan, Justin. *Lincoln Steffens: A Biography*. New York: Simon & Schuster, 1974.

Kepner, Charles David. *The Banana Empire: A Case Study of Economic Imperialism*. New York: Russell & Russell, 1967.

Larson, Keith A. *Public Relations: The Edward L. Bernayses and the American Scene*. Westwood, Mass.: F. W. Faxon, 1978.

Lasswell, Harold Dwight. *Propaganda and Promotional Activities, An Annotated Bibliography*. Minneapolis: University of Minnesota Press, 1935.

——. *Propaganda Technique in the World War*. New York: Knopf, 1927.

Le Bon, Gustave. *The Crowd: A Study of the Popular Mind*. New York: Macmillan, 1896.

Lerbinger, Otto. *Information, Influence & Communication: A Reader in Public Relations*. New York: Basic Books, 1965.

Bibliography

Lesly, Philip., ed. *Public Relations Handbook.* Englewood Cliffs, N.J.: Prentice-Hall, 1978.

Lewis, David L. *The Public Image of Henry Ford.* Detroit: Wayne State University Press, 1976.

Lippmann, Walter. *Public Opinion.* New York: Harcourt, Brace, 1922.

Marchand, Roland. *Advertising the American Dream: Making Way for Modernity.* Berkeley: University of California Press, 1985.

Masson, Jeffrey Moussaieff. *The Complete Letters of Sigmund Freud to Wilhelm Fleiss, 1887–1904.* Cambridge, Mass.: Harvard University Press, 1985.

Matthews, Herbert Lionel. *The Cuban Story.* New York: George Braziller, 1961.

———. *A World in Revolution: A Newspaperman's Memoir.* New York: Scribner's, 1972.

Mavity, Mary Barr. *The Modern Newspaper.* New York: Henry Holt, 1930.

McCann, Thomas. *On the Inside: A Story of Intrigue and Adventure, on Wall Street, in Washington, and in the Jungles of Central America.* Boston: Quinlan Press, 1987.

McNeil, Frank. *War and Peace in Central America.* Scribner's, 1988.

Mencken, Henry Louis. *The American Language: An Inquiry into the Development of English in the United States.* New York: Knopf, 1936.

Miller, Karen S. *Amplifying the Voice of Business: Hill and Knowlton's Influence on Political, Public, and Media Discourse in Postwar America.* Ph.D. diss. University of Wisconsin–Madison, 1993.

Mock, James R., and Cedric Larson. *Words That Won the War.* Princeton, N.J.: Princeton University Press; 1939.

Olasky, Marvin N. *Corporate Public Relations: A New Historical Perspective.* Hillsdale, N.J.: Lawrence Erlbaum, 1987.

Packard, Vance. *The Hidden Persuaders.* New York: David McKay, 1957.

Perera, Victor. *Unfinished Conquest: The Guatemalan Tragedy.* Berkeley: University of California Press, 1993.

Persons, Stow. *American Minds: A History of Ideas.* New York: Henry Holt, 1975.

Pimlott, John Alfred Ralph. *Public Relations and American Democracy.* Princeton, N.J.: Princeton University Press, 1951.

Poole, Ernest. *The Bridge: My Own Story.* New York: Macmillan, 1940.

Rabe, Stephen G. *Eisenhower and Latin America: The Foreign Policy of Anti-Communism.* Chapel Hill: University of North Carolina Press, 1988.

Raucher, Alan R. *Public Relations and Business.* Baltimore: Johns Hopkins Press, 1968.

Ringel, Frederick Julius. *America as Americans See It.* New York: Literary Guild, 1932.

Roberts, Kenneth. *Edward L. Bernays: His Role in the Professionalization of the Public Relations Practice.* B.A. thesis, Rutgers University, 1963.

Samstag, Nicholas. *How Business Is Bamboozled by the Ad-Boys.* New York: Heineman, 1966.

Schlesinger, Stephen, and Stephen Kinzer. *Bitter Fruit: The Untold Story of the American Coup in Guatemala.* Garden City, N.Y.: Doubleday, 1982.

Schneider, Ronald M. *Communism in Guatemala.* New York: Praeger, 1958.

Schudson, Michael. *Advertising: The Uneasy Persuasion.* New York: Basic Books, 1984.

Shank Public Relations Counselors and American Cablevision of Indianapolis, Videotapes with Edward L. Bernays.

Smith, Jane Webb. *Smoke Signals: Cigarette Advertising and the American Way of Life.* Chapel Hill: University of North Carolina Press, 1990.

Smith, Sally Bedell. *In All His Glory: The Life of William S. Paley.* New York: Simon & Schuster, 1990.

Smith, Stephen. *Honest Retailers of Truth: Popular Thinkers and the American Response to Modernity.* Ph.D. diss. Brown University, 1990.

Sobel, Robert. *They Satisfy: The Cigarette in American Life.* Garden City, N.Y.: Anchor Books, 1978.

Spector, Barry and Shelley. Videotaped conversations with Edward L. Bernays.

Stanford University's Hoover Institution Archives, Joseph Freeman Collection.

Stanley, Diane K. *For the Record: United Fruit Company's Sixty-six Years in Guatemala.* Guatemala City: Centro Impresor Piedra Santa, 1994.

State Historical Society of Wisconsin. Papers of Scott M. Cutlip, T. Stacy Capers, and others.

Stauber, John Clyde. *Toxic Sludge Is Good for You: Lies, Damn Lies, and the Public Relations Industry*. Monroe, Maine: Common Courage Press, 1995.

Tedlow, Richard S. *Keeping the Corporate Image: Public Relations and Business: 1900–1950*. Greenwich, Conn.: Jai Press, 1979.

Travis, Helen Simon. *The Truth About Guatemala*. New York: New Century, 1954.

Trotter, Wilfred. *Instincts of the Herd in Peace and War*. New York: Macmillan, 1916.

Upward, Geoffrey C. *A Home for Our Heritage: The Building and Growth of Greenfield Village and the Henry Ford Museum, 1929–1979*. Dearborn, Mich.: Henry Ford Museum Press, 1980.

Vercic, Dejan. *Modern Public Relations: Edward L. Bernays and After*. Ljubljana, Slovenia: Pristop Communication Group, 1996.

Walker, Stanley. *City Editor*. New York: Frederick A Stokes, 1934.

Walker, Strother Holland. *Business Finds Its Voice*. New York: Harper, 1938.

Washburn, Charles. *Press Agentry*. New York: National Library Press, 1937.

Weiner, Richard. *Dictionary of Media and Communications*. New York: Macmillan, 1996.

Wilder, Robert Holman. *Publicity: A Manual for the Use of Business, Civic or Social Service Organizations*. New York: Ronald Press, 1923.

Wilson, Charles Morrow. *Empire in Green and Gold: The Story of the American Banana Trade*. New York: Henry Holt, 1968.

Wright, J. Handly. *Public Relations in Management*. New York: McGraw-Hill, 1949.

Wylie, Max. *Clear Channels: Television and the American People*. New York: Funk & Wagnalls, 1955.

Young-Bruehl, Elisabeth. *Anna Freud: A Biography*. New York: Summit Books, 1988.

Acknowledgments

THIS IS MY FIRST BOOK, AND I WASN'T SURE I'D KNOW HOW TO research and write it, not to mention do it all in the one-year leave I had from the *Boston Globe*.

My friends Sally Jacobs and Andy Savitz *were* sure, though, and they gave me confidence. They helped me assemble the proposal and encouraged me through months of research. They edited an early draft and helped me see the difference between newspaper writing and book writing.

The staff at the Manuscript Division of the Library of Congress went beyond any call of duty in helping me pore over their Bernays collection and track down his papers at other libraries. The library also gave me an office and helped me uncover scores of old manuscripts and magazines. Neil Sheehan entertained and inspired me with tales of his days in journalism and his transition to book writing, Kurt Maier helped me with his translations and good humor, and Barbara Kraft taught me how to make the library work for me and how to keep my sanity. Two other librarians also steered me through my research: Karen Summerhill of Georgetown Law Center, who schooled me in computer searches, and Marc Shechtman of the *Boston Globe* library, who helped me answer 101 questions, much as he has done for so many *Globe* projects.

Jill Kneerim did everything an agent is supposed to do by helping me conceptualize and sell the book. Then she stayed on to help me in dealing with legal and ethical questions and in researching the book, writing it, and landing a new editor when my original ones left for another publishing house. Speaking of editors, I define success as my agreeing with half of the changes they suggest. My editors set a new standard, proposing fixes nearly all of which made the book better, and showing rather than just telling me what was wrong. Those editors were Peter St. John Ginna and Allison Arieff, who got me started, and Betty A. Prashker and Donna Ryan, who treated my book with as much care as if it were theirs. Thanks, too, to Crown's KellyAnn Loughran for shepherding the book through its final stages and responding to my endless faxes and phone calls.

Anne Bernays and Justin Kaplan planted the idea of writing the book and were there throughout with recollections and advice, offering suggestions whenever I asked for help, which was perpetually, but never interfering. Doris Held was more reticent at first, understandably concerned about how I would treat her father, but she ultimately shared her memories and insights in a way that opened up aspects of Edward Bernays's character that I hadn't understood. Anne's and Doris's children also were generous in sharing their time and reminiscences.

More than a hundred of Eddie's friends, colleagues, and protégés let me interview them and see his letters. Barry and Shelley Spector did that and more, sharing eighty hours of Eddie on tape, taking me on a tour of places he'd worked and lived in Manhattan, offering pictures and other memorabilia, and generally encouraging me along the way. Eddie's nephew Walter Wiener was equally generous with his time, steering me through the early years and showering me with advice. Stuart Ewen shared his manuscript on the social history of PR before it was published, Scott M. Cutlip offered invaluable historical context, Harold Burson helped me understand the profession as it is today and as it was in the past, and Joan Vondra openly discussed a trying chapter in her life. The Public Relations Society of America also was tremendously helpful, sharing its mailing list and advice, while the editors of all the major PR newsletters and journals offered invaluable guidance.

Jerold Roschwalb was exceedingly generous in opening up to me the research of his wife, Susanne, who died before she could transform her papers and interviews into a biography. Also generous with their time and guidance were researchers at Columbia, Stanford, Cornell, Yale, and Harvard Universities, along with those at the State Historical Society of Wisconsin, the Henry Ford Museum, and the Canajoharie, New York, Library and Art Gallery.

My mother, Dorothy Tye, and the rest of my family were there throughout with moral support and care packages, understanding when I missed family gatherings and accommodating their busy schedules to mine.

Editor Matt Storin of the *Boston Globe* was great to give me a year's leave, considering I'd been back only a year after my Nieman Fellowship. Bill and Lynne Kovach and my Nieman classmates stood by me, as always. So did Tom Palmer, Don Skwar, Steve Kurkjian, and other *Globe* buddies, along with friends in Boston and Washington. I don't know what I would have done if Phil and Tamar Warburg hadn't lent me their home in Washington, along with their continuing emotional support. And while most academic institutions and foundations shied away from a book on public relations, Marvin Kalb and Harvard's Joan Shorenstein Center on the Press, Politics and Public Policy gave me a grant and an equally appreciated Harvard ID card.

Acknowledgments

Index

Index